ALEXANDER A. PARKER

_____

THE PHILOSOPHY OF LOVE

THE PHILOSOPHY OF LOVE

FOR ANTHONY
AND LOUISE
ZAHAREAS

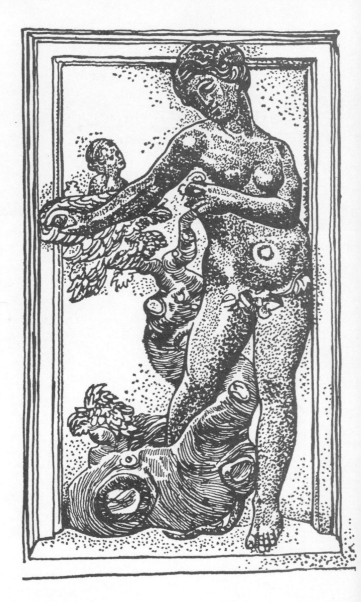

ALEXANDER A. PARKER

THE PHILOSOPHY OF LOVE
IN SPANISH
LITERATURE

♛

1480 — 1680

EDITED BY
TERENCE O'REILLY
FOR THE EDINBURGH
UNIVERSITY
PRESS

PQ
6066
.P36
1985

© A. A. Parker 1985
Edinburgh University Press
22 George Square, Edinburgh

Set in Monotype Poliphilus
by Speedspools Edinburgh
and printed in Great Britain by
Kingprint of Richmond, Surrey

British Library
Cataloguing in Publication Data

Parker, A. A.
The philosophy of love in Spanish literature.
1. Spanish literature—Classical period,
1500–1700—History and criticism   2. Love in literature
I. Title
860.9'354   PQ6066

ISBN 0 85224 491 6

A note on the Frontispiece
It would be automatically assumed that this carving, in the
Italian Renaissance style, represents Venus stepping out of the
sea foam, with Cupid peering over her right arm. But in reality
the waves are the trunk of a tree and the 'Cupid' is the head of a
Serpent, for this is in fact Eve. This carved panel is part of a
choir-stall in the Primatial Cathedral of Toledo by Alonso
Berruguete (c.1490–1561). This juxtaposition or confluence
of the sacred and the profane is a main theme of this book.

CONTENTS

AUTHOR'S PREFACE

This book has grown out of part of the chapter on Spain which was my contribution to *The Age of the Renaissance*, edited by Denys Hay (London 1967). The development began with a lecture delivered in 1968 to the Romance Institutes of Göttingen University and the Free University of Berlin. The subject of that lecture has been expanded into Chapters One, Two and Three. The following year I read a paper at the University of Indiana on the love-poetry of Quevedo, which formed the germ of Chapter Five. When I was invited in 1973 to give a short course of three public lectures at the University of Minnesota, I decided to offer 'The Philosophy of Love in the Spanish Literature of the Golden Age', for which I added new material to the substance of the two early lectures. The invitation came from the recommendation of Professor Anthony Zahareas, at that time Chairman of the Department of Spanish and Portuguese. To him and to his wife this book is dedicated in gratitude for the invitation and their hospitality, as well as in appreciation of a warm and enduring friendship.

Professor Zahareas interested the University of Minnesota Press in the lectures, and an offer was made to publish them as delivered. After some hesitation I decided that I could not possibly publish so short a monograph on so large a subject; instead I offered an expansion. I hoped to write the book after my retirement in 1978, but was intimidated by the bibliographical task involved. This was in any case made impossible almost immediately by my steadily deteriorating eyesight, which left me unable to read and write. It seemed then that the only thing to do was to abandon the scheme or to revert to the original monograph of three lectures.

Two events persuaded me otherwise. The first was the generous offer of Dr Terence O'Reilly of University College, Cork, to edit my manuscript for publication and prepare the bibliography and notes. The second event that made me take up the book was the encouragement given me by my wife, Frances. To this encouragement, and to her early help in reading and writing for me, I owe more than I can say, especially since she soon fell victim to a long and slow illness.

I suggested co-authorship to Dr O'Reilly, but he would not agree to this. His name, however, appears with mine on the title page, for the book is, in fact, a collaboration, without which it could not have appeared. All the views expressed are mine, and it should not be assumed that Dr O'Reilly necessarily shares them.

The 'writing' of the book necessitated adapting myself to an entirely new method of working, from hearing to speaking instead of from seeing to writing. My sister, Mrs Adelaide Burns, deciphered my notes and read them on to tapes. As I was dependent on the kindness of relatives and friends, I could not have read to me all the secondary literature that I had not previously studied. Only the most important contributions made to the subject since my eyesight failed could be read to me. It was necessary, however, to 're-read' some of the literature, and much of this had to be put on tapes for me. From all these tapes I dictated the pages that follow.

Grateful acknowledgements are therefore due to many helpers. In addition to recording my notes for me, Mrs Adelaide Burns wrote down some of this book from my dictation; so too did my wife. The major part of the dictating, however, was done to my friend and neighbour, Mr Denis Aliaga-Kelly, who has given up innumerable hours of his retirement leisure. His forebearance with all my hesitations, changes of mind and other alterations has been beyond praise. He also read to me from Spanish. Books and papers in French and German have been read to me by Mr William Cunningham, who also went to libraries to consult books on my behalf. Francisco García Sarriá borrowed books for me; he has also read to me from the Spanish and has given me the benefit of his advice in many ways. Mrs María Carmen Zamora of University College, Cork, deserves special mention among these helpers. She recorded for me with immaculate diction the plays of Calderón that are here analyzed. A special word of thanks therefore goes to her.

The help of Miss Ann Mackenzie of the University of Liverpool has also been invaluable. She has kept me informed of new publications and has generously supplied me with photocopied material. Dr D. W. Cruickshank of University College Dublin kindly consented to look through my chapter on Calderón and I thank him for his comments and advice. My Editor has occasion to do so also. Parts of the book were submitted to Professors Patrick Gallagher and Ian Macpherson, and I am grateful for suggestions they made which I accepted.

The handicap under which I have laboured in 'studying' my material and in putting the results down in 'writing' means that many shortcomings may have remained which my Editor will not have been able to remove. I would, particularly, ask the indulgence of my readers for the fact that this book falls short of proper academic standards in that it is not based on a full study of all the critical work done on the field. I hope, nevertheless, that it may serve as a guide to further understanding of the Golden Age of Spain's literature. This literature is now better known among non-Hispanists than it was fifty years ago. I should like to think that this book may help to indicate to students of other literatures what Spain has to offer in that particular field. It is impossible, of course, to give adequate thanks to my Editor, as it is impossible for me to know the full extent of the difficulties inadvertently caused him by my method of composition. A final word of thanks is due to Mrs Elaine Edgar for typing the whole of the manuscript.

It would not be out of place for me to acknowledge here the award of a Fellowship from the John Simon Guggenheim Memorial Foundation of New York made to me shortly before my retirement. It was awarded for a project I had submitted on 'The Mind and Art of Calderón', which was intended to be a re-assessment of my ideas on Calderón formed over a period of many years. This will not now be possible as originally hoped, but, *Deo volente*, I may be able to bring out separate parts of the assessment I had in mind. The last chapter is one of these, and I thank the Foundation for the help they generously gave me.

To Mr Archie Turnbull, Secretary to the Edinburgh University Press, I owe apologies as well as thanks. When there was a question of publishing the original three lectures, he accepted co-operation with the University of Minnesota Press for the non-American market, and said that he was prepared to wait for the expansion. My sincere thanks are due to him, for accepting publication so much later than he had expected.

A. A. Parker   Edinburgh, January 1984

EDITOR'S PREFACE

I wish to thank Dr D. W. Cruickshank, who read this book in typescript with meticulous care and made many helpful suggestions; Mr Bernard Bentley, Mr Stephen Boyd, Mr George Every, Professor Patrick Gallagher, Dr Bernard Hamilton, Professor Ian Macpherson, and Miss Jane Tillier, who advised me on particular sections; the Dean and the Faculty of Arts of University College, Cork, who awarded me a grant towards expenses; my sister, Mrs Mary St Clair, who kindly began the task of typing, and Mrs Ursula Burke who completed it; Fr Jock Dalrymple and Fr Tom O'Riordan; Professor A. I. Watson; Professor Terence Folley, of University College, Cork, who was encouraging at every stage; and my wife, Jennifer, for her constant help and support.

T. O'Reilly   Cork, April 1984

ABBREVIATIONS

BBMP *Boletín de la Biblioteca de Menéndez Pelayo*

BHS *Bulletin of Hispanic Studies*

BSS *Bulletin of Spanish Studies*

DS *Dictionnaire de Spiritualité*

Fi *Filología*

FMLS *Forum for Modern Language Studies*

FS *French Studies*

HR *Hispanic Review*

KRQ *Kentucky Romance Quarterly*

MLN *Modern Language Notes*

MLR *Modern Language Review*

PMLA *Publications of the Modern Language Association of America*

PsR *Psychoanalytic Review*

RCEH *Revista Canadiense de Estudios Hispánicos*

RFE *Revista de Filología Española*

RH *Revue Hispanique*

RLC *Revue de Littérature Comparée*

RPh *Romance Philology*

INTRODUCTION

The title of this book will seem pretentious. In our day many philosophers will be surprised at the suggestion that philosophy has any important connection with literature. And recent theories of literature would not concede that literature has any significant connection with philosophy as traditionally understood.

The fragmentation of disciplines in the modern world has led into a seemingly chaotic labyrinth in which the physical and social sciences appear to be at odds with each other. The need to find some unifying principles, to seek for unity through multiplicity, has produced structuralism, a methodology which can be applied to the analysis of human thought and behaviour as well as to the organization of the material universe. The laws of thought can thus be seen as the same laws which govern physics and human society. 'The age in which we live is characterized by the tendency in all scientific disciplines to replace atomism by structuralism and individualism by universalism (in the philosophical sense of these terms).'[1] In linguistics it is held 'that all men share an innate predisposition to organize their possibilities in a certain way. Thus all men participate in knowledge of some "universal grammar" that enables each one to learn his own language creatively, generating new grammatical sentences to suit his own communicative ends.'[2] And in literary criticism Formalism has attempted to isolate the formal principles that govern the structures of literary language and literary forms. This type of literary criticism holds hands with contemporary Anglo-Saxon philosophy, which, if the generalization may be permitted, is concerned primarily with the meaning of statements organized in sentences. Linguistics, which analyzes the structure of language in relation to forms of communication, is the common ground.

An essential element in structuralist literary criticism is the assertion, necessitated by such premises, that intellectual content

I

is immaterial to literary structure and that values (aesthetic, philosophical, moral) are even more irrelevant because they cannot be tied down to objective laws but only to subjective judgements. This, I believe, is literature deprived of mind and heart. Were it incontrovertible, this book could never have been written in anything like its present form. Structuralism as a methodology has produced fascinating results in the sphere of the organization of language and literature as 'grammar', but insofar as it rejects the traditional humanistic standpoints as unnecessary or as invalid, it goes into another field, in which everything embraced by the traditional concepts (however old-fashioned) of beauty, truth and goodness is very greatly restricted, and in which the idea of value in particular becomes largely materialistic. It is obvious why Marxist philosophy has proved attractive to structuralists, despite what others see as the limitations imposed by its materialism and economic determinism.

These modern theories repudiate, in effect, the traditional views of philosophy and literature that began in our Western civilization with Ancient Greece and that have prevailed until recently. The ideal of a Liberal Education began with the study of Latin and Greek and expanded into the study of 'classical' texts in other languages, even when educational disciplines broadened further into history, mathematics and science with all their multitudinous descendants. The universal aim of education was to teach the young how to read, how to write and how to think. Nowadays it may not appear exaggerated to say that the education of children aims at mastering the use of computers, and it might be considered that the unification of the Arts and Sciences that seems to be theoretically envisaged would turn the world of human thinking and learning into a vast computer program. The danger of the potential 'dehumanization' of our minds and sensibilities has been feared for some time.

This book is not ashamed to belong to the tradition of Humane Studies. It believes that the study of ideas in language and literature, as well as the response to feelings and emotions in literature, are the means to an understanding of human life as it has been fashioned by the development of culture. It believes that this understanding embraces values that can be relevant to the formation of our lives in today's world. It believes that the under-standing of the present depends upon our understanding of the past and of the ideas and values that men considered important. The fact that they did so, if not the ideas themselves, can be important and relevant to us. It believes that literature throughout the ages has been the most vital expression of humanity's experi-ence, the best record of its aspirations, successes and failures.

Literature has always been intimately associated with ideas and emotions that have constituted 'views of life' and therefore, in the broadest sense, with philosophy as the understanding of life. Hence the first dictionary definition of philosophy: 'the love, study or pursuit of wisdom, or of knowledge of things and their causes, whether theoretical or practical'. Hence, too, another of its definitions: 'a system which a person forms for the conduct of life'. In any significant period of our culture it has been impossible for serious literature not to be philosophical in these general, non-specialized senses. Literature cannot be the exploration of human thinking and feeling in relation to the conduct of personal life unless it is permeated with the sense of value, of the rightness and wrongness, goodness and badness of feelings and actions, not in any crude, moralistic way, but in the sense of the refining of intentions and emotions: the sense that 'ripeness is all'. It is hoped, therefore, that the use of the word 'philosophy' in the title may be accepted as legitimate and not pretentious. What may remain pretentious is the belief that the development of a particular 'philosophy' over two centuries can be validly com-pressed in the compass of a short book. The attempt may fail, but it may be worth trying.

Concepts and values have been the traditional matter of philosophy. By the 'philosophy of love' in literature is meant the changing ideas about love which literature has presented in relation to values, that is, to what is good for man, to what furthers or hinders his potential perfection. Philosophers from the time of Plato have theorized about love. So have theologians.[3] During the historical period covered by this book there was more theorizing about love than ever before, not only by humanist philosophers but by writers whose main concern was poetry or human behaviour. This book does not deal primarily with their ideas but with the literature (poetry, drama, prose fiction) which exemplified or drew upon particular theories of love. No writer can remain impervious to the views of life in his society. Up to the end of the sixteenth century, if a writer wished to communicate his own experience, he would generally do so indirectly, using a prevailing philosophy either to criticize it or, more commonly, to make his own personal experience more comprehensible and acceptable by this common standard. Or he would try, in the imaginative way proper to literature, to apply the accepted concepts to his own experience. He would be writing about love as he was experiencing it, or as he had experienced it, or as he would like to experience it. In every case he would be communicating a personal philosophy of love, more or less 'real', more or less theoretical. If 'real', he would be implicitly testing experience by theory or theory by experience. If he were communicating imagined experience with a theoretical orientation, he would be consciously or unconsciously trying to give love the central place in the art of living.

This book therefore deals essentially with literature and analyses it as such, but with literature whose central theme is love, whether human or divine. In endeavouring to interpret the meanings given to love recourse will be had to the ideas of prevailing philosophies of love, but this will be incidental to the primary aim of elucidating the concept of love in any particular work or author. The aim will be to make this elucidation as intelligible as possible despite the differences with the mental and cultural climate of today. If certain concepts were of prime importance to a great writer four centuries or more ago, they should have an intrinsic interest for us. Comprehension will necessitate a sympathetic approach. All literature can be read as if the ideas it expresses are true, which means that they should make sense within a historical context and form a coherent, mature and not childish view of life. It will be hard for many readers to accept as coherent and mature some of the ideas expounded in these pages. But that will most likely be due to their expression by particular authors and not to the 'philosophy'. Many of the expressions of Courtly Love in the Spanish fifteenth century are extravagant, even absurd, but what lies at the heart of the theory they extravagantly try to embody may be a human 'truth'. Truth of this kind is not a matter of philosophically meaningful propositions but something that touches instincts and feelings and makes a significant impact on the mind and heart of the reader.

Such an impact is impossible if sympathy is not aroused. All the systems of ideas expounded here will be presented sympathetically. This does not mean accepting them; it means the realization that they could be acceptable at a certain period of history to men of intelligence, imagination and feeling. Sympathy of this kind means, of course, approaching all such systems from their own premises and within their historical contexts. Thus Courtly Love, however absurd its statements, may become sympathetically intelligible in the light of the special tensions produced on traditional religion by the rise of humanism. Thus, too, sixteenth-century mysticism will be expounded, as St John of the Cross expounded it, within the context of the Christian Faith. This will not mean that any other form of mysticism lacks validity; nor will it mean that mystical experience of the kind described is a necessary accompaniment to religious faith.[4]

The term 'love' is used in this book in its full sense to encompass the love of men and women for each other, as well as the love of both for God. The standpoint followed is the one expressed by George Santayana in *The Life of Reason*: 'There can be no philosophic interest in disguising the animal basis of love, or in denying its spiritual sublimation, since all life is animal in its origin, all spiritual in its possible fruits'.[5] Love therefore means the free fulfilment of man's being in personal self-transcendence towards what is higher, either in an unselfish love of generosity, or in a love of desire which serves as a means to self-affirmation. Hope for personal fulfilment can open into the infinite and love is the means by which infinity can shine through a finite form. The hope for infinite fulfilment, however, must conflict with human limitation. If the two cannot come to terms, aspiration for perfection, or aspiration for the ideal, will come face to face with disillusion. This polarity between aspiration and disillusion, due to the clash between the ideal and the real, will form the continuous theme of this book.

Whatever may be the prevailing fashion of our time, love and idealism have been intimately associated in philosophy since Plato, and in literature most markedly since the rise of Courtly Love.[6] The fashion nowadays is openly to deride all ideals, or to belittle them by ignoring them. If this is an unalterable standpoint in the mind and sensibility of any reader, then he should perhaps proceed no further. Where moral ideals are concerned, the prevailing modern attitude is to be more interested in the breach than in the observance. If the ideal of chastity is professed by anyone, others will look for the secret love affairs that belie it in practice. It seems to be assumed that publicly avowed ideals must be hypocritical. No doubt they sometimes are but the fact that an ideal may not be continually fulfilled in practice is not a sign that belief in it or the intention to live by it are necessarily insincere. The cynical assertion that they must be so shows no faith in human nature and overlooks the fact that the ideals humanity has held to in the past were responsible for whatever betterment there has been in the moral development of humanity: '... he who finds (ideals) divine and congenial and is able to embody them at least in part and for a season, has to that extent transfigured life, turning it from a fatal process into a liberal art. A supreme ideal of peace and perfection which moves the lover, and which moves the sky, is more easily named than understood. The value of the notion to a poet or a philosopher does not lie in what it contains positively, but in the attitude it expresses. To have an ideal does not mean so much to have any image in the fancy, any Utopia more or less articulate, as rather to take a consistent moral attitude towards all the things of this world. . . .'[7] The growth of civilization has been a response to human belief that a state of perfection is theoretically conceivable and that it is possible in practice, under the pressure of this urge, to achieve some measure of success. A particular philosophy of life is to be judged on its merits as a 'philosophy', and not by the characters and conduct of those who profess it.

In the case of literature it is generally possible to detect hypo/ crisy or self/adulation by the quality of the language, which can be expressively powerful or intellectually weak and emotionally flabby; in either case the reader's response to the quality of the thought will be affected. In the selection here made from the Spanish literature of the period covered only good literature is presented unless a particular exception is noted. The selections are therefore presented as intellectually, emotionally and artistic/ ally sincere. A modern tendency in literary criticism is that such assumptions can only be subjective and should therefore not be made. This in itself assumes that thought, feelings and the various means of artistic expression are, or should be, objective in a 'scientific' sense. One may prefer to feed one's mind and sensibility, and form a faith by which to live, from the great thinkers and the great art of the past. The value for oneself of this communication with the past is in no way lessened by the fact that there was inevitably an element of subjectivity in the con/ frontation of all thinkers and artists with human life. Literary criticism that makes value judgements about the merits and demerits of literary works *as literature* cannot be objectively valid; it can only be convincing or plausible to the extent in which it might penetrate the barriers of the subjectivity of others.

A final prejudice that, if not consciously checked, may mis/ represent the aim of this book is associated with the rejection of the 'ideal' in favour of the 'real'. It is the requirement that all the experiences written about by a poet must be 'true' in the sense of actually lived by him. Literature, and particularly poetry, is not 'historically' but 'philosophically' true in accordance with the invaluable distinction made some 2300 years ago by Aristotle. Poetry sifts experience and records it through the imagination. Not only may the imagination transmute a lived experience, it may also invent an experience the poet never had and develop it as if he had lived or were living it. For the purposes of a philo/ sophy of life a poet's imagined experience is no less 'true' and 'sincere' than a 'real' one, and it is likely, indeed, to be far more significant, for the whole of his philosophy of life, acquired by learning, contemplation and living, may be brought to bear upon it.[8] This book has therefore been written on the assumption that the 'sincerity' of any poet, dramatist or novelist has nothing to do with fidelity to the writer's personal experience, but only with the quality of his creative imagination and of the artistry that gives it form. It also assumes that 'truthfulness' is not a question of experience as actually lived but a question of the relevance of the writer's imaginative creation to truth about human nature and about the deeper values of life.

A Wild Man lures men into imprisonment with the bait of an image of Venus, radiating a halo more appropriate to a Saint or the Virgin Mary.

ONE.

THE RELIGIOUS LANGUAGE
OF HUMAN LOVE

Courtly Love. the Courtly Love poetry of Castile. the religion of love.
Cárcel de Amor. Juan del ENCINA. *Amadís de Gaula*. Gil
VICENTE. *la Celestina*. Appendix.

COURTLY LOVE

Courtly Love is a comprehensive term, running from troubadour poetry to the chivalric romances, to the *dolce stil nuovo*, to
Petrarch and on to his influence in the Renaissance. In Spain,
characteristic Courtly Love themes are found throughout sixteenth-century poetry and are still evident in the powerful love
poetry of Quevedo in the seventeenth. The pages that follow
deal primarily with its Spanish form in the period 1450–1550,
but the question they raise for that period is analogous to one
that has been raised for troubadour poetry in the Middle Ages,
and the problems of literary interpretation that are involved are,
I think, similar in both periods. The evidence that Spanish
literature can offer in the discussion of the parallels and simi-
larities in the literary expression of sacred and profane love has
not really been examined in any depth and has therefore not
been given much importance. I shall suggest that literary
history may be the poorer for this.

The Courtly Love of the twelfth and thirteenth centuries is a
fascinating literary phenomenon because of the problems it
brings to the fore. Its sudden appearance in Provence around
1100 raises the question of its sources.[1] Some of the explanations
given relate it to religious, even mystical, traditions. Analogous
concepts were found in Islamic Sufism. Their development in
Arab Spain and their passage to Southern France has been
conjecturally traced.[2] Another theory concerns the influence of
contemporary Cistercian mysticism on the troubadours.[3] These

theories have proved controversial enough, but the most controversial of all is the one developed by Denis de Rougemont in *L'Amour et L'Occident*.[4] The simultaneous appearance in the same area of France of a peculiar type of love poetry and of the heresy of the Albigensians is for him no coincidence. The most peculiar feature of the poetry is that in the midst of an ostensibly Christian culture it sings of an adulterous or illicit love. There is no sign of a morally disciplined human love, socially ordered and fulfilled in Christian marriage; instead love is some sort of dark irrational passion obsessed with death. De Rougemont interprets the poetry as a veiled duplicity that says one thing and means another; as, in fact, references to the Gnostic or Manichaean features of the new heresy, and thus as a form of mystical religion, a devotion to the Catharist Church of Love, and therefore as a perverted and despairing version of the Christian faith. The fatal passion of Tristan he sees as a hunger that refuses everything that can appease it; rather than hunger it is an intoxication and 'tout érotomane est un mystique qui s'ignore.'[5] The true meaning of the images and symbols of the troubadours was later lost, and they became a rhetoric of orthodoxy, in the mysticism of the Franciscans, in the poetry of Jacopone da Todi and eventually, and above all, in the great Spanish mystics of the sixteenth century, St Teresa of Avila and St John of the Cross, whose apparently passionate and erotic language has often been an embarrassment not only to theologians but also to the ordinary reader anxious to read their works as treatises of a purely spiritual love. De Rougemont's paradoxical explanation for this is neatly summed up: 'le langage de la passion humaine selon l'hérésie correspond au langage de la passion divine selon l'orthodoxie'.[6]

I am not concerned with the details of de Rougemont's analysis or with its plausibility, but only to recall this extreme connection of Courtly Love with mystical religion. The theory must exercise fascination for anyone primarily interested in the history of religious thought and feeling, but the literary critic must have very serious reservations. An example of the former is the theologian and scholastic philosopher Martin D'Arcy, in

his magisterial work *The Mind and Heart of Love*.[7] He cannot
accept de Rougemont's theory and indeed he refutes it as
regards the Christian mystics; none the less he clearly remains
haunted by this vision of a passionate, punitive, dark Eros in
conflict with the Christian Agape. What I wish specifically to
call attention to in this theory are the parallels de Rougemont
draws between the concepts and language of Courtly Love and
those of the Spanish mystics: he enumerates fifteen principal
themes common to both. One of these seems to me of primary
importance: the emphasis on suffering and St John of the
Cross's doctrine of the Dark Night. I shall come to this in due
course.[8]

The second problem raised by Courtly Love which is
relevant to this study is whether it is human love idealized, or
whether at bottom it is inherently sensual. For long what was
stressed was idealization: *courtoisie* came to transform the gross-
ness of sexuality into a refined conception of love that stressed
the nobility of chastity. Earlier this century, Edward Wechssler
in his study of German *Minnesang* could seek to bridge the gap
between the worldly and the religious by stressing the non-
sensual element in this poetry, whereby the service of women
was approximated to the service of God by means of analogies
that were idealistic and not irreverent.[9] More recently, however,
scholars have tended to move in the opposite direction and to
deny this idealism by affirming the inherent sensuality of the
tradition. An important work published in 1965 by the Cambridge scholar Peter Dronke placed the Courtly Love of the
troubadours in a wider cultural setting than previously, and
challenged all the assumptions upon which its interpretation
had been traditionally placed.[10] One of these was that the love
the troubadours sing of is quasi-Platonic, a desire that should
remain unfulfilled in order not to lessen its nobility. Dronke
maintained that there is no support in Provençal poetry itself for
this belief and quoted with approval an earlier study by Mrs
D. R. Sutherland in which she wrote:

On the question of pure love eschewing intercourse but allowing everything short of possession, it is true that the poets do not mention possession, but it is difficult to see how they could in a poetry meant for public recital in circles with pretensions to delicacy and refinement, and often in the presence of the *donna* herself; they ask for the favours it is decent to ask for publicly, and they go as far as decency allows.[11]

It may be argued, however, that what is important is not the fact that the poets *could* not mention possession, but that they *did* not: one has to interpret literature by what it says, not by what it does not say. There is surely no reason why the reticence that can be postulated in troubadour poetry should invalidate the interpretation along quasi-Platonic lines of what, in very many instances, the poems actually say. Moreover, while within the courtly manners of life in Provence reticence could be accepted as a convention, in other environments and in later ages the absence of any mention of possession could be rightly taken not negatively but as a positive ideal of self-denial.

One must never forget the dangers of generalizing about Courtly Love as if the concept and its expressions were uniform over four or five centuries: at some times the basic attitude may be idealized, at others sensual. After the crusade that persecuted and massacred the Albigensians, and the consequent establishment of the Inquisition, sensuality had to be veiled, or else the poet hypocritically waved it away. There is the case of Sordello, an ardent champion of chaste or Platonic love, who was a well-known libertine in real life.[12] There thus arises the problem of sincerity. What do the poets really mean? What is the connection between what they appear to say and their own experience? Moreover, the modern tendency to discount all expressed idealization has increased the embarrassment felt at the erotic language of the medieval Christian mystics and the Spaniards. If Courtly Love is inherently sensual, then this mysticism would seem to be at best a self-deluding sublimation of sexuality. The problem of the relation of poetry to experience is thus acute here also.

Provençal scholarship itself, as distinct from the scholarship of the medieval latinist, does reaffirm the tradition of idealization in medieval Courtly Love. René Nelli, in his fascinating work *L'Érotique des troubadours*, made a basic distinction by dividing the theory of love in Provençal literature into two main tendencies or strands: 'amour chivalresque' and 'amour courtois'.[13] The former, which appears first and is presented in the long epics and later prose romances of France, idealizes sexual love by subjecting it to honour and making it dependent on certain masculine virtues such as courage, liberality, loyalty. It is relatively chaste to the extent that it is loyalty to one woman alone but it is not necessarily continence, for the law of chivalry demanded that the lady should eventually recompense her faithful servant by concrete favours. 'Amour courtois', on the other hand, which was confined at first to lyrical poetry, was an attachment by the poet, generally to a lady of the upper classes who was married, and in this respect it was 'adulterous', but only in the sense that fulfilment would have constituted adultery. Fulfilment, however, was not intended or expected. This may have made the attachment more exciting by giving it 'spice', but the relationship does not appear to have been considered morally reprehensible. It meant total submission in service to the lady, and was based on the belief that such love revealed, expressed and nurtured the virtues of the well-born lover, virtues that centred on purity and chastity.[14]

It may be argued that the strands Nelli distinguished in Provençal literature co-exist also in all the literature that derives ultimately from Provence.[15] The 'courtly' and the 'chivalresque' obviously run together, it being the existence of the latter that has made so many critics deny the 'Platonism' of the former, but there is a clear, definable distinction. 'Courtly' is the impossible love for an unattainable woman, in which there is an enforced continence that causes suffering. In 'chivalresque' there is no impossible love; continence is temporary and a service to be rendered in order to merit fulfilment. The modern mind is not likely to see any essential difference, but for literature the distinction is clear in plot and tone. In Spanish literature 'chivalresque' love informs the novels of chivalry and eventually becomes the ideal love of Cervantes, while the Courtly Love of the fifteenth century develops into sixteenth-century Neoplatonism.

The Courtly Love Poetry of Castile

In Spain, the influence of Provençal poetry is visible in Galician poetry of the thirteenth century and in Catalan literature. In Castile itself the characteristic features of Courtly Love do not appear until the fifteenth century. The lyrical poetry of this period was collected in a series of anthologies, called *cancioneros*. In one of the earliest of these, the *Cancionero de Baena*, most of the poems are moral and didactic, dealing with religion, death, the uncertainty of worldly Fortune, and so on; very little prominence is given to the theme of love. But in other *cancioneros* nearly all the poems are love poems of a type new to Castile. There are literally hundreds of these poems and every one assumes or expounds the same conception of human love. Ostensibly and for the most part this is based not on the physical and the sensuous, but on love as the faithful service of a lady who never rewards her servant, a love from which there is no escape and which therefore produces a suffering akin to death; but this suffering is not only accepted, it is actually desired and found pleasurable. The lover is condemned by fate to love faithfully, without hope of happiness; yet better this living death than not to love at all. This form of Courtly Love is frequently expressed in religious terms: for instance, the liturgical prayers of the Church or the psalms of the Old Testament are used as prayers to Cupid, the god of love, the suffering and passion of the lover are even equated with the passion of Christ, and the lover is often presented as a martyr for his faith. In fifteenth-century Spain this Religion of Love takes much more extravagant forms than it had earlier taken in France.

The Courtly Love poetry of the *cancioneros* was not taken seriously by literary critics until fairly recently mainly because it did not conform to the post-Romantic requirement that poetry should be the sincere expression of genuine personal feelings aroused by direct experience. For this late Courtly Love poetry in Spain is conventional through and through. The conventionality of the literary form by itself suggests that this conception of love was an artificial attitude to life, the extravagant expression of an impossible ideal. Such artificiality is significant. The conventions of literature should not be lightly dismissed for they can be seen to have a purpose. Whatever becomes a prevalent fashion must give pleasure to its readers, and therefore the fashions of literature must all in their time have satisfied some need. A poetic convention divorced from reality points to some sort of aspiration or ideal. If fifteenth-century poets found satisfaction in posing as suffering martyrs of love are we not justified in concluding that they would have liked to be such ? In other words, that this convention was a kind of wish-fulfilment, an attempt to envisage a pure and perfect love by conceiving it as a self-sacrificing and therefore ennobling devotion ?

When this poetry was first taken seriously, the element of idealization is what was stressed, notably by Pedro Salinas who, in his book on Jorge Manrique, emphasized the idealism exclusively, affirming: 'Everything, love and suffering, constancy and sadness, is directed to the common aim of elevating the human being to the peak of his capacity for noble living'.[16] But this valuable approach has not been developed further by many subsequent scholars. Instead, the anti-idealistic reaction to Courtly Love has spread to the Spanish *cancionero* poetry. Keith Whinnom, for example, and the late Royston Jones, have both seen the convention of love from afar, unfulfilled and suffering, as merely a hypocritical reticence cloaking ideas and sentiments that are sensual and, indeed, licentious. Whinnom has even suggested that the standard imagery of the poems is a code of *double entendres*, whereby each key-word takes on a directly sexual connotation.[17] To accept most of this poetry as idealistic is in fact far from easy, for if the statements of the *cancionero* poets are taken at their face value one is bound to find them unhealthy and morbid. Love is suffering, but the lover cannot escape because he cannot forsake his lady; forced to love without reward, his life becomes a living death which makes death itself something to be vehemently desired as a release; but from the suffering itself the poets seek no release, on the contrary they welcome it as a means of proving their love. On the purely human level, this cult of suffering, this equation of love with death and the longing for death, represent the abdication of all rationality, the subordination of reason to passion; and this, according to Jones, is because the sensuality inherent in Courtly Love is allowed free reign and is indulged in as an unchecked desire.[18] Courtly Love, in this view, therefore represents a moral disorder and a disease of the mind precisely because it is inherently and unrestrainedly sensual.

If this trend in recent scholarship is well-founded and if the Courtly Love tradition throughout its long history is indeed inherently and essentially sensual, then theologians have had good reason to be embarrassed at the analogies between Courtly Love and Christian mystical literature. But I do not think that this is the case. It is important, in my opinion, to see an essential difference between a poetry that sings of sexual *pleasure* and a poetry that sings of *desire*. Love as desire, in the Courtly Love tradition, is generally presented as continence, but it does not on that account cease to be carnal, since carnal union is what is desired; nevertheless it remains an *aspiration* and does not become *achievement*. This distinction is fundamental.

One of the important Spanish verse anthologies is the *Cancionero de Palacio*, compiled about 1440.[19] The manuscript contains ornamental initial letters with drawings of human figures; these latter have been inked over by a later hand but it is still possible to detect that the drawings are clearly erotic, though not exactly obscene. In discussing the themes of the poems, Francisca Vendrell, their modern editor, wrote: 'The love of the poets was platonic, their waiting endless, and the frequent inaccessibility of the lady made each poet solemnly assert his fidelity and constancy'.[20] Professor Whinnom has maintained that in the light of the erotic miniatures it is absurd and unhistorical to call this poetry 'Platonic'.[21] Obviously, the miniatures place the poems in an erotic environment; certainly they were not presented by the scribe as chaste poems or taken by the owners of the codex to be such. The poems, however, were born and continued to live outside the covers of this codex, and we must guard against allowing external circumstances to make the poems mean more than they say. What they actually say is that the lady is inaccessible and that love remains unfulfilled. It may well be that the absence of chastity in the poets' own lives and the general laxity of the society in which they moved gave these poems a certain piquant ambiguity within that society, but this is a matter of social not literary context, and we are not entitled to say that a poem must always mean a certain thing despite the different social contexts in which it is read.

The difference of social context must be borne in mind when considering the analogies between Courtly Love poetry and mystical literature. This may be illustrated by an episode in the life of St John of the Cross. After escaping from his confinement in Toledo, he journeyed to Andalusia, and stopping at Beas he called to see the nuns at a newly founded Carmelite convent there. His journey and the fact that he had been undergoing a period of intense strain in the affairs of his order had made him very tired. In order to relax him the Prioress told two of the nuns to sing him a song. They sang this:

> Quien no sabe de penas
> en este (triste) valle de dolores,
> no sabe de cosas buenas,
> ni ha gustado de amores,
> pues penas es el traje de amadores.

> He who has not experienced suffering in this (sad) vale of sorrows, has neither experienced the good of life, nor tasted love, for suffering is the garb of lovers.

When they had sung this first verse St John asked them to stop and he gripped the bars of the grille in order to try to prevent the trance that he felt overtaking him. He remained in it for an hour, and on emerging he spoke to the nuns of the spritual value of suffering and of how little he had yet been called upon to suffer for the love of God. This poem has been discovered in a manuscript collection. It is, in fact, a religious poem, and its obscure author has been identified as a member of a religious order, but there is nothing in the stanza that sent St John into ecstasy to indicate this.[22] In fact, apart from the *lira* metre which denotes a later date, there is no reason why this stanza could not be perfectly at home in the *Cancionero de Palacio*, despite the latter's miniatures, because it fits perfectly into the subject matter of Courtly Love poetry.

One further example. Among the poems of St John of the Cross there has always appeared one that begins:

> Un pastorcico solo está penado,
> ajeno de placer y de contento,
> y en su pastora puesto el pensamiento,
> y el pecho del amor muy lastimado.

> A young shepherd is grieving in solitude, bereft of pleasure and contentment; his thoughts are on his shepherdess, and his breast is wounded with love.

It is now known that this is not an original work by St John but his refashioning of a human love poem in the courtly tradition of suffering love. It consists of five stanzas of which St John composed only the last in order to transpose the shepherd's suffering into the Passion of Christ, which is the meaning he read into the first four stanzas that he altered only slightly.[23]

Within the social context of Carmelite convents the poem on the suffering shepherd and the one on the lover's garb of suffering which sent St John into ecstasy meant only one thing. Put into the social context of the *Cancionero de Palacio* they would have meant something quite different and might well have been given a specifically sexual connotation, since nothing is easier than to find *double entendres* of this kind if one has a mind to. The point is that one cannot really appreciate the poetry of the pre-Renaissance if one asserts that the Courtly Love tradition is *inherently* sensual and if one thus ignores the essential ambiguity or ambivalence of the tradition whereby sacred and profane love spoke the same poetic language. Although the poetry of profane love deals with carnal desire it does not on the whole deal with carnal pleasure. It is, in the form in which it is expressed, desire without fulfilment. I repeat that this is an important distinction because it is here that ambivalence enters. Whatever the sexual undertones may be within the social context, the dominant note of this poetry is, in fact, the suffering of unfulfilment. What this poetry actually says is that love is a service which one is not free to reject; that constancy in faith through loyalty in this service ennobles the lover; that the suffering of unfulfilment is akin to death, yet this suffering is not only accepted but desired as a part of this service; and that although death can bring release it is less desirable than the suffering itself, which is desired for its own sake as the proof of love.

Now none of this makes any rational sense in connection with human love, and if this is taken as a statement of actual human loving, then without question it is morbid. Indeed a few years ago there appeared in the *Psychoanalytic Review* an article entitled 'Courtly Love: Neurosis as Institution': It is by Melvin Askew, who calls Courtly Love 'one of the most monumentally neurotic structures in all literature', saying of one of its chief neurotic symptoms:

> the pained pleasure of many courtly lovers, and particularly of the pure ones, is a narcissistic and self-destructive pleasure derived either from separation or from constantly beholding a ravishingly beautiful but unattainable woman or ideal.[24]

The reason why this poetry makes no rational sense for human love is because it uses the concepts and language of something different: of religion. It makes sense all the time in terms of divine love within the tradition of medieval Christianity. The Flemish mystic Ruysbroeck had called the love of God an irresistible desire continually to attain the unattainable, in which the object of desire is neither attainable nor can it be abandoned.[25] Transposed into the context of human love this religious concept becomes a poetic convention.

Past literary conventions of this kind are important. They can

act as wish-fulfilments and mirror either conscious or unconscious aspirations. If the *cancionero* poets took pleasure in
posing as suffering martyrs of love, they must have done so
because they thought it the noblest expression of the highest
form of love. This they had learned from religion not from life.[26]
It is perfectly true to say with psychologists that the human love
so expressed is the negation of positive human values and therefore morbid, but this does not explain the poetry. If it is to be
explained, account must be taken of the ambivalence of the
language of love whereby religious concepts were used for a
human ideal. In the 'Ages of Faith' there was theoretically no
dispute about the order of values: divine love had priority over
human love and the latter was undervalued. It may be held that
the Courtly Love phenomenon was part of a reaction against
this undervaluation, an attempt to give human love a value in
its own right. The fifteenth century witnessed in many sectors a
weakening of religious faith. The humanism of the Renaissance
was not only a revival of classsical languages and literatures; it
was an attempt to rectify the balance of priorities by giving back
to the sphere of the human much of what, it was then felt, had
been unjustly arrogated to the sphere of the divine. No speedy
revaluation of sex could be attempted; a beginning had to be
made by placing love between man and woman only a little
above animal instinct. The language whereby woman was
'deified', and man gave her total submission in 'faith' was a
metaphorical expression of this ennoblement.

THE RELIGION OF LOVE

Cárcel de Amor. The most striking example of this humanistic
Religion of Love in Spanish literature is a novel that was an
international best-seller: *Cárcel de amor* (Prison of Love) by
Diego de San Pedro (1437?–1498?), published in Seville in
1492.[27] It is perhaps the most remarkable example in all
European literature of the confluence of the sacred and the
profane. In the novel love, being without hope of fulfilment, is
presented as *faith*, a faith and a consequent suffering which,
fully accepted, ennoble the lover. Woman, aloof and unattain-

able, is the source of grace, infusing into the lover not only the cardinal virtues but also the theological virtues of faith, hope and charity. Since woman is the object of the lover's faith, the supreme value in which he believes, human love is unequivo-cally associated with the mystical union of the soul and God and the martyrdom of love is explicitly associated with the stigmata, namely the representation of the wounds of Christ that appear on the hands, feet and side of some mystics. For the lover is presented as a martyr for his faith, and what is more, his martyrdom is identified with the passion of Christ. When the hero of the novel falls in love he is symbolically crowned with thorns and scourged. In order to prove his love by the supreme sacrifice he chooses death after having attained a eucharistic communion with his beloved by tearing her letters into pieces, placing them in a chalice and swallowing them.

The vogue enjoyed by this novel[28] points to the widespread popularity of a spiritualized mystical conception of human love, of an attempt to centre the highest values of life in the love of man for woman. Because this was remote from actual experi-ence, the plot of the novel is unfolded in an unrealistic setting, in a largely allegorical form. The basic divorce from reality lies in the separation of love from the physical, for this particular idealization of love in religious, mystical terms could find no room for sensuality; it aspired, in fact, not to refine the sensual but to transcend it. The suffering of the literary lovers is the flesh seeking to assert itself against the ideal of a spiritualized and therefore chaste love.[29]

Such an equation of love and religion is, if taken literally, the height not just of extravagance but of blasphemy, but it de-mands to be taken seriously as an attempt to raise human eroticism onto a plane of positive value away from its century-long association with the capital sin of lust. The extravagant form that this took is understandable in a period marked both by the decline of religious faith in the direction of secularism and by its counterpart, the revival of religion in what was to become a militant form. The end of the fifteenth century saw the estab-lishment of the Inquisition in Spain on the verge of the country's unification. In a country divided for centuries into three religions, and now with dissatisfied and resentful Moslem and Jewish minorities, unity was sought by the repression of heresies, which were suspected, above all, among the nominally Christianized Jews. Diego de San Pedro felt obliged to write a recantation of his *Cárcel de amor* and other works, which he came to stigmatize, whether sincerely or not, as 'salsa para pecar', namely, a spice to stimulate a sinful appetite, and the novel was eventually condemned by the Inquisition.[30] Nevertheless the *Cárcel de amor* was not deliberately or maliciously blasphemous, but a serious though misguided attempt to conceive and express a perfect love, or the perfectability of man through love, which is what the poetry of the age was also trying to conceive and express.

To be shocked at this literature because of its irreverence or hypocrisy, in the belief that the authors who wrote like this could not seriously have believed in the claims of religion, is a modern attitude and unhistorical. By equating human love with the values of religion, they were seeking to praise and exalt love, not to decry or mock at religion. Everybody, theologian and poet alike, sincerely believed that human salvation was to be achieved through love. The question was at what point down the scale of Being did love cease to be redemptive. The Inquisition and San Pedro himself decided he had gone too far, but in the direction not of belittling religion but of extolling woman too highly.

Juan del Encina. With the revival of classical studies and the liberal, tolerant mentality that this new education fostered, praise of love could still take an irreligious form but one that was less reprehensible because it was now endowed with the aura of the classics. Juan del Encina (1469–1529?) began by writing, for performance in the household of the Duke of Alba, Christmas and Easter plays of the traditional liturgical type in which secular elements came to predominate. He finished his career by writing two eclogues, pastoral plays in which the 'paganism' of the Italian Renaissance left its mark.[31] The first of these is the *Égloga de Cristino y Febea.* Cristino, disillusioned with the world and its illusory pleasures, decides to seek spiritual perfection in the penitential life of a hermit, from which he will not permit himself to be dissuaded, but Cupid is angry when he hears of Cristino's desertion and orders the nymph Febea to win him back to reason. She proceeds to tempt the new hermit who, unable to resist her charms, abandons the ascetic life in order to return to the service of the god of love. The theme is the repudiation of Christian asceticism, the triumph of the flesh over the spirit, with the assertion of the superiority of profane over sacred love: the hermit's life is fit only for centenarians who cannot feel the call of love; the shepherd's life, on the other hand, should be one of joyful pleasure. Though common enough in Renaissance literature this theme is rare in Spain. There is no reason to suppose that it was taken very seriously by Encina's aristocratic patron: the play could well be produced as a comedy.

The second play is perhaps another matter. In the *Égloga de Plácida y Victoriano* two lovers quarrel, and the shepherd tries to forget his shepherdess by turning to other women. He finds, however, that he cannot ignore the love he feels for her, and so he decides to return; but he learns that she, in despair, has committed suicide, unable to overcome the unhappiness of losing him. When he discovers her dead body he decides to commit suicide too, but he is prevented by the sudden appearance of Venus who says that his shepherdess will be restored to life. The lovers are thus reunited in happiness. The conception of love as a tragic nemesis, characteristic of Spanish literature in the fifteenth century, is overcome here by the intervention of the 'supernatural', represented by a pagan divinity who rules in the affairs of men not malignantly but beneficently and who rewards her faithful servants with happiness. This play continues the Religion of Love, though in an altered form, in that the pagan gods are invoked in words that directly echo Christian prayers.

In these eclogues of Encina the element of profanity has mellowed, and is much less surprising than in the previous generation. It fails to 'shock' and is an unsubtle way of exalting the rights and values of erotic experience, but insofar as it does this it is a facet of expanding humanism in the widest sense: not just the revival of the classics but the transference of ideal values from the exclusively supernatural sphere to the natural.

Amadís de Gaula. This concern with purely human values rather than divine or religious ones is also apparent in the novels of chivalry. Chivalry and Courtly Love, though distinct, are aspects of the same cultural development. The ideal knight was also the ideal lover; both represented the ennobling of humanity through the altruistic ideal of service and the rejection of self-seeking. *Amadís de Gaula* is not the first Spanish novel of chivalry, but it initiated the great vogue of this *genre* in the sixteenth century, and, like the *Cárcel de amor*, it became known and influential abroad.[32] The form in which we know it dates from 1508 and is the recasting by Garci Rodríguez de Montalvo of an earlier work, of which only some fragments survive.[33]

The world of chivalry in *Amadís* is one that never existed nor could have existed in space and time, and the novel may be considered as a narrative form of myth in which the main concern is 'the imitation of actions near or at the conceivable limits of desire'.[34] The birth and upbringing of Amadís follow the mythical patterns of the birth of the hero, and his story follows a heroic sequence of winning for himself a name, territory, a crown and a queen, all this in the fight for justice against oppression and treachery. This pattern is archetypal, and the symbols and archetypes which fill the novel have been given a most interesting interpretation by Yolanda Russinovich de Solé who argues, in accordance with Jungian theories, that the work draws on a deep-rooted tradition with its origins in the Unconscious.[35] But although this approach is convincing in symbolical and allegorical terms it would be mistaken to conclude that the compilers of the *Amadís* material, ending with Montalvo, were mere instruments through which the Collective Unconscious found expression. They were consciously using the underlying pattern of heroic story for a particular purpose, that of representing the human ideal as they and their times saw it, the ideal of the perfect knight and the perfect lover, the two all-embracing aspects of human activity.

Despite the complete unreality of its setting, *Amadís* does present a certain ideal of personality. There is a nostalgic idealization of the virtues of bravery, magnanimity, loyalty and abnegation, and these chivalrous virtues are presented almost exclusively in relation to love. When Amadís is knighted (Chapter 4) the event is a symbolical rite of transition from adolescence to manhood. He keeps a vigil of his arms before the altar, and this ceremony, the outward sign of his dedication to God, is analogous to that of ordination to the priesthood. His arming is performed at the special request of two young women, Oriana and Mabilia, and it is witnessed by them, and by all the Queen's handmaidens, with delight, for Amadís is to be the ladies' champion.

When Amadís sets out in search of adventures it is significant that his first one does not concern injustice but one of the evils that threatens ideal love, namely adultery. In a forest he finds a dead knight; another is wounded, and a woman is trying to kill him by thrusting her hands into his wounds to prevent them from closing (Chapter 4). The wounded man is her husband and the dead man her lover whom her husband has killed. The third adventure takes place at the Castle of Galpano, a very proud knight who prefers the service of the Evil Enemy to that of the Higher Lord (Chapters 5 and 6). He represents another of the enemies of love, sensuality. All women who pass by are invited into his castle and forced to swear that they will never have relations with another man; if they refuse they are beheaded. Amadís kills him, and absolves his last victim from her oath. In Chapter 73 there appears the most hideous of the enemies of love, the Endriago, a monster born of a woman who had seduced her father and then murdered her mother in order to continue relations with him. This represents lust in its most brutal form.

The concept of love is chivalresque-courtly throughout. Amadís is the perfect knight, devoted and self-sacrificing in relation to his beloved. Despite the passion felt for him by the young and beautiful Briolanja he never accedes to her open requests and remains faithful to his lady.[36] She, Oriana, implicitly usurps the place of the divine: it is she who calls forth adoration and devotion in the knight, it is for her sake and to prove his faith that he lives ascetically and even undergoes penance. Love and the adoration of women are the centre and circumference of life, and true love is imbued with an aspiration to chastity and purity which makes Oriana, in effect, equivalent to a goddess placed high on a pedestal.

The description of how Amadís, aged 12, and Oriana, aged 10, fall in love at first sight (Chapter 4) is a strangely touching episode in this idealized world. Their unspoken and therefore uncorresponded love brings to the man a torment akin to death, and must strike a modern reader unfamiliar with this convention as languid and unreal. There is in fact an extraordinary disparity between the unlimited bravery of the knight in the midst of ferocious fighting and his unmanly bearing where love is concerned. This is due to the reversal of the male and female roles: the lady is the lord and master, the lover is the servant and the slave. Hence the weeping and the swooning which are the reactions of Amadís when he hears Oriana's name, or receives a letter from her breaking off relations: he faints on his horse and is carried away senseless (Chapter 45). The medieval warrior has become a man of excessive sensibility.

Moreover, although lovers consummate their passion, usually taking secret vows, they do not always marry and they never disclose their attachments.[37] Amadís is born of an overwhelming passion that his mother, Elisena, feels for Perión when he visits the Court of Little Britain. They separate, to be reunited and married only several years later. Similarly Amadís and Oriana, who consummate their love relatively early (Chapter 35), keep their relationship secret until they are married at the end of the work. The primitive version finished with the death of Amadís at the hands of his own son, Esplandián, and this was followed by the suicide of Oriana. Montalvo removed this ending and his story ends happily with the marriage of Amadís and Oriana. Yet Amadís never asks Lisuarte for Oriana's hand, and he does not think of marrying her until her father's decision to give her to the Roman Emperor precipitates the final crisis between the King and himself. Even then this possible reason is never actually mentioned. These are the conventions of Courtly Love and chivalry: marriage has nothing to do with love, it is a duty and not, like love, a voluntary submission that holds the will.

Gil Vicente. Knight-errantry enters the early drama with the distinguished Portuguese court playwright, Gil Vicente (1465?-1536?), a splendid lyrical poet well known for his comic genius, which was certainly in advance of his times. This quality, together with the fact that the late form of Courtly Love strikes the modern reader as absurd, and therefore funny, has made a modern editor conclude that Gil Vicente was ridiculing this particular philosophy of love and the whole heroic ideal in his own *Amadís de Gaula*, which deals with the most dramatic part of the novel, the rift with Oriana over the knight's supposed infidelity.[38] The concepts of fidelity, suffering and penance can be readily, even sympathetically, understood in the light of sixteenth-century literature and its ideals, but they can be easily misunderstood in terms of modern views of love. Thus T.P. Waldron interprets the play as an ironical, even satirical, treatment of the heroic theme. Nobody had noticed this before, however, and it is arguable that the comic element of ridicule is centred in secondary characters who exemplify the ways in which men fall short of, or oppose, ideal values.[39]

A second play on a chivalresque theme by Vicente is far superior to his *Amadís*. This is *Don Duardos*, which contains a Don-Quixote-like parody of a knight errant.[40] It was probably written between 1521 and 1525, and is based on an episode in the second novel of the *Palmerín* cycle, *Primaleón*, a famous work in its day, published in 1512. Duardos, a Prince of England, comes to the court of the Emperor at Constantinople to challenge Primaleón, the Emperor's son, to combat for having killed the knight loved by a certain lady, Gridonia, whom Duardos has promised to avenge. They begin to fight, but the Emperor orders his daughter, Flérida, to separate them. Duardos is at once smitten with love for her, and withdraws.

Fearing that Flérida will be very hard to win he accepts the advice to disguise himself as a gardener in order to work in her garden where he will be able to see her and talk to her. He gives her water in a magic goblet in order to make her fall in love with him, a scene in Vicente's source to which he gives no actual dramatic function: it is merely symbolical of the power of love. Flérida, by a series of delicately rendered emotional graduations that are perfectly natural, gradually falls in love with Duardos.

A princess, of course, cannot love a gardener, yet she cannot resist her destiny. Love makes her think that he must be more than a gardener, and she sends one of her maidens to discover who he really is, but he refuses to disclose his identity, insisting that even though he be a villain his love is noble and she must love him for his own sake. Later, when Duardos defeats the Quixotic knight who has meanwhile insulted Flérida, he can appear before her in his true colours as a prince, but he still refuses to reveal who he is and where he comes from, asking her to sail with him for a destination he will not disclose. She consents, acknowledging that her love for him makes it immaterial who he is or where he lives, and so she does launch out into the unknown in answer to the call of love.

This play, more a dramatic poem than poetic drama, is a moving expression of the concept of love as an ineluctable destiny. Flérida does not actually have to choose whether to abandon her love or to marry far beneath her social status, for it would have been impossible to make marriage with a real gardener acceptable in that age to any cultured audience, let alone to the court, but the problem is posed and the overriding compulsion of love is powerfully affirmed. The impediment of social class to the free acceptance of destiny was to become a standard theme in Spanish literature, in the drama more frequently than in the novel, but in this case the problem was in principle non-existent. Social conventions and prejudices might intervene in reality, but this would be an outrage against human nature. Obedience to the call of destiny lies for Flérida in the insistence of Duardos that she love him for his own sake, which she finally does. Love is not presented as a destiny that offers only a vocation to suffering. In this respect the difference between *Don Duardos* and the *Cárcel de Amor* is striking. The concept of ideal love can now embrace the prospect of happiness in sexual union and in marriage.[41]

La Celestina. A powerful counterweight to the Religion of Love appeared in the *Tragicomedia de Calisto y Melibea* by Fernando de Rojas (d. 1541)[42] This famous work is a master-piece of European literature. Calisto, a young nobleman, well-to-do, well thought of and in no way personally reprehensible, falls in love at first sight with Melibea, the young daughter of a merchant. Instead of seeking her hand in marriage he exchanges messages and secretly gains access to her through the mediation of Celestina, an old bawd, who has a reputation for practising witchcraft.[43] Melibea falls as passionately in love with him as he with her. Her seduction is quickly accomplished and is followed by secret nightly meetings in the garden of her home. Calisto, climbing over the garden wall after one such meeting, falls and is killed. The disconsolate Melibea commits suicide by throwing herself from the top storey of her house.

Calisto's reactions and his words when he first sees Melibea are those of an impassioned devotee of Courtly Love. The equivalent of the stage directions state that he sees her when he follows his falcon into her garden, but the dialogue clearly indicates that they meet in a church.[44] His first words to her are that he now has proof of God's greatness when he sees her endowed with every perfection of beauty, and in the fact that he has received the great reward of being able to declare to her in person his suffering love. This reward is incomparably greater than any he could hope for, in this particular place, from devotions, prayers, pious practices and charitable good works. His body now is more glorified than any human body has ever been. Not even the saints in heaven, who enjoy the vision of God, can equal his glorious happiness; the difference between them and him, however, is that they cannot fall from their state of beautitude, while he fears to fall into the direst torment when she absents herself. Later, when describing his new passion to his confidential servant in equally blasphemous language, the latter, shocked, retorts '¿Tú no eres cristiano?' [Are you not a Christian?] and Calisto replies, 'Melibeo soy y a Melibea adoro y en Melibea creo y a Melibea amo' [I am a Melibean, and I adore Melibea, and I believe in Melibea, and I love Melibea] (Act I, pp.49–50).

This uncompromising assertion of the Religion of Love does not occur in an allegorical or a socially idealized setting. Calisto and his servant are inhabitants of the real world and they speak the language of everyday life. Calisto, like his literary predecessors, is making his love for a woman usurp the place of the Christian Creed, but he cannot raise his servants and his environment to such a level. For the first time in Spanish literature the Religion of Love is confronted with the world of sordid reality.[45] His servant scoffs at his ridiculous folly and tears away the covering of idealization by recommending Celestina as the mediator between him and his love, thus placing this love in its natural setting. He makes no attempt to disguise what she really is, but paints her and her prostitutes in their true colours. Calisto will not or cannot heed this, and when she appears he praises her and honours her and is immediately free with the gold that will merit his heaven. The gulf between the ideal and the real is stark. The desire for a woman, paraded as equivalent to the adoration of God, is in fact a venal offering to the world of prostitution, and the god-like Melibea is degraded accordingly. Thus when their first meeting materializes, Calisto's love is far from ideal: it finds expression in impetuous seduction, and after this event Melibea's passion for him settles on the same level.

This is neither an ironical nor a cynical exposure of the self-deception of idealizing the human; it becomes a deeply pessimistic view of human love. Melibea is not swept off her feet by any divine rapture: when she hears of Calisto's death she cries out '¿Cómo no gocé más del gozo?' [Why did I not enjoy my enjoyment more?] (Act 19, p.225) although she had enjoyed it to the full. Sexual passion does not destroy human longing for the absolute and the enduring, but human nature can conceal its disfigurement. 'Why did I not enjoy my enjoyment more?' is a humanistic cry of despair in face of death. There is no beneficent power shaping ends for the two young lovers; there is only a void into which Melibea unhesitatingly hurls herself.

Pessimism shapes the tragic utterances of Pleberio, her father, as he gazes on the broken body of his only child. This is what her passion has brought her; this is what his fulfilled love in a hitherto happy marriage has brought him. The happiness, however, has been a delusion for behind it there has lain his own guilt demanding expiation:

> ¡Oh amor, amor, que no pensé que tenías fuerza ni poder de matar a tus sujetos! Herida fue de ti mi juventud, por medio de tus brasas pasé. ¿Cómo me soltaste, para me dar la paga de la huida en mi vejez? Bien pensé que de tus lazos me había librado, cuando los cuarenta años toqué, cuando fui contento con mi conyugal compañera, cuando me vi con el fruto que me cortaste el día de hoy. No pensé que tomabas en los hijos la venganza de los padres.

> Oh Love! Love! I never thought you had the power to kill your subjects. You wounded me in my youth; I passed through your fires. Why did you set me free, only in my old age to punish me for my escape? I confidently thought that I was freed from your shackles when I reached my fortieth year, when I found contentment in the companionship of my wife, when I saw myself blessed with the fruit of our union, which you have cut down today from its tree. I never thought you took revenge on parents through their children.

Then comes this shattering remark, one of the most devastating attacks ever made on Love: 'Haces que feo amen y hermoso les parezca' [You make men love in an ugly fashion, yet you make it seem beautiful to them] (Act 21, p.235).[46]

The existentialist pessimism of the *Celestina* is summed up in one of Pleberio's images: life baits men with the promise of pleasure and happiness, but swallowing the bait they find themselves writhing on the hook.[47] The pessimism is explicitly associated with love, which by its idealization tempts men to swallow the hook, but this need not have been, indeed was probably not, its cause. It has been more often attributed to Rojas's Judaism, first to a long-standing tradition in this culture, and secondly to the fact that in 1492 Ferdinand and Isabella, in the effort to forge unity out of kingdoms deeply divided by race, religion and culture, had put before Jews the alternatives of accepting Christianity or banishment abroad. Those who accepted enforced conversion became subject to the Inquisition and to persecution if suspected of secretly clinging to their ancestral faith. No Jew, in Rojas's lifetime or later, could have an optimistic view of life in such conditions. But although pessimism about life in general could have engendered pessimism about love and sex in particular, the theme and structure of the work, outside its author's biography, place it squarely in the historical context of the idealization of love in literature, and make it an important part of the 'philosophies' inspiring this literature. When, one hundred and thirty years later, Lope de Vega, meditating on a lifetime of dedication to the love of woman and to the idealization of life in a prolific poetic output, confronted his experience of love and poetry with real life in his loosely autobiographical *La Dorotea*, he turned to the *Celestina* as the only literary precedent. In the main outlines of the plot, in the dialogue form of a long and unactable prose play, he drew on Rojas, although he turned the latter's pessimism into sad disillusionment.[48]

Despite its long-term influence, and its literary qualities, the *Celestina* remained outside the main stream of the literature of its age. Though it had a number of successors that tried to imitate it, these were insignificant and uninfluential.[49] It could not divert the continued flow of Spanish literature from the channel of idealism. In the sixteenth century the literary development of this idealism took two directions. One was 'philosophical' and led to Neoplatonism, which became allied with mysticism. The other, an attempt to express the human ideal in terms that involved the moral and social preoccupations of real life, led from a romantic conception of love in its chivalresque form directly to the works of Cervantes.

APPENDIX

The Courtly Love Poetry of Castile

The account of Castilian fifteenth-century Courtly Love poetry given in this chapter was sent some years ago to Professor Keith Whinnom in its earliest draft as the first part of three lectures of which this book is an expansion. In a work published in 1981 Professor Whinnom criticized my views.[50] Since it does not correctly represent my ideas I think some comments are in order.

I referred to Professor Whinnom's inaugural lecture[51] in which he put forward the view that this late Castilian Courtly Love poetry could only be properly understood as covertly sexual, disguised behind a sort of code. No examples were given to support this and I questioned it, since the implication was that the style and language of all these poems are exclusively of this kind. In the second chapter of his book, which is headed 'El "idealismo" del amor cortés', he states that though much has been written on Courtly Love he proposes to concentrate only on my (unpublished) views, and he affirms that I defend the idealizing interpretation of Courtly Love by maintaining that its late Spanish form is a 'perverted' type of religion which seeks to deify woman and which finds satisfaction in the suffering caused by fidelity to an impossible love.[52] I hope that no reader will have taken my statements in this sense, for it is certainly not what I have ever intended. In view of this misunderstanding I may recapitulate my argument.

The Courtly Love phenomenon may be interpreted as an attempt (which I have called a 'confused' attempt) to ennoble human love. The metaphorical language whereby woman was 'deified', and man gave her total submission in 'faith', was extravagant from the point of view of analogy, and thus perhaps a 'perversion of values' in the strict sense, but it was not the invention of a new *religion*. It was merely that religious love comprised a series of words and concepts ('faith', 'constancy',

35

'long-suffering', 'abnegation' and so on) that had given to the concept and practice of religion what were held to be the highest moral and spiritual values in human experience. The concepts, and with them the words, were transferred to what had been considered the lower experience in order to raise and dignify it.

The traditional function of metaphors was to 'praise' or to 'blame' the objects they represented. This kind of language was intended to praise human love instead of continuing to blame it. The process was natural, albeit extremist, and although the result appeared blasphemous to those who could not accept the need for praise, I have never suggested that the *intention* was necessarily blasphemous on the part of any writer, despite the palinodes or recantations which a particular writer might later feel the need to publish. When religious faith grows weak or disappears a man must normally find something to take its place as a goal of worthy endeavour and the source of happiness; love and sex will naturally be among the many alternatives to religious faith and experience.

I have never called Diego de San Pedro a 'mystic who went astray' although it is not clear from Professor Whinnom's words whether he is actually attributing this to me.[53] The word 'mystic' is often applied haphazardly, but I would not wish to employ it in any sense other than the one used in this book.

Professor Whinnom calls it a 'curious coincidence' when the language of human love is used to express divine love, a coincidence which he implies does not require the 'transcendental explanation' I have given it.[54] What I had said in the lecture he saw, and what I have repeated in this book, is that the language of human love is the *only* language in which to express the love of God. What needs explanation in Spanish fifteenth-century literature is not this coincidence, but the really curious one that the language of religion should have been used to express human love.

This is what lies at the root of Professor Whinnom's misunderstanding of me, for when he talks of 'language' he means words, whereas I in this context mean ideas and concepts. It is the difference of approach between a 'linguistic' critic and a 'philosophical' one.[55] When I wrote that this Spanish poetry had a morbid, neurotic view of human love, I said that this could be explained only by the fact that it was not using the language of human love but of something very different, namely an experience requiring such concepts as 'mortification', 're-demptive suffering' and 'martyrdom'. It should be clear that by 'language' here I mean 'the phraseology or terms of a science, art, profession, etc., or of a class', whereas Professor Whinnom means the vocabulary.

Professor Whinnom refers to the semantic range of such words as 'passion', 'fidelity' and 'death' and stresses the possible plurality of meanings and the ambiguities that can arise (23). He acknowledges, of course, that phrases can have an innocent or obscene connotation, but he states or infers that in this type of poetry the latter will be the 'correct' meaning. If 'correct' means the author's real intention this will be difficult to guess at, or impossible in the case of *estribillos* drawn from anonymous traditional poetry. While admitting ambiguity as between the religious and the secular, the 'spiritual' and the 'human', I stressed the importance of the 'social context' in which particular poems were read or sung. In his answer to me (21–33) Professor Whinnom ignores the social context and never mentions readers.[56]

For Professor Whinnom the 'idealistic' interpretation of Courtly Love is mistaken because it does not point to the possibility of its 'true' meaning. Going hand in hand with the prurience of critics, editors and publishers this has prevented readers of such poetry from realizing its correct significance. Let us by all means accept the fact that veiled obscenities do exist in some of the Courtly Love poetry of fifteenth-century Castile. However, until Professor Whinnom produces further and more substantial evidence we may continue to hold that the concepts and phraseology of this poetic convention did not owe their origin, acceptance and diffusion to the need to disguise the impolite.

It has, of course, never been my intention to maintain that in using religious language in this type of poetry each poet was intending to sublimate his own erotic experience. Once the tradition became established poets used the convention, consciously or unconsciously, to exalt their human passion, whether a real passion or an imagined one. Human love in general could be exalted, whether or not the particular instance corresponded to real experience. The fact that the convention used the 'language of religion' might well be forgotten, but the intention to praise and ennoble love for woman remained.[57]

Sixteenth-century views of the *existential* relation between sexual and divine love will become more clear, I hope, in the chapters of this book that discuss poetic love in its Neoplatonic form. This was not a question of theoretical sublimation, but one of passing consciously and deliberately from a lower to a higher experience. The fifteenth-century Religion of Love was a quite different phenomenon, a question, namely, of finding a suitable 'language' to express in poetry a moral and psychological revaluation of human love that was part of a larger and complex cultural change.

My concern in this study has not been the range of meaning possible in particular *cancionero* poems, but the origin and nature of the convention itself. Individual poems developing the convention might be relatively close to, or very far from, what others as well as myself have considered to be its origin.[58] Nevertheless there must have been special reasons why the convention came into life in late fifteenth-century Spain. One possible reason, which I have been concerned to emphasise, is the tension between traditional religion and the new humanist spirit, a tension which, to be appreciated properly, must be considered in relation to mysticism and the development of Neoplatonism.

A Knight rescues a Maiden from the Wild Man. Part of a painted ceiling in the Hall of Justice in the Alhambra of Granada. The painting dates from the last third of the fourteenth century, and must be the work of a Christian artist or of a *mudejar* (a Moslem from Christian Spain). Figurative imagery was alien to Moslem theology and art, but it has been argued that this painting owes its genesis to a close alliance between Castile and Granada at this period. (Information supplied by Martin O'Donnell and Angus MacKay).

TWO.

IDEAL LOVE AND
NEOPLATONISM

Neoplatonism. GARCILASO. *Fourth Canción. First Canción. Second Eclogue. First Eclogue. Third Eclogue.* Fernando de HERRERA. Francisco de ALDANA.

Neoplatonism

The idealization of human love in implicit or explicit religious terms became crystallized in Neoplatonism, the characteristic philosophy of the Renaissance, which came to Spain from Italy. Two of the works exemplifying it had a great influence on Spanish literature. They are *Dialoghi d'amore* by the Sephardic Jew exiled from Spain, Leone Ebreo (Judah Leo Abravanel), published posthumously in 1535, and *Il Cortegiano* (1528) by Castiglione, which in its closing section contains an exposition of the Neoplatonist conception of love.[1]

Plato's philosophy of love was based on the ascent from the material to the immaterial, an ascent in which the mind is drawn upwards by the love of beauty. From the beauty of material things the mind is led to the beauty of human bodies, from there to the beauty of goodness, then to the beauty of ideas and from there to the knowledge and love of Absolute Beauty, which is God. This philosophy demanded the elimination of sex from love to the greatest possible extent on the grounds that it distracts from wisdom and can be condoned only as a meaningless biological necessity. Women were thus excluded by Plato from true love, for since they were thought to be not fully rational no man could have an intellectual friendship with a woman. True love presupposed the friendship of men joined in a contemplative pilgrimage toward the highest good, thus coinciding with true rationality in a non-sensuous striving for transcendental insight. Renaissance Neoplatonism by contrast, gave women a more important and more central place in ideal human love. In this respect it was the heir to the Courtly Love tradition from which it drew the idealization of women. The beauty that in the Platonic ascent draws the mind upward is now specifically the physical beauty of woman, and it is in and through human love that man progresses from the physical plane through the intellectual to the spiritual.

The conception of so-called Platonic love which is not found in Plato at all, became the new sixteenth-century ideal of love between man and woman. According to it a man overcomes sensuality when his reason makes him realize that beauty is all the more perfect the more it is removed from corruptible matter. Through this realization love is transformed into a chaste attachment, which is the union only of the minds and wills of the two lovers. Such mutual attachment will lead in both of them to the contemplation of universal beauty and so on to the contemplation of God, which Castiglione expresses in terms of Christian mysticism.

For Leone Ebreo, too, beauty does not reside in matter, which by itself is ugly: the beauty of material things consists in the ideas which fashion matter. Although physical beauty stirs the mind to love it, such love is only fitting if it leads the mind on to love of the beauty of the spirit. The physical beauty of a body is not itself corporeal, it is the image or reflection of spiritual beauty, and it is this essential beauty that the human soul should aspire to know and love. Love for physical beauty is, therefore, a stepping-stone to the ultimate goal of union with the final and only real Beauty, which is God. The physical union of lovers can be transcended and surpassed in the union of their souls through the communication of their minds and the fusion of their wills; and this spiritual union between man and woman leads to union with God. For Ebreo the ultimate nature and purpose of human love is religious. There is no gulf between the human and the divine, but a natural ascent.

The philosophy of Neoplatonism thus placed human love in the setting of divine love and gave it a spiritual value, which is what the love poetry of the fifteenth century and the *Cárcel de amor* had in a confused way been trying to do. Love on this Platonic plane removed, in theory, any conflict between human love and religion, for the subjugation of sensuality meant that the Platonic love of the human lovers for each other carried them up, effortlessly and inevitably, to the love of God. Love of woman was a stage towards, and a part of, the love of God; it was a stage that was not left behind but carried up. This was a philosophy that, in effect, idealized and glorified human love to the highest possible degree within a religious or theistic view of life. As such, by giving a philosophical sanction to the conception of ideal love, it offered a justification for centering the values of life exclusively in human love, to the disregard of all other human values.

In this respect Neoplatonism consolidated and continued the main literary movement in fifteenth-century Spain. At the same time the return to Plato also appealed, as Platonism had always done, to a different type of mind, one whose interests and aspirations were purely religious. This it could do by its emphasis that in the last resort ideal love was divine love, that the response to the attraction of beauty found its complete fulfilment in the apprehension and contemplation of God. Neoplatonism thus pointed in two different directions: ideal love continued to be the main preoccupation of literature, but now, so to speak, on two different levels instead of only one.

Garcilaso

The gradual modification of the Courtly Love tradition by the influence of Neoplatonism may be seen in the poetry of Garcilaso de la Vega (1501?-1536) whose work marks the full impact of the Italian Renaissance in Spain. His poetry in its formal aspects initiated the transformation of Spanish lyrical verse through direct imitation of Italian metres and rythms, a revolution in the craft of prosody that is paralleled about the same time in France and later in England. He added a further new element into the Spanish tradition by adopting the pastoral convention from Virgil and Sannazaro, and he firmly established the practice of making one lady the single subject of a writer's love poems, like Dante's Beatrice and Petrarch's Laura. This lady, generally married to another man, was a poetic idealization, whether real or imagined, of a love that had to remain unsullied. Garcilaso's lady was Doña Isabel Freire, a lady-in-waiting to the Empress, who chose a husband for her. Although Garcilaso himself was married in due course, his wife, in accordance with poetic practice, had nothing to do with his poetic love.[2]

Garcilaso's later poetry is Italianate in its Neoplatonist content as well as in its form, but the content of his earlier poetry still represents the *cancionero* tradition. His poetic experience passes from the suffering caused by the conflict between reason and sensuality to the achievement of a resigned serenity, not in the self-assurance of being in contact with the divine through love of a woman, but in acceptance of the sadness inherent in life through the fact that love and beauty are perishable. The note of suffering and melancholy links him with the fifteenth century; its gentle, more restrained expression within a pastoral setting and the perfection of his craftsmanship is what he owes to the Italian Renaissance.[3]

Fourth Canción. The main elements of the *cancionero* conception of love are condensed in the *Fourth Canción* which deals with the conflict between ideal love and sensual love. Sensuality is presented as fury and madness which drag the lover along in their wake: this is *amor loco*, the 'mad love' of medieval literature. Its counterpart, the only thing that can control it, is the sanity of reason and its judgements. A sensual passion that is stronger than reason is a cause of shame and torment, and ideal love, which is chaste, demands that conscience and reason be obeyed. But is it possible to love the lady with absolute purity, with no hint or trace of impure desire?

The poem opens with the conventional image of two roads that stretch ahead as life opens up for every man and choices have to be made. One is smooth and level, passing through flower-covered meadows; the other is rugged and rocky, full of thorny briars (1–20).[4] This was a traditional way of expressing the choice between the search for happiness through pleasure

and the realization that the path of virtue is the path of pain and
suffering, and it implied that virtue and happiness do not
coincide since the search for happiness through the senses is
inimical to the discipline of self-mortification. Garcilaso alters
the conventional image by presenting the path of sensuality as
harsh. It is harsh because it is the way of mortification. If
sensuality is deprived of its fulfilment it is a martyrdom; yet to
suffer martyrdom is a sign of the most unselfish love. Repressed
sensuality, in short, is the equivalent of virtuous living. This is
a religious form of expression, but here it is inverted and directed
towards the human.

The poet goes on to state that he lives in suffering, but not
from choice, for the awakening of passion is a destiny imposed
on human nature: love assails man and it is not in his power to
refrain from loving (21-33). This awakening of passion con-
fronts the reason with a new problem which it does not see how
to overcome, but it is impelled by shame to struggle, and man
in his innermost being instinctively desires that reason be
victorious (24-40). The lover, however, is ruled by the senses,
not by reason, which becomes, as a result, a prisoner-of-war:
the 'mistress' is dominated by the 'slave', a concrete metaphor
that expressively communicates the sense of shame (49-60).
This captivity is due to the absence of all tranquility from the
moment the lady looked at him; her glance deprived him of his
freedom (61-80). And since love is captivity, the poet's song is
accompanied by the clanking of his fetters:

> De mí agora huyendo, voy buscando
> a quien huye de mí como enemiga,
> que al un error añado el otro yerro,
> y en medio del trabajo y la fatiga
> estoy cantando yo, y está sonando
> de mis atados pies el grave hierro. (81-6)

Now, fleeing my self, I seek her who flies from me like an enemy,
for to the first error I join a second, and in the midst of toil and
strain I am singing to the sound of the heavy fetter on my bound
feet.

The only joy left in life is to endure this anguish. The theme is developed further by another most expressive image:

De los cabellos de oro fue texida
la red que fabricó mi sentimiento,
do mi razón, rebuelta y enrredada,
con gran vergüença suya y corrimiento,
sujetta al apetito y sometida,
en público adulterio fue tomada,
del cielo y de la tierra contemplada. (101–7)

From the golden hair was woven the net made by my love in
which my reason, overturned and bound, to its great humiliation
and shame, subjected and dominated by sensual desire, was
caught in public adultery, watched by Heaven and Earth.

The reference is to Venus and Mars caught in a net and exposed
to the mockery of the gods: from the lady's golden hair was
knotted the net that has publicly exposed the 'adulterous' poet
to the gaze of heaven and earth. Reason subjected to the domination of passion is 'adultery' because it is an act of infidelity to
human nature and therefore seen by God and men. The poet
goes on to express the 'pleasure' he feels in this pain:

¿Quién no se espantará de lo que digo?
que's cierto que é venido a tal estremo
que del grave dolor que huyo y temo
me hallo algunas vezes tan amigo
que en medio dél, si buelvo a ver la vida
de libertad, la juzgo por perdida,
y maldigo las oras y momentos
gastadas mal en libres pensamientos. (113–20)

Who will not tremble at what I say? For it is true that I have come
to such an extreme that to the serious pain I flee and fear I sometimes find myself so well disposed that if, in the midst of it, I look
back on the life of freedom, I consider it wasted, and curse the
hours and moments wasted in free thoughts.

Such sentiments should not be understood literally; they are a
conventional way of expressing the satisfaction felt in the willing
service of Love, a satisfaction which derives, basically, from a
religious conception of the value of suffering for God's sake.

Garcilaso de la Vega

His senses delivered over to suffering, the poet's only consolation is that the lady might see his torment and feel some pity for him, which would be akin to loving him a little; but the thought that she does not even think of him redoubles his pain (141– 160). The poem closes with an *envoi* which gives the promise of faithfulness unto death (161–9).

First Canción. The 'poetic environment' of suffering love is splendidly expressed in the *First Canción*. The abstract landscape it depicts is based on the Petrarchan metaphors of 'icy fire' and 'flames': love makes the poet burn in the ice of the lady's indifference. The metaphor of burning is developed into a desert scene, withered and parched through excessive heat, which is, at the same time, an area of frozen sand. This landscape, which expresses her cruelty, is where he must go to seek her (1–13). Her cruelty, he claims, is due to her 'pride', and he pleads with her to relent and change because he himself is incapable of change and no longer has the strength to bear his suffering. Following the dictate of love he longs for salvation, not perdition (14–19). Yet now he seeks to increase his suffering by the thought that when he dies of his unhappy love she will be contrite and ashamed of the harm she caused him. The prospect of her future pain increases his torment, affecting him more keenly than his own troubles (20–6). But to sharpen the pain of his griefstricken senses is in fact impossible, for the only pain they can feel is that of his perdition (27–31). There is no remedy, he decides, since it is impossible to escape from his plight, a conviction expressed in the image of the lover stretched out, awaiting death, while the lady looks on (32–9). At this point a rational note enters: he realises that if his suffering does not avail to win her compassion his condition does not correspond to his worth and degrades him. His state is not due to what he has considered its cause, namely the lady's indifference, but to his own frailty: he has made his moral weakness the excuse for his suffering (40–52). The *envoi* declares that although he sends her his poem it will win him nothing for she will not receive it as coming from him; but this cannot do him further harm because he is himself the cause of his affliction.

47

Ideal Love and Neoplatonism

A remedy for suffering love was available in the Neoplatonist belief that the mind could subdue sensual desire and thus enable a man to attain some serenity. This recovery of serenity is what happened to Garcilaso in his poetic experience. His poetry emerges from a state of self-absorption, an obsessive and potentially morbid preoccupation with the problems of human love, and enters instead an imaginative plane of universality. The transition is evident in his pastoral poetry, which comprises three eclogues, each of which is set in the artificial Arcadia that Renaissance writers inherited from the bucolic poetry of Greece and Rome.[5] Arcadia was a means of presenting human love, as well as the human environment, in a state of innocence, and it expressed nostalgia foɪ this state which had since been lost. The Biblical myth of the Garden of Eden presented the same state in a benign and beautiful setting: man in perfect accord with his Creator and with his natural environment, his senses and emotions perfectly harmonized under the dominion of reason. It also gave expression to the same longing, for the disruption of this harmony by pride (the desire to know the secrets of life through the experience of evil as well as good) had brought banishment from Paradise, and had turned human life into a ceaseless pilgrimage in search of a perfection unattainable on Earth. Although the return to Paradise could occur only in another state of existence, the yearning for it in this life could not be stilled.

Second Eclogue. The *Second Eclogue* (which was the first to be written) is a long and confusing poem that was generally found difficult to interpret until modern critics clarified its unity of intention and structure.[6] Salicio represents the idyllic pastoral life, perfectly attuned to Nature, because he is exempt from passion, both moral passion, like anger, and sensual passion, such as lust. Albanio, however, who is not exempt, is in a turbulent state of feeling. He recalls his boyhood (which is part of the nostalgia for a lost innocence) recounting his friendship with Camila, itself an example of an innocent and pure love. But the innocence of childhood does not last, and the boy changes. The girl does not understand what has happened, and

48

when she learns the truth she becomes contemptuous of him. Albanio, feeling the first despair of a lover, attempts suicide, and Camila, who still feels affection for him as a friend, grieves at losing him. But as she lies asleep he seizes her in a frenzy of sensuality and is represented as literally mad. His insanity takes the form of thinking that he has lost his body, a delusion that symbolizes the problem produced by the dualism of human nature. This problem could not occur in a bodiless intellectual being like an angel. The cure for sensuality is, metaphorically, the cure for madness by recovering sanity, and, since only a disciplined and active life can prevent the passions from holding sway, the 'doctor' who cures Albanio is aptly named Severo. For reason to control a man's life he must undergo both a moral discipline and an education that trains and broadens his mind. This 'cure' is administered allegorically to Albanio, and passion/ ate love is dispelled by the disciplined training of reason, this being a free life and not one of slavery. The nature of the human soul demands freedom from sensuality, which blunts and dis/ torts its proper operation. In the Neoplatonic ideal the mind quietens the sensual appetite and the human mind can recover, not, indeed, the innocence of childhood, but its tranquility.

First Eclogue. The suffering love that informs the *First Eclogue* is of two kinds: the pain of unrequited love, sung by Salicio (from *salix*, the weeping/willow), and grief at the death of Elisa, who is mourned by Nemoroso (the Latin meaning is 'grove/like' but Garcilaso's use implies 'dark' and 'melancholy'). Although the poem may have been inspired by love of Isabel Freire, and her early death, it does not express a self/centred sorrow. Instead the personal is transcended into the universal. The anguish of the shepherds is the suffering of all men; their grief at the imperfections of life, of which death is the greatest, is a universal sorrow. This suffering love is presented within the sympathetic and enduring peace of Nature, man's physical en/ vironment to which he must respond emotionally and spiritu/ ally. The pastoral imagery here is not essentially descriptive but evocative of moral states, in particular the serenity that comes from conformity with the peacefulness of Nature, an interior

state that implies the rule of reason.[7] Since whatever calms
passion was considered to have moral value, the poems of
Garcilaso that enshrine this serenity had a moral value also in
accordance with the theories of Renaissance poetic.

Third Eclogue. The final stage in the universalization of suffering love is marked by the *Third Eclogue*, in which the memory of
Isabel Freire is presented in a pastoral context extended to
include classical myth.[8] The bucolic *locus amoenus* is beside the
river Tagus. The mood evoked by the scene is one of restful,
even drowsy, tranquility, one of meditative silence with a tone
of melancholy that imbues the whole poem. Here the river
nymphs are weaving four tapestries, of which the first three have
mythological themes: Orpheus and Eurydice, Apollo and
Daphne, Venus and Adonis. These myths do not have a narrative significance, but symbolize instead the theme of the poem.
Each one records a love that is broken by a violent death: a
woman bitten by a serpent, another turned into a tree and a
young man killed by a boar. And in each one the bereaved
partner is left to mourn his lot: a husband whose wife is
snatched away, an unrequited lover, and no less a person than
the very goddess of Love, who loses her young man, all representing the desolation of suffering love. The descriptions of these
tapestries prelude the mood of the central theme: grief at a lost
love, grief for the destructiveness of death. This takes the form
of a meditation on the death of Elisa, the poet's beloved, who is
mourned by the shepherd Nemoroso. Her passing, and Nemoroso's love, are the subject of the fourth tapestry. Isabel's death is
thus compared with that of Eurydice, Daphne and Adonis, and
the poet's grief is the grief of the gods themselves at the inescapable sadness of existence. The poem is delicately but deeply
imbued with the 'dolorido sentir' of human life:

> En la hermosa tela se veýan,
> entretexidas, las silvestres diosas
> salir de la espessura, y que venían
> todas a la ribera pressurosas,
> en el semblante tristes, y traýan

cestillos blancos de purpúreas rosas,
las quales esparziendo derramavan
sobre una nympha muerta que lloravan.

Todas, con el cabello desparzido,
lloravan una nympha dilicada
cuya vida mostrava que avia sido
antes de tiempo y casi en flor cortada;
cerca del agua, en un lugar florido,
estava entre las yervas degollada[9]
qual queda el blanco cisne quando pierde
la dulce vida entre la yerva verde.   (217–32)

Interwoven in the lovely cloth the rustic goddesses could be seen
emerging from the undergrowth and moving quickly to the
riverbank, with sorrowful expressions; they carried white
baskets of purple roses which they were strewing and pouring
over a dead nymph whom they were mourning. All of them,
their hair in disarray, were mourning a delicate nymph, whose
life showed that she had been cut off before her time and just
before she flowered. Near the water, in a place strewn with
flowers, she lay in the grass, drained of blood, as the white swan
lies when it loses its sweet life amid the green grass.

But from the meditation on death one must return to life in the
world. The love that human beings lose is followed always by
the love that others hope for. Youth must love; in its turn it will
suffer and grieve, but until then young men must sing of its
expected arrival, even if the song is sad because love delays its
coming. The poem concludes with the alternating songs of two
shepherds, Tirreno and Alcino. For the former love is joy, for
the latter it is bitter-sweet because it is not yet requited. The joy is
the joy of Spring, the bitterness is Nature's storms. The suffering
love that is the constant theme of sixteenth-century poetry is not
rejected here by Garcilaso as an emotional or moral aberration.
It is, instead, raised to the level of the resignation that life
requires of all men.

Fernando de Herrera

Garcilaso's later poetry is perfect of its kind. Its verbal music
and rhythms are perfectly adapted to the delicacy of sentiment

and the tone of gentle melancholy. Yet, despite its perfection, it is limited in its range of thought and emotion. Later poets continued what Garcilaso had started, namely, the universalization of personal feeling, and the first direction in which they developed it was towards the Neoplatonism on whose threshold he stood.

The main poet in the early Platonizing direction was Fernando de Herrera (1534–97), a careful and skilled craftsman of poetic diction, a precursor of Góngora in the attempt to fashion an elevated language proper to poetry.[10] He was a regular visitor at the Seville home of the Count of Gelves, a great-grandson of Christopher Columbus, where his company consoled the Countess, Doña Leonor, for her husband's lack of affection, and their relationship became a Platonic attachment in the now traditional manner. She was his only poetic love, probably the only one in his life, and there is a tradition that when she died he abandoned poetry and dedicated himself entirely to the study and writing of history. The sonnets that follow have been selected to show the progress in his concept of love.[11]

Sonnet 30 deals with the commonplace of love as despair, giving it a modicum of development:

> Cánso la vida en esperar un dia
> de fingido plazer. huyen los años,
> i nacen dellos mil sabrosos daños,
> qu'esfuerçan el error de mi porfia.
>
> Los passos, por do voi a mi alegria,
> tan desusados son, i tan estraños,
> que al fin van a acabars' en mis engaños,
> i dellos buelvo a començar la via.
>
> Descubro en el principio otra esperança,
> si no mayor, igual a la passada,
> i enel mesmo desseo persevero.
>
> Mas luego tórno a la comun mudança
> de la suerte en mi daño conjurada,
> y esperando contino desespero.

I wear out my life, hoping for a day of imagined pleasure; the years fly by and give rise to much pleasurable suffering which reinforces the error of my constancy. The steps I take in search for happiness are so unwonted and unfamiliar that in the end they only deceive me; and from this deception I start to retread the same path. As I start again I experience a renewed hope, if not greater than the earlier just as intense, and I continue to feel the same desire; but later I suffer once more the common change of fortune, which conspires to harm me, and as I keep hoping I continually despair.

In this poem despair, or 'lack of hope', is not a static or permanent condition as in the purely conventional poets but a fluctuating mood, a constant renewal of expectation followed by disillusion leading to despair. Then hope is once more renewed, hope for some favour from the lady such as a glance, a smile, a touch, the hope for now 'un dia de fingido plazer' (1-2). This hope, however, is a figment of the imagination. The feigning of such pleasure is the only satisfaction to be obtained from love, but such a substitute cannot last long. The imagination constantly evokes new forms of hope, possible fulfilments of what is desired, but always in vain, and the cycle of despair and hope must be started again. The sonnet closes with the paradox, 'esperando contino desespero' (14), namely, that to hope continuously leads to the loss of hope, this being a variant of the commonplace of a 'living death', a circular pattern of experience, always moving forward in retrogression. Sensuous love is a vicious circle, but this is stated without passion or even feeling, for the sonnet is no more than a poetic exercise, one that is certainly well done.

In *Sonnet 18* there is a development of the value of hope constantly reborn. With this new poetic attitude Herrera gropes towards the abandonment of the idea of pain as pleasurable:

> Flaca esperança en todas mis porfias,
> vano desseo en desigual tormento,
> i, inutil fruto del dolor, que siento,
> lagrimas sin descanso, i ansias mias;

Un'ora alegre en tantos tristes dias
sufrid, que tenga un triste descontento;
i que pueda sentir tal vez contento[12]
la gloria de fingidas alegrias.

No es justo no, que siempre quebrantado
me oprima el mal; i me deshaga el pecho
nueva pena d'antiguo desvario.

Mas ô que temo tanto el dulce estado,
que (como al bien no estè enseñado i hecho)
abráço ufano el grave dolor mio.

Faint hope in all my constancy, vain desire in overwhelming torment, useless fruit of all the pain I feel, ceaseless weeping and all my yearnings, permit me a single hour of bliss amid the sadness of so many days; let me have a sad unhappiness and let me suffer, perhaps contentedly, the bliss of imagined joy. It is not just that I should be for ever broken and oppressed by unhappiness, nor that my heart should be hurt by renewed grief at the transgression of so long ago. But, oh!, I am so fearful of the sweet state of happiness that (because I am not accustomed and trained to happiness) I embrace with pride the heavy burden of my pain.

Insofar as this poem may be, to some extent, rooted in experience, it is not likely to impress us, but it does represent a theoretical analysis of the condition of the lover that has a certain psychological validity, even if this is no 'solution' to the underlying 'philosophical' problem. It implies that the only possible relief from the pangs of suffering love is to be sought through the imagination. The poet can rebel against the constant pain he feels on account of a past madness (presumably at having once harboured sensual desire). The continual acceptance of this suffering can have no compensation, for the 'fruit' it produces is only 'useless'. Why does he not permit himself a single hour of bliss by imagining the happiness of a successful love? But no: he is so totally unaccustomed to happiness that he is too frightened to imagine it. All that can be embraced, therefore, is his suffering, and this he does embrace with self-satisfied pride.

Herrera's poetic imagination looked for an answer to the

problem of erotic passion in the exploration of its basic meta-phor, 'fire'. An example is *Sonnet 7*:

No puedo sufrir mas el dolor fiero,
ni ya tolerar mas el duro assalto
de vuestras bellas luzes, antes falto
de paciencia i valor, enel postrero

Trance, arrojando el yugo, desespero;
i, por do voi huyendo, el suelo esmalto
de rotos lazos; i levánto en alto
el cuello osado, i libertad espero.

Mas que vale mostrar estos despojos,
i la ufania d' alcançar la palma
d' un vano atrevimiento sin provecho?

El rayo, que salio de vuestros ojos,
puso su fuerça en abrasar mi alma,
dexando casi sin tocar el pecho.

I can no longer suffer the fierce pain nor withstand any more the harsh attack from the light of your beautiful eyes; rather, lacking patience and valour in the final onslaught, I cast away my yoke and fall into despair; and wherever I escape I adorn the ground with broken fetters, and daringly I lift up my head and hope for freedom. But what is the use of displaying these spoils and of boasting of the victory of a vain and useless daring? The ray of lightning that came from your eyes spent its force in setting my soul ablaze, but left my breast almost untouched.

The fire of passion is lit by the rays flowing from the lady's eyes. They should be rays of light which illuminate, but they are rays that set on fire. The paradoxical term 'abrasar' (either 'to cause to glow' or 'to destroy by fire') points to the paradox of Neoplatonism in the human dualism of body and soul, which can be overcome only by the due subordination of the body to the mind, namely, the complete subjection of the Slave to the Queen.

Sonnet 72 is an attempt to explore the Petrarchan antithesis of the 'icy fire':

Amor en mi se muestra todo fuego,
i en las entrañas de mi Luz es nieve.
fuego no ái, qu'ella no tórne nieve,
ni nieve, que no múde yo en mi fuego.

La fria zona abráso con mi fuego,
l'ardiente mi Luz buelve elada nieve.
pero no puedo yo encender su nieve,
ni ella entibiar la fuerça de mi fuego.

Contrastan igualmente ielo i llama;
que d'otra suerte fuera el mundo ielo,
o su maquina toda viva llama.

Mas fuera; porque ya resuelto en ielo,
o el coraçon desvanecido en llama,
ni temiera mi llama, ni su ielo.

Love is revealed in me as purely fire, and in the bosom of my
Love as snow; there is no fire that she turns not to ice, nor is there
snow which I turn not to fire. I burn up the zone of coldness with
my fire, my Light turns into frozen snow the zone of heat; but I
cannot set alight her snow, nor can she temper my fire's force. Ice
and flame are equally opposed, because if it were otherwise either
the world would be all ice, or all its structure would be living
flame. It would be more than that; because with all my heart
reduced to ice and hers dissolved in flames, neither would she
fear my flame nor I her ice.

This contains an exhibition of remarkable technical skill, inspired by the sonnet of Petrarch on which it is modelled: rhymes
are formed not by syllables but by words, with only two rhymes
in the quatrains, and two in the tercets, four all together. Nonetheless it does not reveal Herrera to be a truly consummate poet
because the technical mastery has no corresponding significant
forcefulness. The lady, it affirms, does not succeed in cooling
the ardour of his passion, nor does he succeed in setting alight
her chastity. The contrast is needed because otherwise the whole
world would be passion or continence; it would be more than
that, because the opposition would cease: if the whole world
were ice she would not have his flame; if all the world were ice
he would not fear her coldness. There are obvious implications

here within the dualistic philosophy of body and soul, but they are not followed up. The sonnet plays ingeniously with the antithetical ideas, but the conceptual argumentation does not add substance to the thought behind it. The metaphor of the 'icy fire' is explored more successfully in *Sonnet 3*:

> Pense, mas fue engañoso pensamiento,
> armar du duro ielo el pecho mio;
> porqu' el fuego d' Amor al grave frio
> no desatasse en neuvo encendimiento.
>
> Procure no rendir m' al mal, que siento;
> i fue todo mi esfuerço desvario.
> perdi mi libertad, perdi mi brio;
> cobrè un perpetuo mal, cobrè un tormento.
>
> El fuego al ielo destemplo en tal suerte,
> que, gastando su umor, quedò ardor hecho;
> i es llama, es fuego, todo cuanto espiro.
>
> Este incendio no puede darme muerte;
> que, cuanto de su fuerça mas deshecho,
> tanto mas de su eterno afan respiro.

I thought I could, but it was a deceitful thought, protect my breast by sheer ice, so that within the ice the fire of Love should not start a new conflagration. I endeavoured not to surrender to the suffering I feel, and all my effort was misplaced: I lost my freedom, I lost my energy, I gained perpetual suffering, I gained a torment. The fire melted the ice in such a fashion that, destroying its liquid, it was turned into burning. And all the breath that I exhale is fire, is flame. This burning cannot bring me death, because the more its strength undoes me, the more do I breathe with its everlasting longing.

The poet thinks that he can protect himself from the heat of the fire by the 'armour' of ice, namely, cool the fire of passion by the mortification of continence, but it proves a delusion to think that passion can be cooled by a compulsory and involuntary abstinence: the fire melts the ice and burns more vigorously than ever. To this commonplace of Courtly Love, which is the ground of the lover's suffering, Herrera adds only the one new idea expressed in the sonnet's last two lines: the fire is the hitherto inescapable suffering of the lover, but it does not kill because the more the blaze is weakened by the ice, the more the poet wishes to live with an 'eternal desire'. The negative, self-destructive concept is replaced by a positive and affirmative one. This eternal longing, which is life-giving, corresponds to the hope and joy expressed in the sonnets previously considered. The poetic metaphor is that the fire has an 'eternal longing', the restlessness of the flickering flames as they grope upwards and disappear. The restlessness of flames is always an upward aspiration, not just a yearning that endures but one that is 'eternal', some sort of aspiration for the divine, a yearning for eternity. This represents a further step towards Neoplatonism.[13]

A breakthrough into Neoplatonism comes in *Sonnet 45*:

> Clara, suäve luz, alegre i bella,
> que los safiros i color del cielo
> teñis de la esmeralda con el velo,
> que resplandece en una i otra estrella;[14]

> Divino resplandor, pura centella,
> por quien libre mi alma, en alto buelo
> las alas roxas bate, i huye el suelo
> ardiendo vuestro dulce fuego enella;

> Si yo no solo abráso el pecho mio,
> mas la tierra i el cielo, i en mi llama
> doi principio immortal de fuego eterno;

> Porqu'el rigor de vuestro antiguo frio
> no podrè ya encender? porque no inflama
> mi estio ardiente a vuestro elado ivierno?

Clear, gentle light, joyful and beautiful, you who tinge the sapphires and other colours of the sky with the emerald veil that glows in one or other star; divine resplendence, pure spark, you who free my soul to soar in lofty flight, as it beats its red wings, fleeing from the earth with your sweet fire burning within it; since it is not my breast alone that I set alight but also Earth and Heaven, fanning in this flame of mine the beginnings of an immortal fire, why cannot I now set ablaze the rigour of your erstwhile coldness? Why does not my burning summer set fire to your frozen winter?

There is still the conventional idea of melting the icy lady with the flame of passion (12-14), but the poem has a new significance. It is no longer a question of complaining at the lover's suffering; it is, instead, a hymn to the lady's beauty. The introspective obsession has now become exteriorized into light, stars, and the heavens (1-4). This resplendence is divine. All beauty is a reflection of the lady's beauty (5-8), as in orthodox Platonism all material beauty is a reflection of divine beauty. Beauty is what gives freedom to the soul to soar into the realm of the spirit and so to approach God. The fire that she has set alight now burns in his soul; it is no longer a torment but an impulse to a spiritual ascent (9-11). This fire, lit by the love of beauty, inflames the whole Earth and Heaven: it is the immortal principal of the eternal fire, divine love. Love is thus the motivating force of all Creation, a characteristically Platonic concept. Neither God nor divine love are mentioned in this sonnet, but they are implicit. The conclusion (12-14) shows, nevertheless, an attachment to Earth, and thus does not reveal the fulness of the soul's potential freedom.[15]

Sonnet 38, however, is pure Neoplatonism:

Serena Luz, en quien presente espira
divino amor, qu'enciende i junto enfrena
el noble pecho, qu'en mortal cadena
al alto Olimpo levantar s'aspira;

Ricos cercos dorados, do se mira
tesoro celestial d'eterna vena;
armonia d'angélica Sirena,
qu'entre las perlas i el coral respira;

Cual nueva maravilla, cual exemplo
de la immortal grandeza nos descubre
aquessa sombra del hermoso velo?

Que yo enessa belleza, que contemplo,
(aunqu'a mi flaca vista ofende i cubre)
la immensa búsco, i voi siguiendo al cielo.

Serene Light, in whom divine love is present and breathing, and which ignites yet restrains the noble breast that, despite its mortal chain, aspires to rise to high Olympus: rich, golden curls which show forth the celestial treasure from the eternal mine; music of the angelic Siren, breathing between the coral and the pearls (of lips and teeth): what new marvel, what example of immortal greatness is revealed to us by that shadow of the beautiful veil? For in that beauty which I contemplate (although it offends and dims my weak sight) I seek infinite beauty, and I follow it to Heaven.

Love is now only divine love, and the lady is the instrument for communicating it as she inflames the 'noble heart' that aspires to ascend to Heaven. Her beauty is a 'celestial treasure', the shadow cast by Heaven (i.e., its reflection). Loving her beauty, and her, the poet is seeking God.

Finally, in *Sonnet 27* the Neoplatonism is quite explicit:

> El color bello enel umor de Tiro
> ardio, i la nieve vuestra en llama pura,
> cuando, Estrella, bolvistes con dulçura
> los ojos, por quien misero suspiro.
>
> Vivo color de lúcido safiro,
> dorado cielo, eterna hermosura,
> pues mereci alcançar esta ventura,
> acoged blandamente mi suspiro.
>
> Conel mi alma, enel celeste fuego
> vuestro abrasada, viene, i se trasforma
> en la belleza vuestra soberana.
>
> I en tanto gozo, en su mayor sosiego
> su bien, en cuantas almas halla, informa;
> qu'enel comunicar mas gloria gana.[16]

The beautiful Tyrian colour of your blood was on fire, and your snow burned in the pure flame when you, my Star, turned on me a sweet look from the eyes for which I sigh unhappily. Vivid colour of shining sapphire, golden heaven, eternal beauty, since I have deserved the attainment of this good fortune, welcome with gentleness my sigh. My soul, aflame in your celestial fire, comes with this sigh and is transformed into your sovereign beauty. And in the midst of such great joy, it (your beauty) gives form, in their deepest tranquility, to all the souls it finds, for it acquires more glory in communication.

This is a hymn to Beauty (5-8), the divine good that gives form to human souls and communicates to them its life (9-14). The communication of this good to the soul through the lady produces a spiritual peace. Does the poetic formulation of the doctrine contain a forcefulness that makes it convincing? Or is it the conventional philosophizing of the age? Perhaps the answer does not matter, for the sheer faith that Herrera communicates carries conviction.

Francisco de Aldana

Francisco de Aldana (1537-78) was a philosopher-poet of a kind that Garcilaso could have become. His verse lacks the technical mastery of Herrera, and he is scarcely, all in all, a poet of the first rank, but one of his poems, the *Carta a Arias Montano* is a masterpiece of Spanish literature, and his work as a whole is crucial for an understanding of Spanish Neoplatonism. The range of his poetic experience, which is unusual for his time, and more characteristic of poets in the next century, includes the two extremes of erotic sensuousness and religious mysticism, though these do not occur together in any one poem. His poetry passes from an assertion of the goodness of sexual love to a realization of its inadequacy to express the deepest longings of the human spirit. It concludes, at the end of his relatively short life, with a desire for mystical love.[17]

Aldana's sensuality is more Italian than Spanish, and could be due to his upbringing in Italy. It is evident in the poetic fragment *Medoro y Angélica* which expresses an innocent delight in the beauty of the human body. Cupid gazes on Angélica asleep:

> La sábana después quïetamente
> levanta al parecer no bien siguro,
> y como espejo el cuerpo ve luciente,
> el muslo cual aborio[18] limpio y puro;
> contempla de los pies hasta la frente
> las caderas de mármol liso y duro,
> las partes donde Amor el cetro tiene,
> y allí con ojos muertos se detiene.   (49-56)

Gently then he lifts the sheet that seems not firmly fixed, and sees
her body like a shining mirror, her thigh like clean, clear ivory;
he contemplates her from feet to forehead, her hips of smooth,
firm marble, and the parts where Love is sovereign: and there,
with deadened look, he pauses.

This subject is alien to the Petrarchan tradition, but Aldana
does not elude it. He uses Petrarchan imagery to express sen-
sualism, with no sense of sinfulness (3–8, 17–24). At the end
of the poem he reflects ruefully on his own misfortune: unlike
Medoro he cannot make love to his lady who refuses him on
religious grounds:

> La paz tomaste, ¡oh venturoso amante!,
> con dulce guerra en brazos de tu amiga;
> y aquella paz, mil veces que es bastante,
> nunca me fuera, en paz de mi fatiga:
> triste, no porque paz mi lengua cante
> (paz quieres inmortal, fiera enemiga),
> mas antes, contra amor de celo armada,
> huye la paz, que tanto al Cielo agrada.   (73–80)

You took (the kiss of) peace, oh lucky lover!, in gentle warfare
in your loved one's arms; and that peace, which a thousand times
suffices, never would suffice to satisfy my pain: I sorrow, not for
my tongue to sing of peace (you want immortal peace, cruel
enemy), but rather because peace, which so pleases Heaven, is
fleeing, for you are armed with zeal against love.

When there is a conflict between religious feeling and sensual
love peace flees and torment assails the lover. This conception
of the peace of mind and body resulting from physical union is
contrary to all the principles of the Courtly Love tradition,
which retained deeper roots in Spain than it did in Italy precisely because Spanish literature could not or did not openly
accept sensual love as a rightful theme.

The physical union of lovers is treated directly in *Sonnet 17*.
Its central metaphor stems from the lover's hyperbolic belief that
the lady is more beautiful than the sun, which is the source of all
life, warmth and joy. Consequently sensuous love is all that and
more; the supreme value in life. The lady attempts to reject the

hyperbole, but she has to yield and accept it. There is nothing violent here in the portrayal of physical love: it is a 'gentle force' (9), 'sweet play' (13). The same notion informs *Sonnet 2*:

> Junto a su Venus tierna y bella estaba
> todo orgulloso Marte horrible y fiero,
> cubierto de un templado y fino acero
> que un claro espejo al sol de sí formaba;
> y mientras ella atenta en él notaba
> sangre y furor, con rostro lastimero
> un beso encarecido al gran guerrero
> fijó en la frente y dél todo colgaba.
> Del precioso coral tan blando efeto
> salió que al fiero dios del duro asunto
> hizo olvidar con nuevo ardiente celo.
> ¡Oh fuerza estraña, oh gran poder secreto:
> que pueda un solo beso en sólo un punto
> los dioses aplacar, dar ley al cielo!

Next to his tender and lovely Venus stood Mars, full of pride, horrendous and fierce, covered in a tempered, fine steel that formed a clear mirror for the sun; while she, thoughtfully noting the gore and anger in him, fixed a warm kiss on the great warrior's forehead, a sorrowful expression on her face, and clung to him completely. The precious coral (of her lips) had such a gentle effect that it made the fierce god forget the harsh subject (of his thoughts) with new and ardent devotion. Oh mysterious force, oh great and secret power: that a single kiss in just one place should pacify the gods, and govern Heaven!

The aggressive brutality of masculine lust is here presented as Mars, the fierce god of war. Love should be feminine tender-ness, *courtoisie* refining passion. This refined sensual love gives light to the heavens and governs the whole Universe. Similarly, in *Sonnet 1* the poet directs his praise to the god Zephyr, im-ploring him to come with his gentle breeze to counter the rough and mad movement of the North Wind. Zephyr is the peaceful gentle breeze from the West, the father of flowers and fruits and the joys of the meadows, while the mad, tempestuous wind from the North is 'the sound of humanity' (6). The latter is obviously lust; Zephyr is sensual love, but soft and gentle, a passion of a different order. This tranquil joy is innocent, the gentle caress of the wind that makes Nature fruitful.

Some of Aldana's poems are informed by a notion of love that is specifically Neoplatonic. An example is *Sonnet 16* which recounts how one day the lover, asleep in the country, is embraced by the lady. Without waking he is transported to Paradise, and his union with her there is expressed in purely Neoplatonic terms. *Sonnet 20*, which plays on the contrast between good and evil, is more enigmatic:

> Es tanto el bien que derramó en mi seno,
> piadoso de mi mal, vuestro cuidado,
> que nunca fué, tras mal, bien tan preciado
> como este tal, por mí de bien tan lleno.
>
> Mal que este bien causó jamás ajeno
> sea de mí ni de mí quede apartado;
> antes, del cuerpo al alma trasladado,
> se reserve de muerte un mal tan bueno.
>
> Mas paréceme ver que el mortal velo,
> no consintiendo al mal nuevo aposento,
> lo guarda allá en su centro el más profundo;
> sea, pues, así: que el cuerpo acá en el suelo
> posea su mal, y al postrimero aliento
> gócelo el alma y pase a nuevo mundo.

So great is the good that your care, pitying my evil, poured into my breast, that never, following an evil, was any good so prized as this one, for me so full of good. May the evil that caused this good never be foreign to me, or stay apart from me; instead, may an evil so good, transferred from the body to the soul, be preserved from death. But it seems to me that the mortal veil (i.e. the body), refusing the evil a new abode, is guarding it there in its deepest centre; so be it, then: let the body here on earth possess its evil, and at the last breath let the soul enjoy it, and let it pass to a new world.

It has been suggested that the poet wrote this while being healed of a wound that had occasioned a lady's pity,[19] but the interpretation of 'evil' as a wound and of 'good' as her compassion does not, I think, provide a complete account of the poem. Within the context of Aldana's developing philosophy of love, 'evil' makes better sense as sensual pleasure. This pleasure is a 'good' but it cannot penetrate into the soul, and the body there⁄ fore guards it in its 'deepest centre' (11). Yet such a good, so deep a joy, must be immortal: at the hour of death it will be transferred to the soul in order to accompany it to Heaven. From the philosophical point of view this poem is remarkable, and very important in the development of Neoplatonism, for it is an attempt to conceive of sexuality as a good of the soul, an attempt to bridge the gulf between body and spirit.

Other poems of Aldana express not joy but anguish, an anguish born of the human condition. In *Sonnet 33*, for in⁄ stance, the mortal body is held to be a wearisome weight to the soul. The only alleviation is spiritual contemplation, which should be desired with a zeal as great as the burden is heavy. The burden itself is inseparable from human existence. How can life be made bearable? It would be better to have no reason with which to pass judgements, in which case pain at the human condition would not be felt, or else to possess only sen⁄ sation, to live exclusively in sensuousness. Which would pro⁄ vide more comfort? *Sonnet 32* continues the exploration. Its subject is *taedium vitae*. The poet is anguished at his inability to give his life an enduring positive value. He feels profound dis⁄ content not only with himself but with life as a whole. This dissatisfaction with oneself at the mismanagement of one's life is the beginning of religious experience, since it means searching elsewhere for the contentment that has not been found in the world. *Sonnet 36* moves further towards a resolution:

> Señor, que allá de la estrellada cumbre
> todo lo ves en un presente eterno,
> mira tu hechura en mí, que al ciego Infierno
> la lleva su terrena pesadumbre.
>   Eterno Sol, ya la encendida lumbre
> do esté mi alegre abril florido y tierno
> muere, y ver pienso al más nevado invierno

más verde la raíz de su costumbre.

En mí tu imagen mira, ¡oh Rey Divino!,
con ojos de piedad, que al dulce encuentro
del rayo celestial verás volvella,

que a verse como en vidrio cristalino
la imagen mira el que se espeja dentro,
y está en su vista dél su mirar della.

Lord, you who beyond the starry vault see all things in an eternal
present, look in me on your handiwork, whose material burden
is carrying it to unseeing Hell. Eternal Sun, already the burning
light in which my happy springtime might flower and be tender
is dying, and I seem to see in deepest winter snow the roots of its
life becoming greener. Behold in me your image, oh King divine,
with a merciful look; when it gently encounters your heavenly
gaze you will see it turn to see itself, as when a man who sees
himself mirrored in a glass looks at the image, and the gaze of the
image is in his eyes.

The key phrase is 'terrena pesadumbre' (4): the noun meant
both 'weight' and 'sadness'. This earthly 'pesadumbre' (all the
burden of materiality) is carrying the poet down to Hell; only
God can lift him up to Heaven if He sees in man not the matter
of which he is formed but the divine image and likeness that
'informs' it. The divine image in man is his intellect and soul.
Youth dies in the consciousness of approaching old age, the
green of summer yields to the snow of winter, but the root of
human experience becomes 'greener': man, contemplating in
maturity the unsatisfactoriness of his life, will be able to produce
the fruit of wisdom. God looks at man as if gazing into a mirror,
and sees His own likeness in him. Aldana's poetry has arrived
at the 'desire for God' which Platonism, followed by much of
scholastic philosophy, considered to be innate in man. From
this realization Aldana moves upward to the desire for union
with Him which is expressed in *Sonnet 37*, *Al Cielo*.

Clara fuente de luz, nuevo y hermoso,
rico de luminarias, patrio Cielo,
casa de la verdad sin sombra o velo,
de inteligencias ledo, almo reposo:

¡oh cómo allá te estás, cuerpo glorioso,
tan lejos del mortal caduco velo,
casi un Argos divino alzado a vuelo,
de nuestro humano error libre y piadoso!

¡Oh patria amada!, a ti sospira y llora
esta en su cárcel alma peregrina,
llevada errando de uno en otro instante;

esa cierta beldad que me enamora
suerte y sazón me otorgue tan benina
que, do sube el amor, llegue el amante.

Clear source of light, fresh and beautiful and rich in lights,
heavenly homeland, home of Truth without shadow or veil,
lovely in its intelligences, tranquil repose: oh glorious body, how
far you are there from the mortal, fleeting veil, like a divine Argos
raised up in flight, free from, and pitying, our human error!
Oh beloved homeland! To you this pilgrim soul in its prison
sighs and weeps, as it wanders from moment to moment; may
this true beauty that enamours me grant me such a kindly fortune
and season that the lover may reach the place to which love rises.

Heaven is first called 'patrio Cielo' (2), and later 'patria amada'
(9). The soul is a 'pilgrim' enclosed in a 'prison', yet a pilgrim
wandering not from place to place but from moment to
moment, a wanderer in life, searching for its native land which
is Paradise (9–11). Now the only beauty of which he is enamoured, a beauty that is sure and certain, awaits him there, and
love precedes the poet in his upward movement.

The gradual emergence in Aldana's work of religious desire
prompts one to ask if his poetic experience confirms the notion
of Neoplatonist theoreticians that love for woman can and does
lead to the love of God. The answer must be that his poetry
does not communicate the final stage of Renaissance Platonic
love. It passes from erotic sensuality to disenchantment and disillusion, and from there to religion. This does not mean, of
course, that for him erotic and divine love are opposed, but that
they are distinct; they are not contradictory, but they should not
be confused. The Reformation and Counter-Reformation, in
reacting to various aspects of Humanism, brought about a
separation of Christian Platonism from Humanist Neoplaton-

ism. This separation occurs in the poetry of Aldana. He obviously came to believe that sensual and divine love are neither
similar nor compatible: in the *Carta a Galanio* he compares
them to parallel lines that can never meet.[20]

Aldana, however, had no hesitation in associating the love of
men who share similar intellectual interests and spiritual aspirations with progress towards the love of God.[21] The magnificent
Carta a Arias Montano is eloquent testimony of this. Here we
leave the sphere of sexual love, whether sensual or Platonic. The
poem develops the basic principle of the Christian Platonism
of the sixteenth century, namely, that to arrive at the contemplation of divine beauty one must begin with the contemplation of
the beauty of Nature. It opens with a reference to the poet's early
years which he calls his lost life, a wasted youth spent in the
pursuit of two follies (10–21).[22] One of these must have been
sensual love and the other the ambition for military and political
advancement. He is now writing at the age of forty, freed from
these follies and able to march unencumbered towards his
rightful native land, by which is meant detachment from the
world but also from the body, the two requisites for a contemplative life:

> Mas ya, (merced del cielo), me desato,
> ya rompo a la esperanza lisonjera
> el lazo en que me asió con doble trato;
>   pienso torcer de la común carrera
> que sigue el vulgo y caminar derecho
> jornada de mi patria verdadera;
>   entrarme en el secreto de mi pecho
> y platicar en él mi interior hombre
> do va, do está, si vive o qué se ha hecho.
>   Y porque vano error más no me asombre,
> en algún alto y solitario nido
> pienso enterrar mi ser, mi vida y nombre;
>   y, como si no hubiera acá nacido,
> estarme allá, cual Eco, replicando
> al dulce son de Dios del alma oído.   (43–57)

But now (thanks be to Heaven) I am breaking free, now I am cutting the bond in which false hope had me doubly bound; I shall turn off the common highway that the rabble follow and travel straight to my true fatherland; enter the secret place within my breast, and there converse with the inner man about where he is heading, where he is now, whether he is alive or what has become of him. And so that vain error may never again take me by surprise, in some high and solitary dwelling place I shall bury my being, my life and my name; and, as if not born in this world, I shall remain there, replying, like Echo, to the gentle call of God that is audible to the soul.

The marvellous image of the human soul as the Echo of the divine Narcissus whom she loves introduces a detailed consideration of the nature of contemplative prayer. Contemplation means abstracting immaterial beauty from the material sense-images presented to the mind (70–5). The poem contemplates the idea of God through the concepts of immobility and absolute tranquillity, and the mystical experience that this can lead to is that of being 'transformed' in the divine life. The senses are suspended in their functions and matter thus becomes subdued and subject:

> Ojos, oídos, pies, manos y boca,
> hablando, obrando, andando, oyendo y viendo,
> serán del mar de Dios cubierta roca.
> Cual pece dentro el vaso alto, estupendo,
> del Océano irá su pensamiento
> desde Dios para Dios yendo y viniendo:
> serále allí quietud el movimiento
> cual círculo mental[23] sobre el divino
> centro, glorioso origen del contento.   (82–90)

Eyes, ears, feet, hands and mouth, speaking, working, walking, hearing and seeing, will be a rock covered over by the sea of God; like a fish in the tall, astonishing glass of the Ocean, its thought will travel back and forth from God to God: there it will find movement to be rest, like a mental circle around the divine centre, glorious source of contentment.

The process of contemplation itself is, first of all, to raise the mind to God. To meditate on His creation of being, out of

nothing, is the contemplation of divine power. This evokes
gratitude for life, and gratitude is the beginning of love (42–
47). The second stage of the process is the meditation on
Creation in general. The soul is asked 'to emerge to see itself
within the current of time' (150). It is 'a line drawn out from
the eternal point' (151–2), and the striking image continues as
the soul, now descended into the body, becomes the 'horizon'
between the pure unchanging world of spirit and the mutable,
defective world of matter, sharing in the nature of each (152–9).
Thirdly, the meditation turns to the contemplation of 'creatures',
the animate or inanimate works of God's hands (160–74).
This leads to the fourth head of the meditation, the consideration
of God's goodness. The fifth stage is the realization that mystical
experience is a waiting:

> Digo que puesta el alma en su sosiego
> espere a Dios, cual ojo que cayendo
> se va sabrosamente al sueño ciego;
>
> que al que trabaja por quedar durmiendo,
> esa misma inquietud destrama el hilo
> del sueño que se da no le pidiendo.
>
> Ella verá con desusado estilo
> toda regarse, y regalarse junto
> de un salido de Dios sagrado Nilo.   (232–40)

I say that the soul, once tranquil, should await God like an eyelid
that as it falls goes pleasantly into sightless sleep; for when a
person strives to fall asleep this very restlessness breaks the thread
of slumber, which is given when unsought; the soul will find that
in a wonderful way she is self-refreshing, self-delighting in a sacred
Nile flowing from God.

The difficulty of communicating mystical experience through
language is insurmountable; words and metaphors have to be
found that suggest, or indirectly communicate, the ineffable.
Aldana, from the basis of the theory of the 'the three styles',
chooses a vocabulary that the theorists of poetry called 'pereg-
rino', meaning 'unusual' in the direction of the 'marvellous'.
The result is a heightening of poetic eloquence (259–76). But
he withdraws from the attempt, fearful of losing himself and

'drowning in the depths'. The exploration of such an experience befits a Montano, not him, and the ideal of Platonic love is now the desire to stand beside Montano on the summit of contempla/ tion (295–351). This will represent victory over sinfulness, victory over the sensitive appetite, namely the instincts and desires of the body. He concludes with an imaginative picture of the ideal setting in which he might live with Montano a life dedicated to contemplation. This would not be among moun/ tains, or in deep valleys (because one must shun extremes) but next to the sea (352–72). Thereupon begins the marvellous exploration of the seashore with the discovery of beauty in the tiniest works of the Creator (373–434). This is an ideal life, as the meadows were for pastoral poetry, a life representing an innocent and pure love; it is thus an ideal setting for the love of Aldana for Montano, in their mutual love for the beauty of the world (436–47).

Aldana's poetry certainly shows a mystical disposition; it may also show that he had progressed part of the way in preparation. Although there is nothing in it that points directly to a clear mystical experience, it demonstrates indisputably that a longing for ideal love, sincerely felt and sought for, could lead under the prevailing influence of Renaissance Platonism to the search for God, and that the love of God, while representing the same human need to break down the isolation of the individual, leads beyond the physical to the spiritual. Aldana's life marks the emergence and the development of Spanish mystical literature which itself expresses a religious movement that had profound effects on Spain's social and cultural life. Spain had individual mystics both before and after this period, but only within it did mysticism constitute a widespread movement. As regards litera/ ture we may assume that the aspiration for an idealized love, culminating culturally in the revival of Platonism, created a tradition and a climate propitious for the emergence of mystical writings.

Saint Francis in ecstacy, by Pedro de Mena (1628–1688).

THREE.

THE HUMAN LANGUAGE
OF DIVINE LOVE

Ideal love and mysticism. mysticism. Courtly Love and mysticism. ST JOHN OF THE CROSS. Divine and human love. a symbolic language. poems and commentary. *Noche oscura. Cántico espiritual.*

Ideal Love and Mysticism

In European literature from the late Middle Ages to the Baroque, three terms are used to denote the different concepts of love that are treated in it: Courtly Love, Neoplatonism and Mysticism. In the sixteenth century no other literature shows the confluence and intermingling of these three more strikingly than that of Spain, which can therefore offer some of the most interesting illustrations of the general problems raised by European love-poetry in the Renaissance. What Spain can show, as no other literature can, is one of the great schools of mysticism in Christian literature. St Teresa of Avila (1515-82) and St John of the Cross (1542-91) are the two leading figures, but by no means its only representatives. The latter has often been called the greatest of Spanish poets, a title given him by such authorities as Marcelino Menéndez Pelayo and Dámaso Alonso. Although a comparative gradation of this kind is difficult, because his poems are unique in both content and style, the title of 'máximo poeta' is one that cannot be easily disputed. It was re-affirmed by the last-named critic not from any prejudice in favour of the poetry's subject matter, but solely on stylistic and aesthetic grounds.[1] Spanish literature in the Renaissance is therefore uniquely placed to offer material for the discussion of the literary-cultural problems raised by mystical poetry. Nevertheless, the particular problem of the relationship between this Spanish mystical literature and the traditions of secular love poetry has never been properly discussed.

73

Mysticism. The word 'mysticism' is nowadays used vaguely to denote any non-rational approach to life, any adherence to principles and values that repudiate reason. I use the term only in the sense of a direct conscious contact of the human soul with God, or with the Absolute, or the Ground of Being, whatever term one may use for ultimate and eternal reality. That is what those who have experienced religious mysticism claim it to be. Naturally the claim is disputed: it *must* be disputed by anyone who does not believe in the existence in any form of an ultimate transcendental Reality.

The older way of discussing these experiences as hallucinations or auto-suggestion used to seem facile to many, but in recent times it has become apparent that states very similar to, at times perhaps even identical with, those traditionally called mystical are produced by the psychedelic or hallucinogenic drugs, such as L S D and mescaline. Alan Watt, in an interesting study entitled 'Psychedelics and Religious Experience', has described the core of this drug-stimulated experience as 'an awareness of eternal energy, often in the form of intense white light . . . one sees quite clearly that all existence is a single energy, and that this energy is one's own being. . . . At root, you are the Godhead, for God is all that there is'.[2] In essentials this would seem to be very close to the summit of the mystical experience recorded by the Spanish mystics: the living in and through the divine life which is frequently called 'divinization', a state of consciousness to which the mystic is suddenly admitted.

The exceptional nature of these mystical-religious experiences is thus no longer an indication of a possible supernatural origin; but neither is it an indication that the origin of such experiences can never be supernatural. If God revealed himself and his nature and purposes to men, as Jews and Christians believe, he had to reveal himself in a way comprehensible to the people receiving the revelation: in the only concepts and through the only emotions that their particular stage of culture permitted them to formulate and feel. Similarly if God can communicate himself to individual men he can do so only through the psychological, intellectual and affective mechanisms which he has himself implanted in human nature. The fact that there is a particular mechanism of sensibility stimulated by a particular type of drug does not mean that this same mechanism does not respond to a supernatural stimulus. We may take the following image as an analogy of a psychedelic experience: you are imprisoned in a windowless house behind a locked door; suddenly the door is unlocked and you step into a beautiful garden. The drug unlocked the door; it did not create the garden. Another key to unlock the door may well come from another source.

However, whether the mystics' claims are true or false does not really matter for the purposes of this study, or for reading their writings as literature. Whether the literary historian is a theist or atheist, mystical literature remains a cultural phenomenon that has to be dealt with historically. What matters is not the actual truth of the mystics' claims, but the fact that they believed them to be true, and were sincere in this belief, and the fact that the particular public for which they wrote, and their age in general, believed it also. There has always been, at all times and in all countries, a certain amount of pseudo-mysticism, but I am taking it as axiomatic that writers like St Teresa and St John of the Cross were not conscious frauds. They were convinced with utter sincerity that their interpretations of their experiences were correct.

What the Spanish mystics claim to experience is actual union with God, the union of spirit with spirit which is achieved by contemplative prayer. St John of the Cross says that this union is an intellectual intuition of the Divinity; but it is at the same time, and above all, an act of love, the supreme culmination of the soul's love of God. He himself calls it 'an amorous knowledge' and a 'divine conjunction and union'.[3] It is a divine embracing, and this is the language of human love.

Courtly Love and Mysticism

When writers influenced by Courtly Love wrote of human love they used the language of religion; on the other hand, when St Teresa and St John of the Cross wrote of the love of God they used the language of human love. To say, as the rationalist does, that the common use of this language is a sign that mystical experience is a deviation of sexuality, may make sense to the psychologist. But on the plane of literature this is no explanation whatsoever of the poetic quality and language of St John of the Cross, or of the experience he and other mystics describe at length, any more than it is an explanation of the psychedelic experiences some people seek nowadays, to say they are produced by LSD. What is actually experienced is what has to be explained, not what causes it.[4]

Any attempt at an explanation of the literary experience of writers like Diego de San Pedro, on the one hand, and St John on the other, must start from the basic yearning in human nature to transcend the isolation of the individual in some sort of ideal. At its crudest, this yearning was manifested in sixteenth-century Spain in that group among the *illuminati* heretics who were accused of having developed the doctrine of Perfectionism, the belief that it is possible for man on Earth to attain to a condition of sinlessness in which actions normally regarded as sinful are not in fact so. The perfect, some of them reputedly held, could indulge in the sexual act as the highest form of prayer because this act was union with God.[5] In its higher forms, however, this yearning for beauty and goodness led others to the religious life in a contemplative religious order. To my mind, there must be something of this behind the conventions of *cancionero* poetry.

The central element in this connection of the late Spanish form of Courtly Love with mysticism is the concept of suffering. On the purely human level the cult of a suffering and despairing love is indeed morbid, and of course the cult of suffering has been morbid in religion itself in some of its forms. But in religious life the central position of suffering is not morbid. The moral value of suffering is seen in the fact that a man who has known and accepted it is more ready with sympathy and less harsh with criticism; his self-importance is muted. By contrast, the man whose life has been easy is often selfish, unfeeling, immature; in short, the 'spoilt child'. This as regards suffering *accepted*; suffering *sought* has another value. It is the self-discipline required by any training, such as that of the athlete and the musician, who must lead lives as ascetic as those of monks, sacrificing their comfort, steeling themselves to endure, in order to obtain perfect self-control. Self-control is necessary for the attainment of any goal, and without it the balanced calmness that should be the ideal of the rational man is of course impossible.

In the light of these general observations what kind of meaning can we give to the suffering that was so essential a feature of the love literature of the 1500s? At its crudest, this is clearly a sham, something indulged in or feigned in order to arouse the lady's pity and make her consent to the lover's desires. On a deeper level, it is something more real, it is the pain of suspended desire, the pain of non-fulfilment. The man who loves must seek to be loved in return; hope of this fulfilment promises joy, but fear that he will not receive it, still more the awareness that he will never receive it, make him suffer to the verge of despair. For the Renaissance Neoplatonists the grief and despair of the unrequited lover were irrational; they were felt only because sensuality was allowed the upper hand. Their philosophy allowed no place for suffering like this, for the rational ideal they pursued was a calm, serene love of the mind. Suffering was thus dismissed from human experience as an unnecessary evil.

There is, however, one Renaissance Neoplatonist from whose doctrine of love suffering is not excluded. Perhaps it was no accident that he came from the Iberian peninsula; certainly he had a much greater influence in Spain than did Bembo. He was the exiled Portuguese Jew, Judah Leo Abravanel, generally called Leone Ebreo, whose *Dialoghi d'amore* were mentioned earlier.[6] He puts the suffering of love on a much deeper level than the pain of unfulfilled desire. Of course the lover suffers if love is not requited; but, says Ebreo, even when it is requited and union is achieved, the fulfilled love of sexual union does not cease to be anguish because love is the desire for total and complete union with the beloved, the merging of one person into the other. This is possible with souls but not with bodies, which must always remain distinct and apart. Hence the body

frustrates the perfect union of love and the lover suffers un/
happiness, for the imperfect union that he does achieve makes
him yearn more and more for the perfect union he is never able
to achieve. There is surely something deeply tragic, something
existential that reaches to the heart of human experience, in this
idea of the body suffering anguish in the only kind of ecstasy it
is able to know. For Ebreo the way out of this suffering is the
Platonic ascent to union with God in contemplation, but by
contrast with the Italian Neoplatonists this ascent implies the
pain of crushing the body's own happiness. Ebreo is thus the
link between Courtly Love and Neoplatonism on the one hand,
and between Neoplatonism and Mysticism on the other.

The first of these links may be illustrated by an example from
the poetry of Aldana. In one of his sonnets his lady asks him
why in the midst of the union of love they are both compelled to
sigh and weep. He replies:

> "Amor, mi Filis bella, que allá dentro
> nuestras almas juntó, quiere en su fragua
> los cuerpos ajuntar también tan fuerte
>   que no pudiendo, como esponja el agua,
> pasar del alma al dulce amado centro,[7]
> llora el velo mortal su avara suerte."

> 'Love, my beautiful Filis, which deep within us has conjoined
> our souls, wishes also to join our bodies so tightly in its forge that
> when he cannot pass, as water passes into a sponge, from our
> souls to the sweet, dear centre (of our union), our mortal veils
> (i.e. our bodies) lament their miserly fortune.'

Aldana had read about this suffering in Ebreo but he gives no
sign of actually having felt it: his statement seems to me purely
theoretical. But can it be anything else? Can this suffering of
the body in the act of love correspond to anything real? The
mystics point to the answer when they undergo the suffering of
the senses as part of their ascesis; in them it is a very real ex/
perience, and one from which they emerge purified. This is
what St John of the Cross calls *la noche oscura del alma* (the Dark
Night of the Soul), and it seems to me to be connected with the
suffering Ebreo speaks of: the having to break the link between

the senses and the soul's functioning so that divine love can reach the mind, which alone has the capacity to receive it. The onset of the Dark Night takes place when the soul realizes that it is impossible to come to the knowledge of God through the imagination and the reason; this brings a sense of absolute and total frustration. Since the senses cannot spiritually love, they must be stilled in subjugation: the mind must therefore be emptied of all sense impressions in order to be able to receive a knowledge that is purely spiritual. It is the eradication in oneself of attachment to anything that is not God. As the mystics describe it, it is clearly a most agonizing experience, a sense of total aridity and dereliction, of being abandoned in utter solitude and total darkness.[8]

Denis de Rougemont asked whether this experience of the mystics was in some way analogous to the experience of love as rendered in the literature of Courtly Love. He himself instanced the passion of Tristan as a denudation of the imagination by means of an obsessive concentration on a single image. To de Rougemont this seemed a nakedness of the spirit, a denudation of the self in isolation with the beloved, both being lost to the world in a spiritual desert that seemed akin to the Dark Night.[9] I myself prefer to see the analogy not in the obsessive self-absorption of passion but in the pain of love as expounded by Ebreo: the anguish of the senses at their inability to consummate the union of two souls. This pain of the senses at their inadequacy to achieve the ideal that the mind yearns for is itself a religious experience; within the philosophy of Ebreo it is the starting-point for the contemplation of God. But going further back there must be a direct link, somewhere deep in human nature itself, between St John's Dark Night and the suffering, despairing, unfulfilled love of Spanish fifteenth- and sixteenth-century poetry. If there is an experiential link, perhaps only the psychologist could tell us what it might be. But I would maintain that even without this explanation the historian of literature must recognize the existence of this link even if he can do no more than explain it in terms of literary tradition. The link within the tradition is perfectly clear, for the most influential form of Neoplatonism in Spain was the philosophy of Leone Ebreo which, unlike the other forms, preserved throughout the sixteenth century the dominance of the concept of love as suffering rather than as a harmonious serenity. This fact, I hold, cannot be an accident in the century that produced a great mystical literature.

Conventional though the expression of this suffering is in the poetry of around 1500, it is a convention that points, however confusedly, to a genuine aspiration and ideal, and it is based, however confusedly, upon the concept of suffering as a valuable experience. The literature of mysticism is what dispels the con-fusion and clarifies the aspiration by achieving it in actual ex-perience. The difference in intensity between the aspiration and the reality can best be shown by a contrast between Garcilaso de la Vega and St John of the Cross. In the fifth sonnet of the former the ideal of human love is expressed in the conventional poetic language which, it has been argued, is basically religious:

> Escrito 'stá en mi alma vuestro gesto
> y quanto yo escrivir de vos desseo:
> vos sola lo escrivistes; yo lo leo
> tan solo que aun de vos me guardo en esto.
>
> En esto 'stoy y estaré siempre puesto,
> que aunque no cabe en mí quanto en vos veo,
> de tanto bien lo que no entiendo creo,
> tomando ya la fe por presupuesto.
>
> Yo no nascí sino para quereros;
> mi alma os ha cortado a su medida;
> por hábito del alma misma os quiero;[10]
>
> quanto tengo confiesso yo deveros;
> por vos nací, por vos tengo la vida,
> por vos é de morir, y por vos muero.

Your look is written in my soul and everything I wish to write about you: you yourself have written it; I read it in such solitude that when I do so I exclude even you. I am and always shall be dedicated to this, for although all I see in you cannot be contained in me, yet I believe that which in such great goodness surpasses my understanding, for I take faith as my guarantee. I was born

only to love you; my soul has cut you to its own measure; I love
you as the clothing of my very soul; everything that I am I confess
that I owe to you; through you I came to life, through you I am
living now, on your account I shall die, and for you I *am* dying.

This sonnet is very beautiful; the fact that its language is mostly
conventional does not, of course, deprive the experience of
sincerity, but it does, perhaps, limit its intensity. St John of the
Cross took over the conventional Courtly Love language of the
flames of love, of wounding, and of suffering as a living death,
but no secular poet, inside Spain or outside, came anywhere
near giving it the experiential reality and tremendous significance that he did as he applied it to his own experience on
emerging from the agony of the Dark Night. The poem that
does this is *Llama de amor viva* (Living Flame of Love):

¡Oh llama de amor viva
que tiernamente hieres
de mi alma en el más profundo centro,
pues ya no eres esquiva,
acaba ya, si quieres;
rompe la tela deste dulce encuentro!

¡Oh cauterio suave!
¡Oh regalada llaga!
¡Oh mano blanda! Oh toque delicado
que a vida eterna sabe
y toda deuda paga;
matando, muerte en vida la has trocado!

¡Oh lámparas de fuego
en cuyos resplandores
las profundas cavernas del sentido,
que estaba oscuro y ciego,
con extraños primores
calor y luz dan junto a su querido!

¡Cuán manso y amoroso
recuerdas en mi seno
donde secretamente solo moras
y en tu aspirar sabroso

de bien y gloria lleno
cuán delicadamente me enamoras!

> Oh living flame of love, that tenderly wounds the deepest centre of my soul; since now you hold back no longer, make an end if you so wish; rend the veil that screens our sweet encounter! Oh gentle cautery! Oh caressing wound! Oh soft hand! Oh delicate touch that tastes of life eternal and the whole debt repays! by killing you have turned death into life. Oh lamps of fire, in whose resplendence the deep caverns of sense—sense which was dark and blind—give back with a strange beauty both heat and light to their beloved. How peacefully and lovingly you awaken within my breast where you in solitary secrecy do dwell; in the flavour of your breathing, full of goodness and glory, how delicately you make love to me!

The Latin languages, like the Germanic, have one word for both the physical organ of perception and for meaning or significance. As St John's own commentary on this poem makes clear, the double meaning of the word *sentido* (15) is essential for its proper comprehension.[11] The suffering of emptiness that produces the darkness of the soul's night, when all sensuousness is stilled and there is nothing left that the soul can love while searching for God, is expressed as dark, deep caverns of meaninglessness: the flame of love is burning and wounding as the senses die, but the flame heals as it kills and suddenly the caverns, in which the soul without God is empty and blind, are flooded with the burning radiance and heat of meaning as God communicates himself. Here, too, there are close links with much Neoplatonist poetry in what follows, for St John goes on to say that the light and heat that God himself radiates in the soul is the only thing the soul can give back to God in the form of love.[12] Of itself the human soul is nothing but an empty, dark cavern: there is nothing that the soul, of itself, can give to God except its capacity to be filled with God's own light.

In the poem by Garcilaso, the poet's soul is a sheet of paper on which he reads only what his beloved has written. St John's image is infinitely more significant: the awakening from the darkness of meaninglessness by being set on fire and being made to radiate the light of the meaning of the universe. Yet for the historian of literature, as distinct from the theologian, there is a connecting link. For a hundred years the literature, and there/ fore the life, of Spain had groped uncertainly towards an aspira/ tion and an ideal, perhaps to some extent intuiting something of an experience that the mystics brought to reality. The mystics brought a whole movement to fruition because they alone could place the concept of ideal love in an object beyond the imperfec/ tions of matter, time and space. They alone claimed to have found and lived the only love that is not stained by passion, withered by age or destroyed by death.[13] In other words, a love that transcends the limitations of the human condition.

What this meant in practice, as an existential reality, was perfect serenity of mind, freed from all care, with all passion stilled. Whether or not their love was in fact a mystical en/ counter with God, this state of tranquillity which it produced can claim to represent human fulfilment or perfection. After the mystics have passed through the suffering of the Dark Night into the radiant meaningfulness of union with God, they live in a permanent state of awareness of his abiding presence, which is a state of perfect inner peace however much the anxieties of daily living may surround them. St Teresa expresses this state of fulfilment, in her customary practical and realistic imagery, at the end of her *Interior Castle* (*El castillo interior* or *Las moradas*) written in 1577 and addressed to her nuns:

Este centro de nuestra alma—u este espíritu—es una cosa tan dificultosa de decir, y aun de creer, que pienso, hermanas, por no me saber dar a entender, no os dé alguna tentación de no creer lo que digo; porque decir que hay trabajos y penas y que el alma se está en paz, es cosa dificultosa. Quiéroos poner una comparación . . . Está el Rey en su palacio, y hay muchas guerras en su reino y muchas cosas penosas; mas no por eso deja de estarse en su puesto. Ansí acá. Aunque en estotras moradas anden muchas baraúndas y fieras ponzoñosas y se oye el ruido, nadie entra en aquélla que la haga quitar de allí; ni las cosas que oye, aunque le dan alguna pena, no es de manera que la alboroten y quiten la paz; porque las pasiones están ya vencidas, de suerte que han miedo de entrar allí, porque salen más rendidas. Duélenos todo del cuerpo; mas si la cabeza está sana, no porque duele el cuerpo dolerá la cabeza.[14]

This centre of our soul—or this spirit—is something so difficult to describe, and even to grasp by faith, that I am afraid, my sisters, that you will be tempted not to believe what I say because I cannot express myself well. Let me try to give you an illustration . . . The King is in his place, and there is much strife and warfare in his kingdom, but not on that account does he cease to be in his proper place. So it is here. Although in the other mansions there is much tumult and poisonous beasts, and this noise is heard within, yet nobody can enter who could make her leave that place; the things she hears may grieve her, but not in such a way as to perturb her or deprive her of her peace; because the passions are conquered and are fearful of entering lest they be even further subdued. Our whole body may be sick, but if the head is healthy it will not feel pain just because the body hurts.

This union of creature and Creator on a plane of existence that transcends sexuality is the achieved ideal of perfect love of which Courtly Love was the confused aspiration. The literary trajectory from the one to the other cannot be detected, much less understood, if Courtly Love is denied its aspiration towards an idealized conception of love and consigned instead to the sphere of the sensually erotic. To insist that the poetry of the *cancioneros* is only a morbid sensuality is to deprive the poetry of St John of the Cross of the literary tradition which gives it a cultural-historical significance much wider than its value as an exposition of mystical theology. To put it into the context of the literary tradition of its age enables us, if I am not mistaken, to see that the ideal of a perfect, spiritualized love, which has haunted humanity throughout the centuries, can be something existentially and historically real. It became so in sixteenth-century Spain when the search for ideal love broke its links with the human in everything but the *language* of love.

There is an extraordinary difference between the poetry of St John of the Cross and the poetry of the sixteenth century so far considered. Previous poets were conscious of writing within a tradition which indicated the diction and imagery most appro‚ priate to the different types of subject‚matter; these were them‚ selves graded according to quality and value in the experience. In the case of love‚poetry the traditional nature of the subject matter had been reaffirmed and redirected by the philosophical treatises on love. The greatest poets had added to this tradition with originality without denying or distorting its basic features, and not until the end of the sixteenth century, and the rise of the new 'Baroque' poetry with its elaborate images and conceits, was there a marked break away from it. None of this applies to St John, who never intended to be a 'professional' poet or to imitate his predecessors. Some of his poems show the influence of Garcilaso, especially in their metre, but this influence may well have been indirect and is certainly not extensive. It was probably sacred poetry that he normally read, and the poetry he heard recited or sung was probably anonymous poetry in the tradition of the ordinary people.[15]

Despite this lack of 'professional' experience in the reading and writing of poetry, St John was a man with natural poetic gifts of the highest order. His poems were fashioned out of his intense experiences in a rhythm and style dictated by this intensity, and the language and imagery in which his experi‚ ences found expression were determined by his intellectual training in the scriptures, the Fathers and the Scholastics. The principal model he had before him for his treatment of love was the *Song of Solomon* whose influence is pervasive in the *Cántico espiritual*, although St John's poem has an extraordinary originality.[16]

Freedom from precedence, rules and fashions, gives his poetry a special magic of its own, and originality is, in fact, the hallmark of all his poems, each one of which is, in important respects, original in relation to the others.[17] The subject‚matter itself was not original, for mystical poetry in the widest sense was not new to Western Christendom, but his poetic expression strikes a much more intense and much deeper note in every respect, intellectual, emotional and poetic, than any mystical poetry he was likely to have known. It has, in fact, a striking originality in its matter as well as in its form.

Divine and Human Love

In one important particular, St John holds firm to the Christian tradition of the West: in his use of the concept and language of human love to express divine love. For a Christian writer there is no way of escaping from this, except by abstract symbols rooted, like Dante's final vision of God, in cosmic forces. The advantage of love imagery over cosmic lies in the fact that it is personal, the relation of the soul to God as a personal one being essential to Christianity. It also has its linguistic justification. In the Indo-European languages, the words for 'God' are masculine nouns, and those for 'soul' are feminine. This makes the analogy psychologically appropriate, for in the union of love man possesses and woman is possessed; in the spiritual relationship God must be the possessor and the soul the possessed. The metaphor is universal and unalterable, no matter whether the person recording the spiritual union be a man or a woman.

The fact that the lovers in the *Song of Solomon* were originally conceived only as human beings in a poetic pastoral setting does not affect the later tradition that interpreted them as God and the soul, or as Christ and the Church.[18] When the lovers speak to each other, one of the main forms of address used in the Latin Vulgate is the same for each, *dilectus*, and subsequent Latin commentators referred to *sponsus* and *sponsa*. St John makes his lovers address each other as *amado* and *amada* and after the mystical union they call themselves *esposo* and *esposa*. Although these terms are applied univocally to God and the human soul, they are, of course, used analogically in the case of God and with reference to his union with the individual.

This language of human love means that St John's poetry can be read as the love of a man and a woman for each other, and presumably the majority of his readers in modern times have read the poems in this way. Distinguished and sensitive literary critics have maintained that it is, in fact, impossible to read them in any other way. Whether this is indeed the case is a problem for the literary critic and perhaps the psychologist; it is not a problem, or has not been one, for believing Christians and even theologians who can readily distinguish the univocal and analogical uses of words. All languages are constantly changing and the original non-literal senses of words become forgotten by frequent use: when, for instance, we refer to an event as 'disastrous' or call somebody 'jovial', 'saturnine' or 'ill-starred', we are no longer aware of employing the concepts and terms of astrology. In mystical literature the transference from the natural level to the spiritual and supernatural levels must be made, either automatically by those to whom it is quite familiar, or else consciously by those who are not accustomed to it. The opening sentence of the *Song of Solomon*, 'O that you would kiss me with the kisses of your mouth!' (1:1) will be solely sensual for many modern readers, as it presumably was for its author. But for the Fathers of the Church and for the biblical commentators, it had only a spiritual or mystical sense, and one that through long familiarity would have seemed perfectly natural to them.

When St John was a novice in his Order and attending lectures in the University of Salamanca, he must have sat at the feet of one of its most distinguished professors, the scriptural scholar Luis de León (1527-91) who was also, like St John, one of the great poets of Spain; a poet, moreover, who wrote almost entirely in the *lira* metre, which St John used in two of his major poems and which he slightly modified in the third.[19] In 1583 León published *Los nombres de Cristo*, which no doubt contained much material from his Scripture courses. It is a treatise expounding the metaphorical and symbolical meanings of the names given to the Messiah in the Old Testament and to Christ in the New. Among the names there are two metaphors whose erotic content cannot be disregarded, *Amado* (Lover or Beloved) and *Esposo* (Bridegroom or Spouse).

In discussing these León does not seek to elude the specifically

87

physical connotations. He derives the name Spouse from *Ephesians* (5:28–33), where Paul compares the love of husband and wife to the love of Christ for his Church. León says that there are three things to be considered in the marriage of Christ and his Church. The first is the 'uniting and close union' and the word he uses for 'uniting' is *ayuntamiento*, which was the word for copulation. The second is 'sweetness and delight' that results from this union. The third is the circumstances in which marriage finds its expression. Since, he continues, Christ is the husband not only of the Church as a whole, but also of each one of its members, these factors must all combine in the relation of the believer to Christ. The marriage bond is a tight knot tying two different beings together, a tying which is preceded, accompanied and followed by an ineffable sweetness. There are, he adds, many kinds of unity in human society, including the family unity of parents and children and the political unity of king and subjects, but the union of husband and wife is greater, not only because it is so much tighter, but also because it produces a far greater joy. The application of the human experience to the spiritual does not, however, cover the total and absolute unity of Christ and humanity, for husband and wife remain distinct beings, while, on the other hand, human nature, through the Incarnation, provides the body for the Divine Person, which in its turn becomes the Bread that gives men their spiritual nourishment by merging into the substance of their bodies. The extension of the original metaphor into the Incarnation and the Eucharist does not depart from its erotic basis, because León continues his exposition in this way:

> así como por razón de aquel tocamiento son dichos ser una carne Eva y Adán, así y con mayor razón de verdad, Cristo Esposo fiel de su Iglesia, y ella, Esposa querida y amada suya, por razón de este ayuntamiento que entre ellos se celebra, cuando reciben los fieles dignamente en la hostia su carne, son una carne y un cuerpo entre sí. Bien brevemente Teodoreto sobre el principio de los *Cantares*, y sobre aquellas palabras de ellos: 'Béseme de besos de su

boca', en este propósito dice de esta manera: 'No es razón que ninguno se ofenda de aquesta palabra de *beso*, pues es verdad que al tiempo que se dice la misa y al tiempo que se comulga en ella, tocamos al cuerpo de nuestro *Esposo*, y le besamos y le abrazamos, y como *Esposo* así nos ayuntamos con El.[20]

Just as Adam and Eve are said to be one flesh because of that physical contact, so for the same reason, and more justly, Christ the faithful *Spouse* of his Church, and she, his dear Bride and beloved, form together one flesh and one body as a result of this union between them that is celebrated when the faithful worthily receive his flesh in the host. Theodoretus, commenting on the opening words of the *Song of Solomon*, 'O that you would kiss me with the kisses of your mouth!', writes very well and succinctly as follows: 'It is not right for anyone to be offended by this word "kiss" because it is true that when we celebrate Mass, at the time when we receive Communion, we touch the body of our *Spouse*, and we kiss him and embrace him, and thus we unite with him as with a *Spouse*.'

In the treatise on *Amado*, León goes further and asserts that all Creation, and not only man, has an innate thirst for God through love's yearning. To the religious mind, in whatever well-developed religious system, the thirst for God is a perfectly intelligible expression of man's yearning for love, and for the Christian it must mean, specifically, an innate longing for Christ, for the love that moves the whole of Nature. León, a confirmed Christian Platonist, writes most eloquently and movingly of the longing that the whole of created Nature has for Christ;

las (cosas) que ni juzgan ni sienten, las que carecen de razón y las que no tienen ni razón ni sentido, apetecen también a Cristo y se le inclinan amorosamente, tocadas de este su fuego, en la manera que su natural le consiente. Porque lo que naturaleza hace, que inclina a cada cosa al amor de su propio provecho, sin que ella misma lo sienta, eso obró Dios, que es por quien la naturaleza se guía, inclinando al deseo de Cristo aun a lo que no siente ni entiende.[21]

The things which neither judge nor feel, those things that lack reason and those that have neither reason nor feeling, also desire Christ and incline towards him lovingly, touched by this fire of his, in the way that their nature permits. For what is done by Nature, which inclines each thing, without it realising, to love its own good, is worked by God, by whom Nature is guided, and who inclines even things without feeling and reason to desire Christ.

The fact that the Christian God is revealed in the human Christ gives an inevitable human dimension to the expression of mystical love, which need not be there in the language of non-Christian mystics, and in describing this innate yearning for love and perfection, in its most intense form, León, a Christian Platonist, gives an account of mystical experience as an ardent longing for goodness and redemption from evil, a burning thirst for love to permeate one's being.

A Symbolic Language

It is within this dimension of analogical and symbolical thinking and feeling that St John's poetry must be read. He has not, however, been well served by his translators, with the exception of one.[22] Many special effects that poetry produces in one language are, admittedly, untranslatable in another. For instance, the *Cántico espiritual* begins with the soul, who is filled with yearning for God, being dissatisfied with the knowledge of him given by faith. Longing for more, she goes out into the countryside asking Creation to tell her more about him; but the natural world can tell her only that God is beautiful and good, for these are the qualities he has impressed upon it. She cries out to God that all his creatures who wander through the world keep praising his beauty a thousandfold, which only increases her longing to know him more closely. This she expresses as: 'I am left near to death by an I-know-not-what that they keep stammering'. This means that Creation can offer men only the most fleeting glimpse of God which is equivalent to an incoherent and incomplete statement. St John phrases this as follows:

Y todos más me llagan,
y déxame muriendo
un no sé qué que quedan balbuciendo. (Stanza 7)

That Nature's revelation of God is no more, or can be no more, than a halting stutter is a fine concept; St John makes it something finer by reproducing the stutter in the threefold repetition of the stressed syllable 'que', preceded by the stressed vowel 'e' of 'sé', itself part of the three halting monosyllables that follow. St John not only tells us that our natural knowledge of God is dim and faltering, he makes us hear and feel the stutter itself. Peers's translation is:

> Each deals a deeper wound
> And something in their cry
> Leaves me so raptur'd that I fain would die.

It would be too much to expect the sound of the stutter to be conveyed, but it is unpardonable that the concept of a stutter should disappear. What replaces it is a complete misinterpretation, for the whole point is that the answer of Creation to the desire for God can cause no rapture; unsatisfying 'rapture' caused by natural beauty or by human art is what the soul's yearning strives to transcend. Campbell is better, but still too far away:

> All those that haunt the spot
> Recount your charm, and wound me worst of all
> Babbling I know not what
> Strange rapture, they recall,
> Which leaves me stretched and dying where I fall.

'Babbling I know not what' is near to an inarticulate stammer, but the rest is gratuitous embroidery, which weakens the whole concept. Both Peers and Campbell are apt to alter irresponsibly the terms of St John's metaphors if they do not think them appropriate.

The special problem of St John's poetic images is that his elucidation of them in the commentaries depends on the precise words used in the poems. These must therefore be translated as literally as possible. A free translation of the poems will make nonsense of the commentaries. We may take as an example an astounding metaphor which occurs in the *Cántico espiritual* when the soul and her Spouse are united. The soul wishes nothing to intrude upon their union, and conjures the threatening tres-passers to remain at a distance. She does so in these words:

> ¡O ninfas de Judea!,
> en tanto que en las flores y rosales
> el ámbar perfumea,
> morá en los arrabales
> y no queráis tocar nuestros umbrales. (Stanza 18)

> Oh nymphs of Judea! while the amber is scenting the flowers and the rose trees, live out in the suburbs and do not try to touch our threshold.

To read this as part of a dialogue between two human lovers makes one ask what can it possibly mean? 'Nymphs of Judea' is a haunting image that seems totally out of place. What are nymphs with all their sensual associations in pagan literature doing in this poem of divine love? In any case, what have nymphs got to do with the Jews? And how can nymphs live in the suburbs of a town? The commentary not only explains the startling image, but also reveals the extraordinary control of a disciplined mind over the splendid intuition of poetic genius. The nymphs are the distractions of the imagination that con-tinually arise unbidden to disturb our concentration and that are so difficult to suppress. Being images, they are mental pictures that summon our attention, and being distractions (the com-mentary does not add this, but we should) they entice us away like nymphs. Because these fancies of the imagination are so hard to control, they are capricious and wayward, as were the Jews in their dealings with Jehovah.[23]

Once the metaphor is grasped through the relationships of the literal terms to the figurative, 'Oh nymphs of Judea!' is felt to be poetically so marvellous an image that it becomes impossible to think of it in any other way, and this applies as much to its literal translation as to the original. Yet Peers has 'daughters of Jewry' and Campbell (only one degree better) has 'Oh daughters of Judea'. But what daughters?[24] Through the avoidance of the 'nymphs', with all its associations of sensuous enticements, 'daughters of Jewry' becomes pointless as a metaphor for the fancies of the imagination.

We should also note the special significance of the word 'suburbs'. The word referred to the outlying parts beyond a city's walls, separate, but governed by the same municipal laws. Intellect and will are the spiritual powers of man and constitute the centre of the human city, separated from the physical senses, functions and instincts. Where else should the imagination's capricious nymphs dwell but outside the walls? There they have their proper place, governed by the city centre (i.e., reason and will) though separated from it. The English 'suburbs' does not, of course, have the melodious assonated sound of the Spanish *arrabales* whose melody no translator would willingly forego, but 'suburb' cannot, on that account, be dismissed as 'unpoetic'. Aiming at 'poetic' affects, Peers 'recreates' the stanza into pseudo-poetic triviality, once again missing the contact between poem and commentary:

Daughters of Jewry, stay!
While choicest amber-perfume doth invade
Rose-bowers and blossoms gay,
Rest in their outer glade
And come not to disturb our holy shade.

Campbell, as nearly always, is better: he has 'outskirts' which will do, though rather less concrete and precise than 'suburbs'.[25] He writes, however, 'But keep the outskirts clear', without intruding into the city centre: the point is that the sensuous images of the imagination must keep their place without disturbing or hindering the non-physical working of the mind.

'Nymphs of Judea' is not a descriptive metaphor but rather a symbolic one. This is the principal key to St John's poetry, for in it objects are constantly being raised from their literal dimension into a higher one. This is often brought about by a linguistic connection, and here too, translations must generally fail, for the particular link is unlikely to exist in another language. A very significant example of this symbolical language occurs in the second stanza of the *Cántico*. The soul searching for her Beloved, whom she has glimpsed only by faith, sends him the ardour of her emotions by means of prayers containing messages of anguished love. She bids the shepherds to carry this message of her malady up the hillside. The hill is God; but this is no ordinary hill. Of the various Spanish words for hill, St John chose *otero*, which means a single hill rising abruptly out of a plain. From this noun there was formed a verb *otear*, which means to command a view on all sides from a height. This, says the commentary, is how God looks at his creation: he commands it all, on every side, from his lofty eminence (as one would say in Spanish, 'otea el mundo'). He is therefore an *otero*, a symbol which also occurs in stanza 13 as the lovers climb the mountain where their union will be consummated.[26] In stanza 2 St John wrote:

> Pastores los que fuerdes,
> allá por las majadas al otero,
> si por ventura vierdes
> aquel que yo más quiero
> decilde que adolezco, peno y muero.

> Shepherds, you who go up through the sheepfolds to the hill, if by chance you should see him whom I love most of all, tell him that I am ill, that I suffer, that I am dying.

Campbell translates:

> O Shepherds, you that, yonder,
> Go through the sheepfolds of the slope on high,
> If you, as there you wander,
> Should chance my love to spy,
> Then tell him that I suffer, grieve, and die.

This is, perhaps, as adequate a rendering as one has the right to expect, but the absence of a specific noun as the termination of the mission impairs the symbolical sense. The fact that the soul's message consists of three words describing her condition is a further indication of St John's exact thinking, for traditionally the human soul had three powers, memory, understanding and will, and each suffers by having no direct experience of God, each in a way appropriate to its function.[27]

Poems and Commentary

These few examples will have illustrated the nature and the range of St John's symbolical language, and they will have shown how the poetry is enriched, not weakened, by the symbolism, since it denotes how thought and language are unified in the poetic experience, whose intensity of feeling has been universally acknowledged. The reader who has no Spanish must take this unification of thought, feeling and poetic imagery on trust. They will also have shown how impossible it is to grasp the precision of the poet's thought without the explanations supplied by the commentaries. These commentaries did not follow any literary tradition but were entirely in the line of patristic and medieval exegesis of scripture.[28] St John, however, when commenting on his poems, was explaining personal experiences, which the biblical commentators did not have to do. How the metaphorical meanings of his images, with their extraordinary precision, were present in the act of composition, whether intuitively or consciously, is a mystery.

The commentaries place the mystical states in their scriptural, theological and philosophical context; they also consider the poetic expression itself, the words and images in which it consists. This latter function, which is important for the layman, is crucial for the literary critic. It has been difficult, however, for most critics to accept the fact that precision of thought can fire feelings and emotions without depriving poetic diction of its glow. But, then, St John's poems are not ordinary poetry. It has also been difficult for them to accept the fact that the link between poems and commentaries is a very close one. The most distinguished Spanish literary critic of recent times, Dámaso Alonso, has asserted that the commentaries were an inevitable failure and by their very nature far removed from the poetic experience. That is, of course, strictly true. The commentaries,

while they fill in the whole mystical experience within a complete theological framework are, for this very reason, not the
experience itself nor the poetry. The poems alone come as close
to the experience as it was possible for the poet to convey it;
he could do it only in poetry, which was language burnished
and refined by the white-heat of an overwhelmingly intense
experience.

The commentaries did not aim to be poetry but treatises on
mystical theology through exegesis of the poems, but as such they
are an indispensable guide to the poems unless, of course, one
maintains with so much modern literary criticism that what the
poet meant to say in each of his images is irrelevant to the poetry
and, in any case, unknowable. All poetry, it would be claimed,
once written down and delivered by the poet begins to exist
independently in its own right, and to attempt to reconstruct the
original meaning constitutes 'the intentional fallacy'. The fact
that St John's commentaries tell us what the poems meant to *him*
would not affect the argument of such critics, because as Alonso
says, the poems were composed in the intense glow of inspiration,
and the commentaries were a rationalized analysis *a posteriori*,
which the poet manipulated to make the inspired poems mean
what he, as a theologian, later wanted them to mean.

Arguments of this kind cannot be discussed on any satisfactory
terms. Our only test for the legitimacy of the commentaries as
vehicles for the intrinsic meanings of the images must be, first,
that the revelation of the meanings prove entirely illuminating
within the context, and, secondly, that they in no way go counter
to the poetic emotion and tone. It is being suggested here that
'ninfas de Judea', in their 'arrabales', and 'otero' can, in their
contexts, mean only what the commentaries disclose, and that
their full meanings, with all their expounded associations, are
fully satisfying both intellectually and emotionally. It seems
impossible that the poet composed these poems in the fire of
poetic intuition, and only later worked out meanings for them.
The examples given of these images and their analyses surely
demonstrate a necessary and not an arbitrary relationship between
the word and the concept.

Perhaps familiarity with the various commentaries on Virgil, Dante and many other poets automatically causes modern critics to be repelled by commentaries as such, with their mass of often pedantic detail. As theological treatises, St John's commentaries go beyond the poetic experience to a large extent, but insofar as, in the course of the theological exposition, they explain individual words and phrases, they are intrinsically linked to the poetic experience. These explanations are the jewels buried in material that is of primary interest to theologians; the jewels themselves are of primary interest to literary critics and should be dug out by them.[29]

Noche oscura. To read St John's poetry as human love-songs in the manner of the *Song of Solomon* leaves the larger part of its imagery unintelligible, and the poems themselves, with one exception, enigmatic; it also robs it of much of its magic by depriving it of its air of mystery. If, however, we read the poetry sympathetically we can allow ourselves to be given a glimpse into another plane of experience. The erotic human language will succeed in conveying this other plane in the measure that it succeeds in awakening in us a sense of mysteriousness and wonder. In this it will be aided by the strangeness of the symbolic language which itself elevates us above the world of normal communication.

The one 'major' poem that could be read as a human love-poem is *Noche oscura* (Dark Night). Even in this case a feeling of strain to some extent remains if it is read as a meeting of human lovers, for there is more in the imagery than such a meeting can encompass. The soul tells how she left her house at dead of night, when all the house was quiet, leaving it in disguise and by a secret stair, going to where her Lover was waiting for her. On the ramparts they are united, the soul reclines her face upon the Lover, all else is forgotten and the yearning of her love is left among the lilies. The setting could not be more appropriate for a lovers' tryst: night-time, stillness and silence, disguise, a secret exit down a secret stair. It is also a most appropriate symbolical setting for the mystical union.

The soul apostrophizes the Night, calling it more lovable and loving than the dawn, for it is the Night that transforms the soul into her Beloved and the Beloved into her. This too is fully human in itself, but what is unusual is that only the Night is addressed by the soul; she never speaks to her Beloved nor does he speak to her. The Night is the Dark Night of the soul. It is the result of the soul's denudation, of her stripping herself of all attachment to the world of sense, of her breaking the links that bound her to all sensation, and rooting out from her mind and imagination every image, for images recall sensuous experiences. This state of total emptiness is the only route to her divine Lover, for he cannot meet her through the bodily senses. The denudation of the mind is for her, a 'disguise', and a 'secret stairway' out of herself, because it is the break with normal experience. The process is agonizingly painful, but once it is completed, it proves totally 'lovable'.

It would be only natural for the experience of human love to have suggested to the poet the symbol of night, but it is also perfectly natural that the secrecy and stillness of this prelude to full mystical union, with its detachment of the soul from everything visible and tangible, should be conceived as Night. As always with St John's major symbols, there is a perfect fusion of both the human and the mystical levels of experience, as well as a fusion with the word that represents the symbol. All that the word connotes on both levels of experience becomes relevant to the symbol.

The Night in *Noche oscura* not only unites the lover with the Beloved, it also 'transforms her into him'. On the human level of the poem 'transformed' is a metaphor, not a literal description. The concept of transformation is central to the experience of mystical union: in the commentaries St John says that the soul comes to be 'transformed' into God. By this St John does not mean any ontological change, any alteration in the soul's being and faculties; he explicitly excludes any possible pantheistic interpretation. God and man are infinitely distinct beings, the one uncreated, eternal and infinite, the other created and finite, and the likeness that union produces can only be on the level of accidents, not substance. The union of the soul and God is a union of love, and the universal principle that governs love is that it creates a likeness or a similitude between the two persons who love: the more perfect the love, the more perfect is the likeness. Likeness means conformity of wills in a mutual benevolence, in the impossibility of not desiring the total good of each other, and conformity and likeness is what St John calls 'the transformation of the soul into God'. A man becomes what he loves: if he loves matter he becomes a materialist, if he loves lust he becomes lustful, if he loves wisdom he becomes a philosopher, if he loves the spirit he becomes spiritual, if he loves God he 'becomes God'.[30] All true love brings a rupture with self-interest; a perfect love makes a person die to self. That is why, in order to attain to a perfect love of God, the soul must die in the pain of the Dark Night to all attachment to the sensible world, to everything that is not God. The Dark Night, transformation, and the healing flame of love are the cardinal elements in St John's mystical philosophy as they are in his poetry.

Cántico espiritual. The *Spiritual Canticle* is the longest of the poems of union and the one that in its linguistic technique lies half-way between the human setting of the *Noche oscura* and the non-human, solely transcendental, fire of the *Llama de amor viva*. It describes all the gradations of the mystic way, from dissatisfaction with a world that cannot reveal God to final union with him. In much of its imagery, and in the way the lovers address each other, it is close to the *Song of Solomon*, and it has therefore a link with scriptural and theological tradition that the other two poems, which are more original in their conception, do not show.[31]

The theme is the soul's search for God and her eventual union with him. She knows God only by faith, which means belief in what one has not experienced directly. Moved by the desire for a direct knowledge, she wanders through the countryside, imploring Nature to reveal him, as she seeks for visible evidence of his presence. In her search she exclaims that she will shrink from no hardships, she will cross all rivers and all frontiers, she will pass without fear by all fortresses in her way and face every assault.[32] Nature, however, can offer no more than transient testimony:

'He moved through these groves with haste, and looking on them as he passed, he left them clothed with beauty' (Stanza 5). The beauty of Nature makes the soul yearn for the transcendent beauty of its Creator. Although this beauty is testimony to God's existence, Nature cannot disclose his actual presence. The soul must have recourse to faith. God is revealed in Christ, and the soul gazes intently into the 'cristalina fuente', in which she hopes to see his reflection:

> ¡Oh cristalina fuente,
> si en esos tus semblantes plateados
> formases de repente
> los ojos deseados
> que tengo en mis entrañas dibujados!   (Stanza 12)

> Oh crystal fountain! Oh that I might see in your silvered images the longed-for eyes that are imprinted within me!

The waters of faith reflect the 'faces' of the Divine, but these are silvered only, indistinct and misty. Faith only produces know-ledge that is as blurred as the halting stammer of Creation. With the expression of this ardent yearning to see the mirrored reflection of the Beloved's eyes, she cries out with dramatic suddenness, 'Take them away, Beloved, for I soar in flight!' (Stanza 13). The first sight of his eyes is more than the soul can bear.[33]

Up to this point in the poem the only speakers have been the soul and 'creatures', but now there begins the dialogue between the soul and God, who are named bride and Bridegroom. The soul sings of her love by ennumerating the beauties of nature: 'My beloved, the mountains, the lonely wooded valleys, the unknown islands, the murmur of the rivers, the whistling of the enamoured winds; night which is still and silent at the approach of dawn, the silent music, the resounding solitude, the supper that strengthens and brings love' (Stanzas 14–15). We must note how different this is from conventional pastoral poetry. Here Nature is mysterious: darkness, solitude, sound; nothing is seen, it is only heard and felt. It is a mysterious music that is silent, a silent solitude that is full of sound. This music is, as the commentary says, the 'harmony of the Universe, silent to the

senses, heard only by the spirit'.[34] In detachment from the senses
the soul is aware of the mysterious music of Creation which can
only be 'heard' in darkness and solitude and among the islands
of still uncharted seas: 'God is all the unknown strangeness of
islands that have never been seen'.[35] Read as pastoral poetry, these
lines do not reveal their conceptual profundity, although they
would indicate an element of mystery in their paradoxes. In the
light of the commentary they point to depths of feeling and
experience.

The senses are cut off from these depths. They, together with
the image-forming fancy, are the foxes that would eat the flowers
of the vineyard and prevent the harvesting of the grapes (Stanza
16); that is to say, they would break God's communication with
the soul. With the marvellously unconscious disregard for the
conventional decorum of rhetorical theory St John continues to
mix his metaphors: the nymphs of Judea have become foxes, and
the flowers of the vines, which are the grace with which the
'perfumed amber' has scented the life of the soul, now become
flowers that are plucked to form not the commonplace garland
of poetic tradition but a startling 'pine-cone of roses'. As always,
the image is not descriptive and can have only a conceptual
relationship with what it symbolizes. The meaning, according
to the commentary, is that the life of the soul has now acquired
perfection and solidity.[36]

Behind the transformation of the garland of ordinary poetry
into a pine-cone of roses there lies a significant thought. In our
ordinary everyday lives, our experience is fragmented, the
external world is presented to us in disconnected fragments: our
senses, feelings, passions, reason and conscience all pull us in
different, often opposing, directions. Our experience is thus disorderly, lacking a unifying discipline, but the life of the mystic, as
St John expresses it, becomes quite different from this. All his
reactions, spiritual, intellectual and physical, are ordered into a
tight unity (a pine-cone). This unification of experience is the
ideal of human perfection; according to the mystic, speaking out
of his own experience, it is attained only when sensuous feelings
and passions are subjugated and silent: 'You swift-winged birds,

lions, deer, and leaping bucks, mountains, valleys, river-banks, waters, breezes, stifling heat and fears felt in sleepless nights: through the gentle music and the sirens' song, I conjure you to cease your anger and not to strike the wall, so that the Bride may sleep in safety' (Stanzas 20–21).

The Lovers' marriage-bed is described with a series of symbols:

> Nuestro lecho florido,
> de cuevas de leones enlazado,
> en púrpura tendido,
> de paz edificado,
> de mil escudos de oro coronado. (Stanza 24)

> Our flowering bed, interlaced with lions' caves, spread out on purple, built with peace, crowned with a thousand gold escutcheons.

Other animals are said, according to St John, not to penetrate into the caves where lions dwell. The union of bride and Bride-groom, on a bed that is girt around with lions' caves ('interlaced', because there is no gap through which disorder of any kind could squeeze) is immune to any assault from without; the spouses are totally secure. The bed, defended by the king of beasts, is adorned with all the accompaniments of majesty and nobility. The escutcheons are also defensive shields. In the intimacy of this impregnable fortress the soul has found security from the attacks of evil and therefore the perfect peace which human beings have always longed for.

The mysterious imagery continues through the stanzas denot-ing the union:

> A zaga de tu huella
> las jóvenes discurren al camino,
> al toque de centella,
> al adobado vino:
> emisiones de bálsamo divino. (Stanza 25)

> Following your footprints, the girls move along the road, to the striking of the spark, to the mulled wine, to the outpourings of the divine ointment.

In the midst of her ecstasy the soul is conscious that her experience is not exclusive to her, but something available to all humanity. The women are the other contemplative souls who have progressed thus far along the mystic way and cannot now turn back. They are 'young', because the striking of the spark brings spiritual rejuvenation; the wine they have been given to drink is mulled because warmed and spiced by the joy of God's love. This wine is drunk in her Beloved's 'interior wine-cellar' (Stanza 26). Once more St John does not shirk the concrete word that all poetic theory would have considered completely 'unpoetic' in such a context, nor does he shrink from introducing, with the wine-cellar, the fact of intoxication:

> En la interior bodega
> de mi Amado bebí, y cuando salía
> por toda aquesta vega,
> ya cosa no sabía
> y el ganado perdí que antes seguía.   (Stanza 26)

In the interior wine-cellar of my Beloved I drank, and when I emerged wandering through all this valley, I knew nothing any more, and I lost the flock which previously I followed.

From now onwards the soul is totally absorbed in God. She has no other profession, she has no flock to tend; now her one and only task is love (Stanza 28).

The stanzas that follow have a passionate tenderness which can readily suggest the love of man and woman. They climb the mountainside to lose themselves in its innermost caverns. The emphasis is not so much on their companionship as on solitude:

> En soledad vivía,
> y en soledad ha puesto ya su nido,
> y en soledad la guía
> a solas su querido,
> también en soledad de amor herido.   (Stanza 35)

In solitude she lived, in solitude she has already built her nest and in solitude she is led all alone by her lover, himself also wounded in the solitude of love.

Human love is companionship and communion, it is the way men escape from their solitude and loneliness, and go outside themselves. In the love of God, on the other hand, a human being must enter inside himself, he must search for solitude within himself. Thus the mystic way carries man away from the populated highways of the world, away from the trodden paths of experience, to make him climb up to the secret caverns in the mountain-top.

In the final stanza the characteristic type of imagery recurs, with a meaning that can scarcely be guessed at without the clue provided by the poet:

> Que nadie lo miraba . . .
> Aminadab tampoco parecía;
> y el cerco sosegaba,
> y la caballería
> a vista de las aguas descendía.[37]   (Stanza 40)

For no one saw their love . . . nor did Aminadab appear; the siege was quietened, and the cavalry descended within sight of the waters.

The intensely intimate seclusion of the spirit with God is rendered first by the absence of any witnesses. Aminadab appears in the Vulgate version of the *Song of Solomon* (6:11) where he is a driver of a four-horse chariot who is disturbing the Bridegroom; traditionally he was taken to represent the Devil. This is St John's source and the meaning he gives to this unknown personage. The cavalry, or horses of the chariot, symbolize the passions, the senses and the images of the fancy. All these sensitive faculties have been totally subjugated in the ascetic discipline of the Dark Night. The soul is now utterly safe from all the assaults of the world, the flesh and the devil. No disorder or evil can teach her in the impregnable peace into which she has sunk with her Beloved. Every human soul is permanently besieged in its fortress, not so the mystic who has achieved union with God.[38]

St John uses this symbol with his customary exactitude. The waters of the spirit, in the soul's communion with God, cannot be drunk by the horses because the senses, being material, cannot be 'transformed' into God. Yet the total peace that fills the soul is felt, at a distance so to speak, by the senses, for they too are purified and stilled into rest, and are no longer a hindrance in the soul's search for her Creator; this means that though they cannot drink the waters, they come 'within sight' of them and so feel their indirect effect. The commentary goes on to say that the word 'descended' is used rather than any other (e.g. 'approached' or 'came') because this restfulness is a cessation of their natural operation, and cessation is a lowering, not a heightening.[39]

This, the summit of the mystical experience, is the ancient Platonic ideal, in which the intellect moves freely towards Love without the impediments imposed by the material body. And it achieves what has always been the ideal of human life: complete serenity, absolute self-control, a perfect ordering of experience in a harmony of the personality whereby intellect and will are totally in control of all sensible faculties and operations. It is clear from the mystical literature, as we have seen, that such serenity of spirit, impervious to disillusion, was no private experience personal to St John but an enduring quality in the lives of other sixteenth-century Spaniards who were ardently committed to the quest for ideal love on this plane.

Platonic Love Disillusioned. To save himself from confessing that he had lied to Don Quixote when reporting his visit to the lady Dulcinea del Toboso, Sancho Panza compels the Knight to kneel before a peasant woman on an ass, persuading him that this is Dulcinea transformed by the magician who is persecuting him. Don Quixote sees the reality but cannot believe it. (An engraving from the Spanish Academy's edition of 1780.)

FOUR.

IDEAL LOVE AND
HUMAN REALITY

Neoplatonism. the pastoral novel. the Counter-Reformation. *la perfecta casada. la conversión de la Magdalena.* CERVANTES. *Don Quijote. la Galatea. la ilustre fregona. Persiles y Sigismunda.* LOPE DE VEGA. the lyrical poetry. *la Dorotea. la comedia nueva.* TIRSO DE MOLINA. GÓNGORA.

Neoplatonism

In Spanish literature of the late sixteenth century the idealization of love is confronted increasingly with the moral and social demands of everyday life. The reasons for this lie partly in the philosophical limitations of Italian Neoplatonism. It is difficult to take Platonic love, as expounded by Castiglione, or even Bembo, seriously as a practical moral ideal. Within the cultured and elegant way of life portrayed in *The Courtier* there is a certain smugness in the way Platonic attachments to other men's wives are surrounded with an aura of religious mysticism. This is not so, however, with Ebreo, whose deep earnestness is unquestionable. This is apparent, above all, in the note of suffering that runs through his presentation of human love, to one aspect of which I have referred already. Human love, for him, is imbued with an underlying sense of anguish, a real existential hurt that it can never, in this life, fully be what the human mind and heart are compelled to yearn that it should be: even the body is hurt at the imperfection of the only love it can achieve. For the Italians, on the other hand, suffering in love can only result from a disordered reason. The grief and despair of Courtly Love for them, as for modern psychoanalysts, were irrational, and irrationality becomes dominant in man's experience only if sensuality is allowed the upper hand.

Bembo, in *Gli Asolani*, denounced specifically the literary tradition of love-as-suffering and denounced all the disorderly emotions and the riotous behaviour that follow from sensual passion: the sighs, tears, pining, jealousy, anger, rivalry, duelling and so on. He denied that the god of Love was a cruel tyrant because he denied that man was incapable of resisting passion: he held, on the contrary, that passion could be subjugated by reason if the mind were intent only on the spiritual and moral beauty of the beloved. This is why human lovers were supposed to be able to rise so easily to the love of God.[1] The assumptions behind this theory were not to remain unquestioned in Italy itself, for the Counter-Reformation was not to leave the optimism of the Renaissance intact. Writing his treatise on human love in 1569, Flaminio Nobili stated that the concept of Platonic love was incomprehensible to him, since if one wants to rise by contemplation from the beauty of creatures to the beauty of God, it is better to contemplate the beauty of stars than the beauty of women.[2] This, of course, is because sensuality cannot so easily be curbed by an act of the will on the command of the reason.

What strikes us about Bembo's Neoplatonism is precisely the assumption that self-control can be achieved without a discipline involving suffering, the smug way, in fact, in which suffering is dismissed from human experience as an unnecessary evil. If the Neoplatonists were right in considering Courtly Love to be an irrational disorder (and, of course, on the surface they were) we may well ask whether their own Platonic love did not go to the other extreme, becoming so rational as to cease to be real. Is it so easy, without suffering and struggle, for a human being to overcome sensuality merely by reasoning that it is better to do so? If Christian theology is to be believed, this was possible for Adam and Eve before the Fall; it certainly has *not* been possible for the general run of mankind ever since. As we have seen, the mystics tell us that the direct experience of God can only be reached by passing through a period of intense suffering, thus showing how purely theoretical was the mystical experience that the Neoplatonists placed as the crown of human love, obviously never having experienced it themselves.

We are therefore face to face once more with a concept of love divorced from life. But there is a difference this time. Whereas the convention of suffering, unfulfilled love endured for at least two centuries, thus proving that it appealed to and satisfied some need in writers and readers, Neoplatonism in its complete form scarcely took root in Spanish literature; where it exercised influence it was in a modified form. Only in mystical literature does ideal love appear as an experiential reality; by contrast, Neoplatonism never achieves in literature the intensity of a lived experience, and it seems to me that this is because it deliberately turned its back on suffering as a stage in the struggle towards an ideal love. A serene, non-sensual, non-passionate love, formulated by the reason and achieved by merely willing, is an ideal that, however theoretically desirable, has never formed part of human experience, and can therefore scarcely inspire a literature that seeks to have a significant contact with reality. The poets of Courtly Love, Leone Ebreo and the Spanish mystics all knew that the senses and passions are not so easily subdued and pacified; and the great writers of the next century were to know it also.

The Pastoral Novel. The contrasts and tensions within Neoplatonism are evident in the Renaissance *genre* of the pastoral novel which was established in Spain in 1559 with the publication of the *Diana* of Jorge de Montemayor. This was followed in 1564 by a second novel, the *Diana enamorada* of Gaspar Gil Polo.[3] The first of these works draws on Leone Ebreo, but more heavily on the earlier tradition. It distinguishes two kinds of love, 'good love' and 'false love'. The former is a form of reason but not subject to it, it aims at spiritual union with the beloved; the latter springs from base appetite and desires physical satisfaction. In either case, the nature of the resulting feeling is equally passionate and beyond the control of the lover's reason; love is a doom against which it is useless for the lover to struggle. Suffering is inseparable from love and an ennobling aspect of it. Fulfilment is therefore not desirable, since it would put an end to the exquisite, ennobling suffering of suspense.

Gil Polo's continuation shows the influence of the Italian Neoplatonists and is very different. It seeks to make the point that lovers by surrendering to passion are responsible for their own suffering. Love can hold no sway over men except insofar as, of their own accord, they place themselves in its power. The impure love of sensuality may claim to be spiritual and chaste, but it can always be known by the suffering it produces. Truly spiritual love, however, causes no suffering but brings joy: it is a love in which the will remains free and reason remains in control. The contrast with Montemayor therefore lies in the rationality and happiness of true love, and in the rejection of suffering as being against the order of nature.

This is pure Italian Neoplatonism; but, doubtless conscious of its impracticality, Gil Polo departs from his Italian mentors by not seeking to go beyond the human sphere into mystical com-munion and, more important, by giving love a fulfilment which includes the senses, namely marriage, something by its very nature unideal and therefore excluded from nearly all the mani-festations of Courtly Love and certainly from all the Neoplatonic ones. We have, then, love guided by reason, with marriage as its natural, joyful fulfilment. This is something new; the rejection of the basic positions of both Courtly Love and Neoplatonism, it marks the beginning of the attempt to bring love down to reality from the clouds of idealization.

The Counter-Reformation

The confrontation of literary idealism with reality was greatly advanced by the concern of churchmen after the Council of Trent to imbue literature with religious and moral values. In the early sixteenth century humanists like Luis Vives and Juan de Valdés had attacked the novels of chivalry for portraying improbable or impossible situations far removed from human nature and experience. Their criticisms were taken up by church-men of the Counter-Reformation who, eager to christianize humanistic literature, condemned the literary tradition of ideal-izing human love not only for not being religious but also for being irresponsible in its unreality since, by failing to show its readers what the main problems of life were, it encouraged them to take refuge in what we now call escapism. Fray Luis de Granada, for instance, attributed the popularity of the novels of chivalry to the fact that women identified with Oriana and other heroines, and secretly felt worthy of the services and heroic deeds of knights, while men enjoyed the vicarious excitement of witnessing heroic deeds, if only in their imagination.[4] These churchmen advocated replacing the 'untruthful' chivalric and pastoral novels by a literature that would be 'truthful', by which they meant one that would promulgate a Christian view of life and a sense of moral responsibility by presenting human nature as it actually is instead of idealizing it.

La perfecta casada. This concern with 'truth' in literature may be observed in *La perfecta casada*, a prose work by Luis de León.[5] It is a treatise in praise of women, which had been a favourite topic in the literary tradition of Courtly Love. In the numerous works treating of this subject woman had, of course, been idealized as a sort of goddess, and was not a creature of flesh and blood with a real life to live in the material world. In *La perfecta casada*, however, she is, as the title indicates, a married woman, and at once the idealized feminist literature is brought down to the plane of social duties and moral obligations. Luis de León takes us through the practical tasks of daily routine (the stocking of the larder, the making and mending of clothes, the looking after the servants and so on) insisting all the time that it is in a busy domestic life and not in idle luxury that women find their fulfilment. Yet this does not mean that he considers women to be inferior drudges. A good woman, he says, is something finer than a good man because ultimately it is upon her that human society depends. The goodness of a woman is creative, and communicated to others: it is not in her nature to attain to a self-centred perfection, but to give. For this reason, the love she inspires in man is, or should be, the love of reverence, based upon the realization of her unique worth in the task and art of living. In this way the ideal of woman and the ideal of human love are brought down from the clouds to reality and are, in fact, ennobled in the process, for this is a work that retains all that is best in Renaissance idealism: a belief in and an emphasis on what is good and noble in human nature.

La conversión de la Magdalena. Luis de León was only one of a number of Counter-Reformation theologians who were Platonists. Although they directly attacked humanistic secular literature, they at the same time continued and brought to fruition the philosophy on which its conception of ideal love was based. In them Platonic doctrine found its proper fulfilment in divine love without being led astray by the unreal illusion of a spiritualized human love.

A representative example is *La conversión de la Magdalena* (1588) by the Augustinian friar, Pedro Malón de Chaide (d. 1589).[6] This is a treatise on love; its first part is in fact the clearest and simplest exposition in Spanish literature of the Platonic doctrine of love, which Malón presents as a cosmic circular movement from God down to creatures and back to God, the unbroken circle being the ideal of love. In this first part of his work Malón is the pure Platonist, and as such a man of the Renaissance; he becomes the Christian Platonist, and a man of the Counter-Reformation, by his later insistence that this ideal is not just lying at one's feet ready to be picked up and absorbed without difficulty. The tragedy of man lies in the fact that since in his nature spirit is compounded with matter, he is strongly impelled to break the cosmic circle of love by remaining bogged down in an imperfect and inferior love.

In his preface Malón attacks Garcilaso, *Amadís de Gaula*, and *Diana* for being unaware that they are representing a broken circle. By contrast the figure of the lover that he puts forward is the historical Mary Magdalen. A repentant prostitute becomes a heroine of love to replace Oriana and the shepherdesses of the *Diana*. In that she was a sinner she represents, unlike the heroines of fiction, the reality of human experience; yet in her answer, through repentance, to the call of a higher love, she also represents the ideal. In Malón's presentation of the Platonic doctrine of love the emphasis therefore shifts away from the confident pursuit of divine beauty through the beauty of woman, away from the confident reliance on the spiritual nature of human love, to the recognition of the essential weakness of human nature, a weakness which is such that men can have no natural confidence in their ability to attain to the divine, but can only seek to love

God through the plea for his forgiveness and mercy.

It was in this way that the religious literature of the Counter-Reformation brought the ideal of perfect love down from the clouds, while at the same time retaining the vision of the ideal: the union of the soul with God. It counteracted the prevailing idealistic humanism by placing the ideal where it properly belonged, in the realm of the spiritual, and by laying stress on the real world, on the reality of human nature, and on social obligations and moral duties.

MIGUEL DE CERVANTES

Don Quijote. The assumption that ideal human love must be non-passionate, disembodied so to speak as regards both the lover and the beloved, created and kept in being only by the mind, received in Spain its most devastating attack in *Don Quijote*.[7] He, it will be remembered, is a country gentleman who is so avid a reader of the idealistic literature of his age that he fails to make the distinction between literature and life. Fired with the ideal of heroism in the service of justice, he determines to put into practice the literary convention through which this ideal was expressed: knight errantry. Part of the convention was that the ideal knight had also to be the ideal lover, a Platonic lover. Consequently his imagination creates his love on only the most tenuous basis of experience, and acts as if he were really in love, and as if his lady really existed. This, in principle, is passion under the control of reason. He chooses a farm girl, Aldonza Lorenzo, who lives near by, and wishing to find a name that would convey the suggestion of a princess or a great lady, he resolves to call her Dulcinea del Toboso. Later, when he orders Sancho to deliver a letter to her, and gives him information about her for the first time, Sancho guesses her identity and proceeds to describe her appearance and her habits: far from beautiful, far from delicately feminine, far from modestly secluded. But Don Quixote remains unmoved:

> Así que, Sancho, por lo que yo quiero a Dulcinea del Toboso, tanto vale como la más alta princesa de la tierra. Sí,

que no todos los poetas que alaban damas, debajo de un
nombre que ellos a su albedrío les ponen, es verdad que las
tienen. ¿Piensas tú que . . . fueron verdaderamente damas
de carne y hueso, y de aquellos que las celebran y celebraron?
No, por cierto, sino que las más se las fingen, por dar subjeto
a sus versos, y porque los tengan por enamorados y por
hombres que tienen valor para serlo. Y así, bástame a mí
pensar y creer que la buena de Aldonza Lorenzo es hermosa
y honesta; y en lo del linaje importa poco, que no han de ir a
hacer la información dél para darle algún hábito, y yo me
hago cuenta que es la más alta princesa del mundo . . . Y para
concluir con todo, yo imagino que todo lo que digo es así,
sin que sobre ni falte nada, y píntola en mi imaginación
como la deseo, así en la belleza como en la principalidad, y
no la llega Elena, ni la alcanza Lucrecia . . .[8]

And so, Sancho, as regards my need of Dulcinea de Toboso, she
is worth as much to me as any highborn princess in this world.
For not all the poets who praised their ladies under names of their
own choosing actually had such mistresses. Do you think . . . they
really were flesh-and-blood women who belonged to those who
sang their praises? Certainly not; most of the writers merely
invented them to provide themselves with a subject for their
verses and in order that they might be considered lovelorn swains
and respected as individuals. And so it is enough for me to think
and believe that the good Aldonza Lorenzo is beautiful and
modest; and as far as her lineage is concerned, that is a matter of
little importance, for no one is going to investigate it with a view
to conferring on her robes of nobility, and I consider her the most
highborn princess in the world . . . In short: I imagine that
everything I say is true, with nothing added or left out, and in my
imagination I paint her as I would have her be, in beauty as in
nobility, unequalled by Helen, unrivalled by Lucretia . . . .

The Neoplatonic victory of reason over passion is here depicted
as in fact the subjugation of reason to the imagination: 'Imagine
that everything I say is true . . . in my imagination I paint her as I
would have her be'. This, of course, is precisely what ideals do
when they take no account of human limitations. The Neoplatonists imagined that all they said about human love was true.
But while Cervantes can laugh at the unreality of ideal love in its

Platonic form, he cannot laugh at the existence of ideals as such. However absurd, Dulcinea is the ideal woman who arouses Don Quixote's devotion; she does come to symbolize for him his self-imposed mission. However vaingloriously and extravagantly this mission is conceived, it is yet something to live by, something that justifies Don Quixote's existence in his own eyes. But since he has not cut it to the measure of his human limitations he is bound to face disillusion.

In Part 11 Dulcinea clearly represents not Aldonza Lorenzo absurdly idealized, but his mission. If he can see her and obtain her approval he will know he is the real knight errant that he claims to be. At the beginning of Part 11 he sets out to visit her but is frustrated; at the end he is still hoping to find her but never does: in between, his self-confidence declines until he loses all the arrogance he possessed in Part 1 when he was confident that Dulcinea existed and was reachable. He cannot reach her in Part 11 because he is forced to think her enchanted: from that moment his confidence in himself begins to wane. When he penetrates into the Cave of Montesinos and falls asleep, his dream brings his subconscious unavowed fears to the fore. In the dream he enters the ancient world of chivalry that he has always idealized, but he finds nothing heroic about it. The knights are old and tired; everywhere there is an atmosphere of psychological depression and physical decline. Finally Dulcinea appears in the form in which he believes her to be enchanted, as a coarse peasant girl (like Aldonza Lorenzo, in other words). He addresses her, but she does not answer and turning her back on him she runs away so fast that he cannot overtake her. Shortly afterwards her companion returns, tells him that Dulcinea is in dire financial straits and asks her knight for the loan of six *reales*. Don Quixote cannot grant her this favour since he has no more than four *reales*. Consider what has happened to ideal love: the lady who is the object of worship needs a trifling sum of money and her heroic and faithful knight is unable to meet her needs. When ideals come to this, disillusion is pathetically sad and no longer funny. Later, Don Quixote, deceived into thinking that Sancho can disenchant Dulcinea, and then deceived by Sancho into thinking that she is at last disenchanted, peers eagerly ahead along the road as he journeys home, expecting to see her appear at any moment. But he reaches his village without sight of her and then occurs one of the most touching incidents in the whole book:

A la entrada del cual, según dice Cide Hamete, vió don Quijote que en las eras del lugar estaban riñendo dos mocha⸗ chos, y el uno dijo al otro:

—No ten canses, Periquillo, que no la has de ver en todos los días de tu vida.

Oyólo don Quijote, y dijo a Sancho:

—¿No adviertes, amigo, lo que aquel mochacho ha dicho: 'no la has de ver en todos los días de tu vida'?

—Pues bien, ¿qué importa—respondió Sancho—que haya dicho eso el mochacho?

—¿Qué?—replicó don Quijote.—¿No vees tú que apli⸗ cando aquella palabra a mi intención, quiere significar que no tengo de ver más a Dulcinea?

Queríale responder Sancho, cuando se lo estorbó ver que por aquella campaña venía huyendo una liebre, seguida de muchos galgos y cazadores, la cual, temerosa, se vino a recoger y a agazapar debajo de los pies del rucio. Cogióla Sancho a mano salva y presentósela a don Quijote, el cual estaba diciendo:

—*Malum signum! Malum signum!* Liebre huye; galgos la siguen: ¡Dulcinea no parece![9]

As they entered the village, according to Cide Hamete, Don Quixote noticed two boys on the communal threshing floor who were having an argument. 'Don't let it worry you, Periquillo', one was saying to the other, 'you'll never see her again as long as you live'. Hearing this, Don Quixote turned to Sancho: 'Did you mark what the boy said, my friend?'. 'Well', answered Sancho, 'what difference does it make what he said?'. 'What?', said Don Quixote, 'Don't you see that, applied to my love, it means I shall never again see Dulcinea?'. Sancho was about to reply when his attention was distracted by a hare that came flying across the fields chased by a large number of greyhounds and huntsmen. The frightened animal took refuge by huddling under the donkey. Sancho reached out his hand, caught it up and presented it to Don Quixote who was muttering, '*Malum signum, malum signum*! A hare flees; hounds pursue it; Dulcinea appears not!'

Though both incidents turn out to have a natural explanation, nothing can remove from Don Quixote's mind the effect they had when he took them for omens. Dulcinea has not appeared: he will never see her again. His ideal love is a trembling hare pursued by hounds. What little faith he still had in himself is shattered. Tired and melancholy he retires to bed never to rise again. Ideal love is an illusion; nonetheless, reality without the illusion may provide no inducement to go on living.

La Galatea. The burlesque of Platonic love in the unreal character of Dulcinea does not mean that Cervantes came to reject the literary idealization of love with which he began his career in his pastoral novel, *La Galatea*.[10] In the sixteenth century Platonic love had come to be an *absolute* ideal; only a spiritual love could be a truly human one. This disembodied spirituality may or may not have been an ideal in everyday life, but in literature, as we have seen, it was generally accepted without question: hence the convention for every poet to have an ideal lady. This absolute ideal, divorced from any social values, was what Cervantes could not take seriously. But in *La Galatea* love is always directed in intention towards marriage: until the lover marries he must be, and remain, a chaste lover, devoted and loyal.

The narrative of *La Galatea* has the traditional episodic structure, but with a special modification due to the influence of the so-called Byzantine novel: various love stories are interlaced, interrupted, and later continued. The tone, or literary atmosphere, is lyrical rather than prosodic: there is a mixture of prose and verse, and songs sung every time a shepherd or shepherdess appears or returns are the divisions marking the progress of the narrative. It is not a work that has found much commendation, but perhaps its literary defects lie more in the poetic mediocrity of its songs than in the pastoral convention itself. In actual fact the pastoral element is minimal, and all the different stories could, with little modification, have appeared in a further collection of Cervantine *Exemplary Novels*. They are idealistic love stories within the frame formed by the story of Galatea and the two shepherds who love her, a story that remained unfinished since the promised continuation of the work never materialized.

The interest and importance of *La Galatea* does not lie in its fictional material but in the manner in which the fictional material clarifies its philosophy of love, and in the fact that it presents all the ideas of love held in the sixteenth century. The central theme, and the centre of the work's structure, is the debate on the nature of love between Lenio and Tirsi. Such debates were themselves a traditional form for expounding the concept of love, developments of an earlier theme, typical of the fifteenth century, expounding feminist or misogynist standpoints. Naturally, since all literature was written by men, women were praised or despised according to whether love was experienced as beneficent or morally harmful. The basis of the attack was the experience of love as a turbulent passion that profoundly perturbs those who feel it: it holds the will in thrall and disorders the reason, it breeds jealousy and provokes to hatred, vengeance, duelling and killing, only because man desires a sensual experience which puts him on the same level as an animal and so brutalizes him.

The debate occurs in Book IV. Lenio is the attacker. He holds that it is, in fact, impossible for man to attain the love of incorporeal beauty, because bodily beauty grabs his senses and drags him along the ground. The result is hatred, discord, vice and crime, all the violence that waylays and ensnares mankind. This attitude of Lenio's is a pessimism that despairs of humanity which keeps recurring throughout the work. It is a puritanism that condemns everything in human life which permits of abuse, a rigorist, authoritarian cast of mind that binds freedom in chains and leads to tyranny. Against this, Tirsi's argument is as follows: love is an instinct which cannot be evil in itself because it is the work of Nature. Nothing natural is evil as such; it can be perverted, but good must not be shunned out of fear of evil.

For medieval religion the only love that was entirely good was the love of God, and human love could not be entirely good, because reason cannot be in control when erotic passion dominates a man. But with the coming of the Renaissance and before the Age of Disillusion, all love could be conceived as good, including sexual love which appeared purified by Neoplatonism. Cervantes was heir to the optimism of Renaissance humanism. He sincerely believed in the efficacy of the two remedies for disorderly passion, namely, marriage and reason, and that, in consequence, one must not reject the good for fear of abusing it; one must not restrict or destroy freedom in order to prevent the evil it might commit.

La ilustre fregona. It was for long incomprehensible that the same man could have written both *Don Quijote* and *La Galatea*; still more incomprehensible that after the triumphant success of the former work, he could revert to the idealistic vein in *Persiles*, his last work which he claimed was his best. It was not to be possible much longer for a literary artist to show this conscious ambivalence which was itself the result of the overlapping of the new age with the old. Cervantes's realistic writing was essentially comic, and his humour, satirical and ironic, was directed at the weaknesses and affectations of human beings. His idealistic writing after *La Galatea* remained concerned with the serious, namely, the nobler aspects and the profounder emotions of human life. It was easy for readers around 1600 to make the automatic shift of style, tone and literary technique from the serious to the comic and back again. This ambivalence can most easily be understood where Cervantes contrasts the serious with the comic in the same work. The best example is perhaps *La ilustre fregona* (*The Illustrious Kitchen-Maid*), one of the collection of his *Novelas ejemplares* published in 1613.[11]

The beginning of the story puts before us a sociological fact, the equivalent of what was called the 'run-away revolution' in the 1950s and 1960s, when boys and girls ran away from home to escape constraint and discipline in the search for a free life. The equivalent in Cervantes' day were the *almadrabas* or tunny fisheries near Seville, an unruly community where young criminals and homeless children and youths congregated in the apparent enjoyment of a free life. Cervantes states that many youths, sons of gentlemen, sought freedom and excitement by escaping there from the rigorous discipline of their homes. One such, in the story, is called Carriazo. After a period of free and riotous living he dresses again as a young gentleman and returns to his parents. Before long, however, he rebels against the bore-dom of a humdrum existence and persuades another young gentleman, Avendaño, to run off with him to the tunny fisheries. On their way they hear talk of an exceptionally beautiful girl who works in the kitchen of an inn in Toledo. Their interest aroused, they make a diversion in order to see this phenomenon. She is indeed extraordinarily beautiful, and Avendaño falls so deeply in love that he refuses to leave the town, working as a servant in the same inn where he can see, from time to time, his beloved. Carriazo lives among the low-life of the town, among the gamblers, the gypsies and the horse-thieves, longing for his tunny fisheries but unwilling to go there alone, since he cannot persuade his friend to resume their journey.

Carriazo feels the attraction of an anarchical life against social stability and order. He is pulled by the urge for social dis-integration. Avendaño, on the other hand, is held back from disintegration by the service, at a distance, of a beautiful, modest and reserved kitchen-maid. The aim of Cervantes is to contrast, remaining on the plain of low-life, the pull of a civilized order with the pull of uncivilized freedom (229–31). The values of civilization are enshrined in this service of beauty, which becomes in the new social realism of the Spanish novel a sort of archetype: a faithful, altruistic and reverential love that seeks no favour for itself.

While Avendaño's love and its object are idealized, the social environment remains real. His idealized love is described as a response to beauty (241); it is the beauty of woman that calls up in a man the values that make civilization, the values that retain men within their spiritual home. In the initial search for freedom, both youths have fallen far below their social status. It is grotesque, says Carriazo, that a gentleman's son should be enamoured of a kitchen-maid, but it is equally grotesque, as Avendaño retorts, that a gentleman's son should be enamoured of the tunny fisheries. Avendaño is right, for the love of beauty carries within it its own justification, a moral force independent of the social class to which the woman belongs, but this love is, of course, the ideal, and must be contrasted with the coarse experiences and behaviour of low-life society.

Costanza, the kitchen-maid, is contrasted in her reserve with the loose attitudes of the other serving-maids. Her purity is not puritanism; it is the sense of personal worth and dignity that holds a woman back from abandoning herself to the desires of men, waiting for the marriage that is the civilized form of loving (264). The opposite is the vulgar promiscuity of the other women servants (256). It was a literary fashion to associate beauty and ugliness with moral qualities pointing to something deeper than physical reality, and Costanza is beautiful, the other women are not (266-7). For Carriazo it is ludicrous that modesty and purity should be found in a kitchen-maid, since these virtues are proper to a high-born lady, but for Cervantes they can exist in any woman, whatever her social station and environment.

Costanza remains uncontaminated by the frivolity and vulgarity of the servants, both men and women, in the public inn, a fact that provokes Carriazo to an ironical remark (264). Avendaño, on the other hand, sees no disparity in this; beauty knows no class distinctions, and it is his destiny to love beauty (264-5). This is the Neoplatonist ideal. Carriazo cynically laughs at it; like many young men, at all times, including today, he does not believe in ideal values because he does not understand them (265-6). Cynicism of this kind befits an educated man who holds to no ideals, whereas the rough, uneducated man will insult ideal love because it is beyond his comprehension: this latter reaction is that of the muleteer when he hears a song serenading Costanza (276).

In an age that knew no universal education and no mass culture, there was no attempt to reduce moral values and social standards to a lowest common denominator; on the contrary, there was the desire to raise the lowly to a higher level. The beauty, virtue and reserve of Costanza, in other words her capacity to inspire in a man an ennobling love, signifies that she lives on a superior plane to that of the other maidservants, despite the fact that they all belong to the same environment. Consequently, her function in this story is to redeem young men from the attractions of the wild, unruly life at the tunny fisheries. In effect, she brings about their return to their parents and to their homes.

The ending of the story is idealized in a way that every modern reader is bound to regret, for it turns out that Costanza is not, after all, a working-class girl but the daughter of a noble lady who came to the inn to give birth to a baby she could not publicly acknowledge. The innkeeper was charged with its upbringing, given funds for it, and told how and when to publish the fact. It was too much to ask Cervantes to make, or his readers to accept, as the emblem of ideal love the offspring of working-class parents reared in the shifting life of a public inn, just as it had been impossible for Gil Vicente to make his Princess Flérida actually marry a gardener. Cervantes even felt the need to make the innkeeper assure everyone present at the disclosure that Costanza had never actually washed any dishes. It was, of course, a pity that a realistic ending was incompatible with literary convention. Nevertheless, the final aristocratization of Costanza may be seen as a symbol of the power of human love, in an ideal form, to raise human beings above the rudeness and vulgarity of un-redeemed low life: in short, to civilize them. Cervantes's heroine is an ideal creation, but she is presented, with literary mastery, in the midst of real life. She is not part of a fantastic or near-paradisiacal setting of pastoral.

Persiles y Sigismunda. Los trabajos de Persiles y Sigismunda (*The Trials of Persiles and Sigismunda*), which was published post-humously in 1617, is a remarkable work that only in modern times has begun to emerge from the cloud in which the realistic canons of literary criticism had hidden it. In contrast with *Don Quijote*, and judged by its standards, it seemed diffuse, formless and a strange medley of fantastic and realistic episodes, devoid of theme and verisimilitude. It was, in consequence, dismissed as a work of Cervantes's dotage despite the fact that he himself presented it as his masterpiece. The trouble was that *Don Quijote* is a totally inapplicable standard of comparison. It is a comic satire and therefore a novel of real life, whereas *Persiles* moves in a different dimension, one akin to myth. It must be read allegoric-

ally and many of its episodes symbolically: in this way its complicated structure and its theme appear meaningful.

Alban Forcione has described the theme as a re-enactment of
the Christian myth: 'man in his fallen state must wander in the
sublunary world of disorder, suffering in the world of human
history, and be reborn through expiation and Christ's mercy'.[12]
This theme is presented in a sequence of adventures that involve
the heroes, Periandro and Auristela (the real names of Persiles
and Sigismunda). Each adventure mirrors the cyclical pattern
of the overall quest in its structure and in the implications of its
theme, and numerous sub-plots present quests of secondary
figures that also mirror the main plot in theme and form. There is,
in other words, a recurring repetition of myth and ritual on the
same level as the main quest for perfection.

This interpretation is enlightening and for the most part convincing. It might be added, however, that the work has a threefold structure in which each recurrence of the pattern of the quest
is enacted in a different dimension of history. The three stages are
first humanity's emergence into primitive barbarism, secondly
the development of civilization, and thirdly the age of Christianity. The last two were traditionally called the Law of Nature
(where reason was the only guide) and the Law of Grace (where
reason is illuminated by Revelation). The pattern is a geograph-
ical one: first a desolate arctic region, then the lands and islands
of Northern Europe, then the journey from Lisbon (where the
travellers land) to Rome. From the North Pole to Rome: that
is the symbolical trajectory of the work. The pattern of the book is
therefore humanity's progress from barbarism, through humanistic civilization, to Christianity, and the lives of the protagonists
demonstrate the same progress in the individual sphere: first the
tempestuousness of passion, secondly the emergence of reason,
and thirdly the acceptance of religious faith.

If one is properly tuned to the symbolical dimension of the
novel, its opening appears powerful: a savage is standing at the
narrow opening of an underground dungeon, 'more the tomb
than the prison of many living bodies buried inside it'.[13] The
savage is shouting with a fearful roar that is nonetheless inaudible

to the captives. His roar demands that a young man, recently captured, be released and with him any woman captive who is worthy of their company. A thick rope is lowered and up is pulled the young man, Periandro, who is to be the protagonist of the story: emerging from the captivity of darkness into a human savagery that demands the company of a woman. This savage world is one of violence and disorder, and in nearly every case the disorder originates in sexual appetite. Escaping from this savagery, the wanderers arrive at the kingdom of Policarpo where civilization reigns and disorder is replaced by a social order imposed by reason, but there remains one disorder which reason is powerless to control: erotic passion. At best, reason can canalize it to some extent in the social institution of marriage, which checks sexual promiscuity and the rivalries this would produce, but in Policarpo's kingdom marriage exists only for sexual gratification, leaving individuals self-indulgent and self-seeking, which is a constant menace to social order.

Cervantes refuses to accept the optimism of the Neoplatonists: passion cannot be subjugated by reason. On the other hand Periandro and Auristela love each other and have vowed to remain faithful. Their fidelity is not broken by trials and tribulations and is a selflessness that contrasts with the prevailing selfishness. It is true love and it does not need, in fact it shuns, sexual gratification. This, however, is not Platonic love: it is a love that is put into its social-cultural setting when the wanderers reach Christian lands. Chastity and fidelity, in other words perseverance, devoid of self-seeking, in one's obligation to the person loved, are the dimension Christianity adds to the social institution of marriage, to which it thus gives stability in a permanent relationship entered into out of loyalty to God in one's permanent relationship to him. This of course reverses the Neoplatonist position: God is not reached through love of woman; respect and devotion for woman are reached from and through God. In Rome, the symbolical centre of civilization infused with grace, Periandro and Auristela deepen their Christian faith, renew their profession of it, and marry.

Through the multiplicity and great variety of adventures, and through the imagery with which these are related, there runs one constant theme: mankind's advance from barbarism to civiliza, tion is the passage from animal lust to devoted and altruistic love that seeks nothing but the good of the person loved. It is the traditional theme of pastoral, but with this important difference: in *Diana* the Wild Men appear only once and are quickly annihilated by Felismena, who represents a pure and chaste love, but in *Persiles* the Wild Men are there all the time. They dominate Book I. Figures representing lust in all its manifold forms run right through the novel. Even in Rome itself, Persiles is tempted to sensuality. The temptation and the danger of succumbing to it are universal in human life, and not a stage that is left behind (as the Neoplatonists would have it) in the pilgrimage of life. The praise of indissoluble Christian marriage, in which husband and wife remain faithful to each other, is sung on numerous occasions. To keep faith before marriage is to preserve one's purity and this in *Persiles* is ideal love, a chaste love until it is sanctified by the marriage vows. Fidelity before and after marriage is the form now taken by the concept of love as destiny. Men should accept their destiny and follow it to the end. Such is the lover's heroic life.

In his presentation of ideal love, Cervantes is faithful to the basic tradition of the sixteenth century, but modified and com, pleted by the new sense of reality that he had helped to introduce into literature in such a marvellous way by his *Don Quijote*. He believed firmly in a pure love, and to that extent in a Platonic love, but directed towards marriage, which gives it dignity and permanence. *Persiles* in this respect, however, looks backwards; now, at the beginning of the seventeenth century, modernity meant something different. It was *Don Quijote*, written earlier, that had been forward-looking.

The new note and tone, as regards the concept and expression of ideal love, lay in its confrontation with real life. The ideal was deeply rooted in the consciences of men; sensuality was deeply rooted in instincts and in the flesh. And the clash between conscience and the flesh produced a tormented anguish, which replaced experientially the theoretical suffering love of earlier literature. Cervantes, on the level of 'philosophy', is old-fashioned because in his treatment of ideal love there is no hint of torment or anguish. Ideal love is threatened from without, not from within. Torment and anguish come from the archetypal witches and wolves, not from the surge of passion and a tortured conscience. Persiles valiantly faces all his tribulations and overcomes them by the mere fact of resistance; on this account he is freed from inner struggles. He is an exemplary character, not a fully human one.

Don Quixote, in contrast to Persiles, is a modern creation, not only because he is more human, but because his humanity is full of the irony of human nature with all its vanity, arrogance, generosity and contradictions. Cervantes's idealism was not ignorant of the meanness and perversity of men; he could present them more powerfully as well as more humorously than any of his contemporaries, but he could not see, as Mateo Alemán saw, that the portrayal of 'real life' with its coarseness and vulgarity could be associated with 'high' artistry and a deep moral earnestness.[14] He was convinced, to the very end of his life, that *Persiles* was his finest work, and in the preface which he wrote for it on his deathbed, he even promised, should he live, a second part to *La Galatea*.

This critical blindness, as it seemed to be, was inexplicable until fairly recently. Nowadays we have a better sense of literary tradition and its various modes, and Cervantes's liking for *Persiles*, which was shared throughout the seventeenth century by the literary public, is no longer so inexplicable. We can appreciate the sweep of its mythic design and the strength of its symbolical and near allegorical conception, but we cannot put it on the same level as *Don Quijote*. We can also appreciate the ideals that Cervantes held to, and we may even see their transcendental value as, so to speak, the magnetic pole of moral endeavour, but we cannot accept them as a pull strong enough to counter the undertow of real life.

The career of Lope Félix de Vega Carpio (1562–1635), a prolific writer in every *genre* and a major dramatist and lyrical poet, covers the period which in the literature of Western Europe marks the transition from Petrarchan and Spenserian idealism to realism, and his work brings to the fore the problem of relating poetry to experience. His own temperament and his private life, which was a practically continuous public scandal, were the greatest possible contrast to the Courtly and Platonic lovers of literary tradition.[15] As a young man he had a passionate liaison with a married actress which led to a libel action, sentence of banishment from Madrid, and enlistment in the Invincible Armada, with a safe return to Spain. Before he enlisted, he eloped with a girl whom he was forced to marry. There were other liaisons, and, when his wife died, another marriage; the early death of the second wife and of a young son contributed to intense remorse and religious fervour. He became a priest at the age of fifty-two. In time he contracted a final liaison with a woman who shared his domestic life until she died. She grew blind and finally lost her reason, but he tended her devotedly till her death three years before his own. Despite the public scandals of his life, he was always a devoted husband and father.

Much of what Lope wrote was basically, if not literally, autobiographical. A man who could experience love without limits, he was a poet who poured out his experiences also without limits. Even when he uses the pastoral convention his 'shepherd' is unidealized, and only a poetic covering for himself. This personal poetry of experience, close to reality in feeling if not always in literary expression, culminated in *La Dorotea*, a work that many critics would consider his masterpiece, which sums up at the end of his life the poetry he had written and lived.

The Lyrical Poetry. Lope's lyrics exemplify two developments that were taking place also in the work of his contemporaries.[16] The first of these was the use by cultured, sophisticated poets of all the forms of popular poetry, especially the *villancico* or folk-song and the *romance* or folk-ballad. Popular poetry had never lost, in form or in theme, its contact with the soil. Lope could write a *romance* on the death of his wife with a remarkable naturalness of expression, devoid of all strong feeling, with nothing approaching hysteria or passionate emotion.[17] This naturalness was inherent in the form and metre of the ballads which Lope, unlike his contemporary Góngora, did not try to adorn. The second development was the acceptance into poetry of lived experience, despite continuing adherence to traditional, even conventional, themes. His lyrics continue the tradition of poetic idealism, but it is no longer isolated from a sense of reality; instead it is pervaded by an awareness of the problems that flow in real life from the absence of idealism in practice. The ideal, to which conscience is still attuned, has to struggle with the reality of passion, a reality that is not shunned, or even glossed over, but presented as personal experience in a much more concrete way than it was in Garcilaso.

A constant note in Lope's lovepoetry is the modification, not to say inversion, of poetic tradition into the reality of lived experience. He does not reject the stylistic features or the emotional aspects of traditional poetry, but he does not permit them to obscure the fact that the love they express is not an ideal one; passionate it indeed is, and on that account glorious, but it is real and natural, and therefore even commonplace. It can at times lead him to a joke that may be somewhat coarse and, in any case, not at all poetical. Even mythology, whose prestige had served to sublimate commonplace ideas and ordinary life, is not spared. The rape of Europa by Jupiter in the form of a bull, a seemingly universal symbol for virility, could be taken to imply that human women are indeed worthy of the love of a god, but in Lope's sonnet on the subject (132) there is no sign of any sublimation of the symbol or the myth. As the wind and the bull raise Europa's tunic, the red roses on her lap fall to the ground, making her exclaim '¡Ay triste, yo perdí las flores!' [Woe is me! I have lost my flowers]. The joke, which is coarse, not subtle, lies in the pun on 'flower', which meant virginity and also menstrual bleeding.

On a more serious level, Lope transformed the convention of the cruel lady, remote, untouchable and unyielding, who causes despairing grief in the lover. In Sonnet 135 of the *Rimas humanas* (140) it is expressed in the images of 'killing' and 'freezing', and in the paradox of 'ice' that sets the lover 'on fire'. These implied, traditionally, that the lady preserved an inviolate chastity but such is not the case here. She is a women of flesh and blood, conscious of her power over the man. Craftily, she teasingly plays about with him, pretending not to understand his language of suffering (11–12). There is no pretence here of any ideal love: the suffering is due to having to wait for the renewal of favours that have pre-viously been granted and that will be granted again. The image of dying in icy fire has been lightly turned into a humorous vein.

Another example is Sonnet 10 (121) in which the suffering of the poet is due to his lady's inconsequential behaviour. At one moment she is ice, at the other she is fire in abandonment to his passion. Whereas in previous poetry the poet suffered from the absence of a reward he had no right to demand, now, realistically and humanly, he suffers from the unpredictable behaviour of the lady in her inconsistency, which now replaces the lover's con-stancy in his unrequited fidelity. A 'philosophy of love' is dis-appearing into the background. Similarly Sonnet 37 (124) is, at first sight, a conventional lover's complaint, but the closing tercet makes it enigmatic:

> que si la viere el mundo transformada
> en el laurel que por dureza espero
> della veréis mi frente coronada.

Literally (but paraphrasing the last line), this would run in translation:

> . . . for if the world should see her
> transformed into laurel, which
> is what I expect from her coldness
> you will see, because of this very coldness,
> my brow crowned with laurel.

The allusion is, of course, to the myth of Daphne who, fleeing from the attempted seduction of Apollo, was saved by being turned into a laurel bush. The difficulty lies in construing the word 'della', which could refer either to the lady or her 'coldness' (*dureza*). To crown a brow with laurel means either to win a victory in war, or to gain renown as a poet. Lope would seem to be running the two senses together: Daphne's chastity won the victory over Apollo, but if Lope's lady resists his advances to the end, it is he who will win the victory, namely fame as a poet, because her coldness is the inspiration for his immortal verses; in effect, it is she who will be crowning his brow and so, with a witty paradox, admitting defeat. Doubtless the despairing poetic lovers of the preceding generations expected immortality from the sufferings they sang of, but few would have ventured to express this as a compensation, certainly not as a victory over the lady. We thus see not only convention being turned inside out, but also idealism on its way out.

In these ways Lope transformed the image of the cruel lady, implying that the rigorous inflexibility of chastity does not exist in reality. What does exist is woman, mutable and unpredictable, and mutability is the hallmark of Nature. The following sonnet expresses this idea:

> Estos los sauces son y esta la fuente,
> los montes estos y esta la ribera
> donde vi de mi sol la vez primera
> los bellow ojos, la serena frente.
>
> Este es el río humilde y la corriente
> y esta la cuarta y verde primavera
> que esmalta el campo alegre y reverbera
> en el dorado Toro el sol ardiente.
>
> Arboles, ya mudó su fe constante . . .
> Mas ¡oh gran desvarío!, que este llano
> entonces monte le dejé sin duda.
>
> Luego no será justo que me espante,
> que mude parecer el pecho humano,
> pasando el tiempo que los montes muda.[18]

These are the willows, this is the stream, these the woods and this the bank where first I saw the lovely eyes and the unfurrowed brow of my sun. This is the humble stream, and this is the current, and this the fourth green spring-time that colours the cheerful countryside, and from within golden Taurus shines forth the burning sun. Oh trees! She has now broken her constant faith . . . but oh! what folly to have left this then uncultivated field without a qualm of doubt. But then, it is not right for me to be surprised that human hearts should change, with time that alters woods and fields.

The lover, faithful unto death, replaced by fickle woman: how blasphemous this would have been in literature's Religion of Love! Yet there can be no escape from the 'ideal woman', however much she has changed. She remains the noblest part of a man's life and it is madness to condemn her as the worst. She is man's life and consolation, yet she is also his poison and his death. To man's eyes, she is an unclouded, brilliant Heaven, yet she can often lead to Hell.[19]

Lope allowed realism to break also into the tradition of love as a cruel destiny from which there can be no escape. There can, says Lope, be no escape because there is no will to escape: man permits his own imprisonment. In Sonnet 162 (145-6) Lope knocks at the door of Disillusion for admission, only to remember that he has left behind certain papers that he must needs fetch; but, he continues, this will be only a self-deception, for if Lucinda knows that he has returned, her lovely eyes will hold him captive for a hundred years. One can will to escape from one imprisonment only if one has entered another.[20]

The unity of lovers despite their separation, with all the paradoxical emotions that absence can arouse, inspired in Lope one of his most moving and powerful sonnets:

> Ir y quedarse y con quedar partirse,
> partir sin alma y ir con alma ajena,
> oír la dulce voz de una sirena
> y no poder del árbol desasirse;
>
> arder como la vela y consumirse
> haciendo torres sobre tierna arena;
> caer de un cielo y ser demonio en pena
> y de serlo jamás arrepentirse;
>
> hablar entre las mudas soledades,
> pedir prestada sobre fé paciencia

y lo que es temporal llamar eterno;
  creer sospechas y negar verdades
es lo que llaman en el mundo ausencia
fuego en el alma y en la vida infierno.[21]

> To go and remain, and by remaining to depart without one's
> soul and to go with another's soul, to hear the sweet voice of a
> siren and be unable to untie oneself from the mast; to burn like a
> candle and to be consumed, building castles on shifting sand;
> to fall from heaven and become a demon in hell, and never repent
> of being one; to speak aloud in voiceless solitude, to ask for
> patience on the pledge of faith, to call what is temporal eternal; to
> believe suspicion and to deny truth, this is what the world calls
> absence: fire in the soul and hell in life.

This is no longer an ironical twist of a conventional philosophy;
it can, in fact, no longer be called philosophy in any conceptual
sense, for it is not an idea of love but a reaction to the experience
of it. It is, however, philosophical in the sense that love as an
experience is problematical and paradoxical. The basic problem
of love is the transcendence of individual loneliness through a life-
enhancing communication. This sonnet has resonances beyond
the fact that communication is ruptured by the enforced absence
of the lover, resonances that raise echoes of what lies beyond
human contact. The fine 'hablar entre las mudas soledades' means
in the first place that the poet, journeying through a lonely
countryside, talks to himself with his thoughts on his absence
from his beloved, but one cannot help feeling, beyond the silence
of loneliness, the loneliness of endless silent space. What communication can there be with another? The resonances become
overtly religious in the imagery of Satan falling from Heaven and
in absence from love being a hell on Earth. This implied association of the erotic with the spiritual is a 'philosophy of experience'
deeper than that of the fifteenth-century Religion of Love because
it is more real and less theoretical.[22]

The concept of love in Lope's lyrical poetry departs from
Renaissance tradition in that neither women nor love are idealized. His lady is always a creature of flesh and blood with human
feelings and failings, but beautiful and desirable always, tugging
endlessly at his heart-strings and grievously hurting his con-

science. There is no cult of a spiritual love in a realm above sensuality, and love is not a martyrdom suffered patiently in altruistic service: Lope could not pay even lip-service to such a literary convention; he would have felt its hypocrisy in his very bones. Love is always carnal, and inconstancy and infidelity are its natural counterparts in that sphere, but in this there is nothing essentially cynical or shameless. Love is not the most spiritual of human experiences, but it is the most glorious in the transitory happiness it can bring. There is implicit a moral philosophy in Lope's love-poetry, and in accordance with it he condemns himself, but he never condemns love or woman, or Nature for having created her and made desire for her the centre of man's experience. Erotic love can clash with a higher duty, which Lope's heart and conscience never deny, however much he failed to heed them, but although his religious poetry is very moving, it is never mystical, just as his love-poetry is never Platonic; it is a poetry of repentance in which the sinner bares his heart and soul. He de-idealizes literary convention because he has no illusions about himself, and because he cannot write poetry that is not rooted in himself and in his experience.[23]

Lope aptly characterized his love-poetry as follows:

> Versos de amor, conceptos esparcidos
> engendrados del alma en mis cuidados,
> partos de mis sentidos abrasados,
> con más dolor que libertad nacidos;
>   expósitos al mundo en que perdidos
> tan rotos anduvistes y trocados,
> que sólo donde fuistes engendrados
> fuérades por la sangre conocidos.[24]

Poems of love, thoughts scattered (to the winds) engendered by my soul amid the cares of life, birthpangs of my burning senses, born of more pain than freedom; foundlings cast into the world, in which, forlorn, you moved so ragged, and with identities so lost that only your begetter could recognise you through the blood you bore.

What end has been achieved by so much loving and so much writing? At the close of this sonnet (13-14) he throws his poems

into the wind, and tells them that there there they will find their very
centre as their final resting place. Wind was a common symbol,
especially in the seventeenth century, for vanity and presumption:
his love-poetry is centred here, not on solid ground. Since it
formed so large a part of his life, Lope may have felt that his life
itself was insubstantial and, to a large extent, wasted. His final
word on this nascent disillusion comes in *La Dorotea*.

La Dorotea was published in 1632. Lope died 3 years later. It
is a long prose work in dramatic form, in five unperformable
acts. It is prolix and diffuse, and its structure is disorganized.
Nonetheless, though difficult to read for these reasons, it is one of
the really remarkable works of Spanish literature. The main
thread of the plot is autobiographical, and in the protagonist,
Fernando, Lope reconstructs his youth, contrasting the idealization of love with reality.[25]

The memory of his first, tempestuous love affair haunted Lope
to the end of his life. He early associated with actors and at the age
of seventeen fell in love with Elena Osorio, an actress and
daughter of an actor, whose husband was absent in the Indies.
She seems to have been a remarkable and intelligent woman.
Both of them entered into the liaison with emotional intensity
which found expression in Lope in a flood of poetry. Her disguise in this poetry behind a pastoral convention could easily
have been penetrated by those who knew of them, for, in accordance with custom, handwritten copies of the poems circulated
in the capital. The affair lasted four or five years until Elena
became the mistress of Francisco Perrenot, nephew of Cardinal
Granvelle. In the *Dorotea* Lope attributes the heroine's desertion
of Fernando to her mother's pressure on behalf of a wealthy
merchant from the colonies. In real life he reacted with scornful
fury, publicly attacking her and her family who then initiated
proceedings against him for libel.

The deep-seated impression which this affair left on Lope was
not erased by the numerous associations which followed. It
became connected in his mind with the *Celestina*, which must
also have impressed him deeply, and when his memories were
finally transmuted by his poetic imagination into literature the

result was a work that recalls the *Celestina* in form and in part of the plot. Rojas had associated the ecstasy of passionate sexuality with the pessimism of guilt. Lope's seduction of Elena and his violent recriminations could never have ceased to trouble his conscience, however much this could be stretched. As he reconstructed in old age the stormy events of his youth, the sense of guilt was present, but it was dimmed by nostalgia for the joy of a passion that had been, and had remained for so long, the source of so much intense poetry.

The lovers in *La Dorotea* live in the beautiful but illusory world of sixteenth-century love poetry, having this poetry and the language of Neoplatonism on their lips. Their endless talking and reciting of poems gives the impression of futility. They never *do* anything. They are the victims of an idealized, romantic conception of love in that they are tied to their own feelings; they cannot escape from themselves but must go aimlessly round and round. Yet both lovers, for all their weakness, are presented understandingly and sympathetically. Love is a beautiful thing, but if pursued obsessively as an all-absorbing ideal, it must, like everything human, come up against sad reality. Neoplatonist love with its worship and exaltation of beauty, may be all very well as an ideal; but men do not live on that plane of idealization. They live in society, which is governed in the last resort by material considerations. One must make a living somehow, and so all men and women, in their relationships with each other, are subject to self-interest. Pure altruistic love is an illusion in practice; self-interest is the sad reality. When compelled to face the practical problems of life, the young couple's ardent love founders in mercenary greed, jealousy and vengeance. Love, like all emotions, if not governed by reason and social prudence, becomes self-frustrating in the inexorable decline to which everything human is subject.

La Dorotea is sad, not tragic. The ideal of love is indeed something beautiful, if only because it can be turned into poetry. The lovers in the work love and cultivate poetry, but this itself removes them from direct contact with reality into the world of illusions and contributes to their lack of backbone. But though the work is disillusioned with the enchantment of poetry, there is all the time a wistful nostalgic glance at the beauty of poetic illusions.

La comedia nueva. Lope de Vega was a major lyrical poet but his fame, and his influence outside Spain, rested on his plays. The drama was the literary genre most closely connected with real life, watched by people of all classes as they crowded into the public theatres. It had to reflect their lives and their problems and could not, therefore, at least in Lope de Vega's generation, deal with love 'philosophically'. Although love was the dominant theme in nearly every play, it had to be presented in the social context of contemporary life. Love, as such, could not therefore have on the stage the kind of treatment it had been receiving in lyrical poetry for more than a century and a half. It had to be love with marriage as its end, love inside marriage or outside it; and if inside marriage it had to be put into the context of what religion demanded and society expected of husbands and wives.[26]

All the moral regulations and conventions with which courtship and married life were hedged around became the stuff of drama. Naturally the infringement of these rules, or pressure to infringe them, was more dramatic than their observance. According to convention arranged marriages were the accepted norm and young women had to be kept as far as possible from meeting young men in order to preserve them from emotional attachments. Their duty was to accept the man chosen by their fathers. Neither were young men themselves free to choose their own brides, although rebellion was less serious with them than it was with women. Once marriage was contracted, fidelity to the spouse became, of course, the expected standard, but the 'double standard' prevailed in Spain as it did everywhere else. In 1636 Quevedo wrote a masterly 'Vision', *La hora de todos* (The hour that strikes for everyone) in which he imagined a parliament of all nations, convoked to discuss and legislate on all the social and political ills afflicting humanity. Women, imaginary precursors of suffragettes and women's liberators, denounce the tyranny of men. Among other complaints they say: 'Adultery for you is an entertaining pastime, but you have made it a capital offence for us.'[27]

Preservation of the sanctity of marriage depended on the stead-fast virtue of the wives. Although moral guilt did attach to adulterous husbands, it was only the wives who incurred punish-ment. But the moral guilt of husbands could add dramatic irony to the punishment of wives because theatrical convention retained the old tradition of giving husbands the right to avenge the dis-honour caused by their wives' misconduct, even if this were only intended or, indeed, only suspected.

These features of the Spanish *comedia* are not directly related to any philosophy of love; rather would they provide material for a study of the ways in which literature presents changing social and moral ideas in human history. Nonetheless they indicate support for two basic principles of natural law and moral theology: first that love between men and women is natural and good in itself, and second that to follow the dictates of one's heart should be a natural right, provided the particular case is not complicated by other issues. In addition to these principles the *comedia* almost always presented love as destiny. This conception lay at the heart of Courtly and Chivalrous Love, but on the stage it was not for the most part presented with the overriding force with which it appears in *Don Duardos* or *Celestina*. There are, however, two notable exceptions in the drama of Lope.

The first is *El caballero de Olmedo* (The Knight of Olmedo) which was probably written about 1621.[28] When the heroine of this beautiful play appears on stage she asserts that the cause of love is held to lie in the stars, but why should they act so caprici-ously? Why should she love so intensely a man she has never met, while disliking her official suitor with equal intensity? She had been watching a civic procession from the balcony of her house and one of the knights riding by had looked up, their eyes had met and from that moment she could love nobody else. Before long she was to learn that he too had met his destiny in that glance. Falling in love at first sight is a convention of the Spanish drama. It is unrealistic only in the speed with which it happens, but this is a time-saving device for telescoping an action into its essentials. Young people do fall in love, and it is immaterial for dramatic purposes whether the process takes one minute or one

year. The suddenness with which it happens powerfully reinforces the theme of destiny. From the moment their eyes meet,
each can live only for the other and their love becomes for them
an overwhelming joy that cannot be gainsaid. They brush aside
all obstacles unheedingly, swept away by a carefree joyousness.

Such love is outside the control of reason. This was why
theologians had looked askance at or openly condemned erotic
sensuality when expressed outside the restraints of marriage. Even
within these restraints it meant that sexual love could never be
the highest expression of human desire for fulfilment, because
the swamping of reason by instinct was not proper to men, the
dominance of instinct being proper to animals alone. Alonso
and Inés never stop to consider the most suitable ways of furthering their attachment. Their delight in each other sweeps away all
prudence. Had they proceeded with due regard for the conventions, all would have ended well, but Lope directs the plot
into the *Celestina* situation, to which he makes several pointed
references. Alonso obtains access to Inés through the mediation
of an old bawd, he being blind, like Calisto, to her true character.
Inés, for her part, willingly connives at deceiving her father by
feigning a vocation to convent life. Their conduct is imprudent
and underhand, although never otherwise dishonourable,
because Alonso never aims at anything but marriage. His rashness and impetuosity, themselves the fruit of a love that is
inherently noble, make his death inevitable at the hands of his
rival, the official suitor of Inés. Despite omens and foreboding
dreams, he allows selfconfidence to destroy his love. The play is
lyrical throughout with nothing of the stark realism of *Celestina*,
but from the moment that the two lovers allow their love to
smother reason and conscience, their fatal destiny is sealed.

The destiny to which Love summons human beings is powerfully presented as fatality in another of Lope's masterpieces, *El
castigo sin venganza* (Punishment without Revenge), written in
1631.[29] A young couple consciously allow themselves to be
caught in the web of a passion that is itself entangled in a complex,
threefold relationship. The young man, Federico, is a son of the
Duke of Ferrara. He is illegitimate, but his father loves him so

dearly that he does not allow this to bar his succession to the Dukedom. The Duke is a womanizer, who has never married in order to be free to carry on his amours, but when his subjects petition him to marry in order to give them a legitimate heir, he chooses the young and beautiful Casandra. Her bridegroom's reputation and age make her dislike this prospect. The Duke's heart is not in the marriage, and he deserts his wife's bed after the first night.

Federico intensely resents the marriage because it is likely to deprive him of the succession, yet he is captivated by his step/ mother's youthful beauty. She, also captivated by him, is so out/ raged by the Duke's insulting treatment of her that she desires vengeance on him, and therefore offers no resistance to her mounting love for his son whom she seduces, thus paying her husband back in his own coin. Federico's passion for his step/ mother makes him enter into the adulterous and incestuous union as a morbid death/wish because of his neurotic obsession at being supplanted.

This complex situation has nothing crudely melodramatic about it. The two lovers are caught in the net that Fate has cast for them. Nature has made them for each other and impels them into each other's arms in what can only be a hopeless struggle against conscience. When the Duke discovers the liaison, he realizes that his own loose living has ultimately been the cause of the whole affair. As chief magistrate of his State he is compelled to punish the crime of adulterous incest by 'executing' his son and his wife; but as a dishonoured ruler he is also compelled to execute the sentence in such a way as to hide its real motive and its real cause. He orders his son to kill someone whom he has condemned as a traitor, and when Federico discovers that he has killed Casandra, he is immediately accused by his father of murdering her in order to prevent an heir to the Dukedom. Allowing him no time for any explanation, the father has his son killed on the spot.

Nature is thus thwarted by Civilization. The two lovers are destined for each other, and rightly so, but their union is the opposite of joyous. Their social circumstances entangle their natural passion in psychological and political dilemmas that, in effect, cause them to seek death, rather than find life through their union. This terrible irony culminates at the close in the Duke claiming to be the minister of divine justice: he had allowed love (not destiny but pleasure) to obscure his social, political and moral duty, with the result that he is left at the end with no wife and no heir to succeed him, neither legitimate or illegitimate. Within the social conditions of the age the problems posed by human love could scarcely have been more powerfully presented.

TIRSO DE MOLINA

The concept of natural law in jurisprudence and theology had nothing to do with nature as the setting for rural life. Yet in an age that had become conscious of the corruptions of urban living, it was natural to contrast the terms 'nature' and 'natural' primarily with the 'artificiality' of sophisticated and luxurious living, although the contrast between 'natural' and 'contrary to nature' in the moral sense was never lost. The social contrast had been explicit in the literary convention of pastoral, and the superiority of country over town became a motif of the new drama, adapted as closely as possible to the conditions of everyday life. Where peasants and nobles appear together in plays which contrast the manner and traditions of their life-styles, it is the peasantry who are presented as the more upright, honourable and loyal class of citizens.

Such plays do not directly concern the theme of this book, except in the case of the dramatist Tirso de Molina, a younger contemporary of Lope de Vega who used a pseudonym for his plays. His real name was Fray Gabriel Téllez (*c.* 1581 – 1648).[30] Several Spanish dramatists were priests or, like Lope and Calderón, were ordained late in life, but Gabriel Téllez was exceptional in being a member of a religious order, a friar of the Order of Ransom (Orden de la Merced). His plays present peasants, both men and women, with a sense of moral integrity but without idealizing them as natural ladies and gentlemen. He portrays them as down-to-earth, lively, humorous, even witty and with a racy command of language. They have no sense of inferiority, but know their place and have no desire to ape the upper classes. The women generally resist the wooing of gentle-men who fall in love with them, but these gentlemen, however, often come in the end to marry them.

The exaltation of the peasantry as the equals, indeed as morally superior to the upper classes, is genuine enough in Tirso, but behind it there lies a political intention. This, though not apparent in the plays themselves, is connected with one of the least edifying aspects of Spanish civilization in this period. A racially mixed society with three different religions on its soil, followed by the attempt after 1492 to impose uniformity by banishing Jews and Moslems who would not accept baptism, had created a society of 'Old Christians' and 'New Christians'. The former could claim 'orthodoxy' by reason of birth; the latter, up to the fourth generation, could be suspect 'heretics'. Access to the professions and the higher positions in the administration of the State were closed to the latter. Jewish and Moorish blood was therefore considered a tainted inheritance.

Such laws produced an exaggerated sense of social 'honour', fanned by the award or sale of titles of nobility, and such equiva-lent distinctions as knighthoods in the Military Orders, now only sinecures. Legally, only Old Christians could aspire to, or petition for, these honours, but it was popularly believed, often with justification, that the men who could afford to buy titles of nobility were frequently of Jewish stock. Some notorious examples of benefits given to ministerial favourites caused much popular discontent, and since the public stage was, to a certain extent, a forum in which grievances of a national kind could be aired, some dramatists made themselves the spokesmen for this resentment, though naturally in an implicit and indirect way. Thus, the marriage on the stage of members of the upper and lower nobility to peasant women, or the corresponding enoble-ment of peasant men as a reward for services to the King, was the people's voice telling the Crown that admission to the aristocracy should be granted to country people who could alone be sure of an untainted ancestry, since Jews had been bankers and mer-chants, but never farmers.[31]

Tirso shows himself to be no admirer of the aristocracy. Perhaps the most striking example is *Antona García* (1620–5?), a play set in the wars which Queen Isabella the First of Castile had to wage in order to ensure her succession to the throne.[32] Her opponents were the Castilian feudal nobility who supported another claimant to the throne, who actually had a better 'legal' right to it, her niece, Princess Juana. In the play this historical setting is of first importance. The Portuguese occupied the town of Toro on the invitation of the local nobility who had declared for Juana, and they were not defeated until 1476. Tirso makes the townspeople, under the leadership of a local woman, Antona García, rise in revolt and take control of the town in the name of Isabella, to whom they deliver it. The aristocrats are corrupt, traitors to the State and cruel to the townspeople.

Tirso's feminism is portrayed in three strong women who dominate the action. First, María Sarmiento, widow of the head of the aristocratic party, the ringleader of the feudal rebellion and commander of the usurping forces; secondly, Queen Isabella, a forceful leader and a just and prudent ruler; and thirdly, Antona García, who restores the town to its rightful sovereign. Antona, a woman from the common people, possesses instinctively the virtues of political loyalty and resoluteness in defence of the law, as well as a physical strength that can cow men and an unflagging bravery that belies her sex. She would be a caricature of a masculine woman, had Tirso not endowed her with a lively, down-to-earth humour and cheerfulness. He also makes her attractively feminine with the necessary quality of great beauty, but she has nothing of the swoonings, tears and fickleness supposedly characteristic of her sex. She is as loyal to her husband as to the Queen, and makes no more fuss of giving birth to twins than she does of wielding a sword. Despite all these extremes, she is a very human and attractive creation, and obviously for Tirso she enshrines a symbolical quality, a forthright adherence to all natural values and a cheerful acceptance of the hardships this may involve.

These qualities are evident in her attitude to love. Struck by her beauty and fascinated by her temperament, a Portuguese Count, a member of the invading army, declares his love for her. He does so in the poetic imagery of romantic love, at which Antona can only laugh, vigorously but with no touch of mockery. The gulf between two class cultures is marked by the artificial and the natural attitudes to love and sex. After the death of Antona's husband, the Count offers her marriage and sincerely endeavours to win her. Though she continues to poke fun at the idea of their marriage, she is touched by his constancy and sincerity, and feels a certain tenderness towards him. This open ending leaves the superiority of country life over urban life, and even of woman over man, undimmed. It is possible, however, as the plot really requires, that a second part was intended, which would portray their marriage and the exploits of the new Countess in a very different sphere of life. Over this she would clearly rise superior, as she does when faced with the political corruption of the nobility.

All through Tirso's comedies there run witty remarks and jokes about sex, generally put into the mouths of his female characters. These used to be considered on the borderline of the salacious, and it has never failed to cause surprise that they should have been written by a friar. But the cheerful, carefree attitude to sex as a natural and wholesome part of life is, in the whole context of Tirso's humour, actually far from salacious. This is evident above all in two things: the human superiority of his woman characters and the fact that this is generally rooted in country life and the peasantry.

Tirso's best-known play might appear an exception to this. *El burlador de Sevilla* (The Libertine of Seville) is the first example on the European stage of the legendary Don Juan theme.[33] The swaggering seducer of women moves with panache through its three acts and all the women in his path become his victims. The plot requires the women to be, uncharacteristically for Tirso, easily deceived, but this is no exaltation of *machismo*. Don Juan Tenorio does not seek sexual pleasure as such, but the dishonouring and vilification of women. This abuse of women is part of a moral anarchism that threatens to overturn the whole structure of society, for Don Juan also shows no respect for King or for the sanctity of marriage, and no respect for the dead any more than he has respect for human life itself; he has no loyalty to friends and feels no gratitude for the saving of his life and for a hospitality that nurses him back to health. This 'masculine' attitude to sex is the negation of civilized values and contrasts with the 'feminine' attitude that Tirso's women protagonists invariably portray.

One example of a natural attitude to sex and a resoluteness in facing the dangers with which society hedges it round, is an early play entitled *El vergonzoso en palacio* (The Timid Man in the Palace).[34] Two women are contrasted. Serafina repels the advances of her suitors because, as events disclose, she is frightened of sex through a combination of narcissism and homosexuality: she loves to dress as a man and to play male roles in amateur theatricals; so dressed, she falls in love with her own portrait, painted without her knowing. Magdalena, her sister, is determined to win the man she loves. She is a Duke's daughter and the man is her father's secretary. No servant, however well-placed, could propose to such a mistress but she, slowly and ingeniously, compels him to do so and accepts him.

Situations of this kind in which women overturn convention in order to win the men they want abound in the comedies of the period. But this play of Tirso's is different in a very important respect. Daughters withstand their fathers and after they have made their point the fathers generally submit with as good a grace as they can command. But Tirso's Magdalena, to make sure of winning her husband, actually seduces him and presents the Duke with the *fait accompli* of her and his own dishonour, knowing full well that this may mean her death. The secretary is the husband Nature has destined for her, and to win and keep him she bravely faces moral and social disgrace and possibly death, for no gentleman could ever accept a dishonoured woman as his wife. Her death is prevented by a surprising twist in the plot, but the point is made: Nature should rule, and it is woman who serves and safeguards Nature.

These few plays represent Tirso's most characteristic output, but others present different facets of society. One such play, which deals with the contrast between divine and human love, is *La ninfa del cielo* (The Nymph of Heaven), subtitled 'The Bandit Countess', which was written in 1613.[35] It shows that Tirso's firm adherence to the natural values did not blur his sense of the supremacy of supernatural values. Ninfa (that is not a metaphor, but the heroine's first name) is a countess who shuns the frivolity of city life and the amours it encourages, preferring to live in seclusion in her country estate near Naples, away from the company of the male sex because she has too strong a sense of her dignity as a woman. A chance visitor to her house is the Duke of Calabria, who hides his real identity. He is accomplished in all the arts of seduction and is able to arouse all the passion and tenderness Ninfa has suppressed, to which she abandons herself on his solemn promise of marriage, only to find herself in due course betrayed and dishonoured. Feeling deeply this outrage to her woman's dignity, and vowing to hate all men from now onwards, she conforms to an already developed dramatic type by becoming a bandit-chief, sparing all women but killing all the men who fall into her power in order to make the whole sex pay for the treachery of one of its members.

This fierce and violent reaction to personal dishonour was the normal response of a spirited woman on the Spanish stage. Dishonour of this kind robbed her of her self-respect and made it impossible for her to face the scorn of her community. Outlawed by this moral ostracism Ninfa seeks refuge and revenge in social rebellion. Meanwhile the Duke, tired of the company of his wife, longs to return to the Ninfa he had seduced. While searching for her he is captured by her bandits, but she cannot consummate the act of vengeance on the man she loves while he still protests his passion for her. Finding out who he is, she makes him promise to kill his wife so that they may marry.

Pursued now by the troops sent to apprehend her, they become separated and Ninfa finds herself alone and lost in the wilderness. Realizing the horror of her situation, she is overwhelmed by remorse, and becomes a public penitent as a kind of anchoress, rejecting all the Duke's attempts to win her back. The Duchess, aware of her husband's continuing infidelities, comes searching for him; seeing movement in a bush and thinking it an animal she strikes at it with her hunting spear, to find that she has mortally wounded Ninfa, who acknowledges the special justice of death at the hands of the woman she had wronged. The Duke, arriving as she lies dying, passionately wishes to hold her in his arms, but she will not let him touch her, saying that she must go into the arms of Christ. The ending makes it clear that this is what happens as her soul ascends to heaven. Deeply moved by all this the wayward Duke promises his wife to change his life.

There is much in this play that is melodramatic, but it is, nevertheless, profoundly interesting in its attempt to portray mystical experience on the stage, and to contrast mystical love with human love. In the first act Ninfa speaks to the Duke in a poetry full of tender amorous feeling; in the last act she addresses Christ with the same lyrical tenderness. At the beginning she abandons herself to a human embrace, at the end she yearns only for the divine embrace. The same love language is used through-out, what changes is the object. Ninfa's peculiar name, Nymph, is of course intentional: it denotes the sensuousness, the tender-ness, of this woman's nature, which needs expression in a way that will not degrade her dignity.

The point of the play is this: woman's sensuality is subject to man in courtship and marriage, but the human male is sexually promiscuous in his desires and unfaithful. The two women in the play, Ninfa and the Duchess, are the victims of the same man's infidelity, both of them are dishonoured and degraded. Ninfa's love for a man is born in his deceit and spurned by his betrayal; her love for her Creator is born in suffering and consummated in faithfulness unto death, and this is the only love in which woman's dignity is safeguarded and fulfilled. Previously women had been presented as aloof, indifferent, unattainable and men as the victims of their unhappy love. Now in the moral and social evils that bedevil the sphere of love, women are recognized to be the victims: victims of lust, of oppression, of male tyranny, of male infidelity, of jealous and revengeful husbands, of a social code that severely limits their freedom. They are invariably the ones who suffer. This leads in the drama to an awareness of women's social rights.

Tirso's presentation of sex as wholesome within the supremacy of country over city is a realistic conception that is found idealized, but within the same system of values, in the most sophisticated poetry of his age. The idealization of love in earlier Spanish literature had stressed the spiritual and intellectual values that love can foster. It had, however, tended to overlook, minimize or denigrate the sexual fulfilment that gave so great but so fleeting a joy to the heroine of the *Celestina*, despite moments, prior to 1580, as in the early poems of Aldana, when suggestions are made that this physical joy is the central value of love. In the poet Luis de Góngora (1561–1627) sexual love, when it appears, is presented as beautiful and joyous within the natural order, free from the self-seeking, mercenary, lustful and violent aspects that urban civilization gives to its expression in real life.

It may be granted that Góngora's *Fábula de Acis y Galatea* is the most deeply erotic poem in the Spanish literature of this period.[36] It would also probably be granted by most literary critics that it is also the most beautiful presentation of erotic love, delicately sensual without the intrusion of any suggestion of lasciviousness. This was made possible, within the moral standards and literary conventions of the age, because its subject and treatment were sanctioned by classical antiquity. In the Renaissance period the story of Polyphemus and Galatea, found in Ovid's *Metamorphoses*, was a popular one. Ovid makes the Cyclops, with his destructive wooing of the nymph, the dominant element in the fable, whereas Góngora makes the central episode the successful wooing of the nymph by Acis. In the midst of a Nature prolific in beautiful and life-preserving vegetation and fruits Acis represents the beauty of youthful strength, and Galatea's feminity represents the summit of all natural beauty: she is the divinity whom all the inhabitants of Sicily yearn for and worship from afar. The setting of the poem is the classical world of fable, which gives to its human and semi-human inhabitants a natural innocence that can cause no offence. The offence to the beautiful island of Sicily comes not from human lust but from Nature's storms and rivalries, and from the violence she inflicts on humanity by the inescapability of death. The grief of Galatea over the crushed body of her lover is the grief of Nature herself, but it cannot destroy the joy and fulfilment that Nature can give to human love.

In the first of the *Soledades* (Solitudes), a long, unfinished poem, a young nobleman is swept ashore from a shipwreck, a castaway from the urban civilization that has brought him only the despairing unhappiness of an unrequited love. As he moves through the countryside he joins the peasants, men and women, who are making their way to a wedding. He contemplates the beauty of Nature, which in Góngora's elaborate descriptions has all the grandeur of Renaissance art, and his sick spirit is slowly healed as he becomes aware of a purposeful form of life within the permanent rhythm of Nature. The young men are strong and excel in athletic sports; the young women are all beautiful, and woman's beauty is fulfilled in marriage. Marriage is a cause for festive rejoicing, and the simple joys of the peasantry in their songs, dances and competitive sports, do not yield to those in the palaces of nobles. The *Soledad primera* concludes thus:

> En tanto pues que el palio neutro pende
> y la carroza de la luz desciende
> a templarse en las ondas, Himeneo
> —por templar, en los brazos, el deseo
> del galán novio, de la esposa bella—
> los rayos anticipa de la estrella,
> cerúlea ahora, ya purpúrea guía
> de los dudosos términos del día.
>
> El juicio—al de todos, indeciso—
>   del concurso ligero,
> el padrino con tres de limpio acero
> cuchillos corvos absolvello quiso.
> Solícita Junón, Amor no omiso,
> al son de otra zampoña que conduce
> ninfas bellas y sátiros lascivos,
> los desposados a su casa vuelven,
>   que coronada luce

de estrellas fijas, de astros fugitivos
que en sonoroso humo se resuelven.

Llegó todo el lugar, y, despedido,
casta Venus—que el lecho ha prevenido
de las plumas que baten más suaves
en su volante carro blancas aves—
los novios entra en dura no estacada:
que, siendo Amor una deidad alada,
bien previno la hija de la espuma
a batallas de amor campo de pluma.

While, with the prize in doubt, the car of day
descends to where the ocean's waves allay
its fire, Hymen anticipates the haste
of gallant groom and lovely bride, embraced
in straining arms, to allay the fire of love,
and sends the planet which presides above,
cerulean first, and then with purple light,
over the dubious bounds of day and night.

No certain verdict on the hard-run race
the wavering public gives,
but now the father, with three curving knives
of shining steel, resolves the doubtful case.
Juno and Love, mindful of every grace,
while beauteous nymphs and lusty satyrs dance
behind the music of another flute,
crowned with the radiance
of many stars, some fixed and some that shoot
like meteors and in sounding smoke explode.

When all who followed on their way had sped,
and Venus had prepared the marriage bed
with plumage from the softest wings of white
which beat the air before her car in flight,
the lovers to no hurtful lists she brings,
for, since her Cupid is a god with wings,
the daughter of the foam has wisely found
feathers are Love's most fitting battle-ground.[37]

The *Soledades* are very elaborate poetry in the 'high' style.
Góngora has many beautiful poems in what was technically the
'low' style, though it is not at all 'low' in his hands. These are the
metres of popular poetry, the *romance* and the *villancico*, both of

which were vehicles for pastoral and peasant themes. Here, too, Góngora introduces sexual attraction and love, but because of the countryside setting he can present it as joyful and innocent. The ballad *Angélica y Medoro*, taken from *Orlando furioso*, may serve as an example. It also illustrates how the Renaissance literature of Italy, like classical mythology, provided a distancing that could imbue sex with innocence. Angélica, who had shunned men, is won for love by nursing the wounded Medoro, and a rustic hut and the caves on the sea shore contain their marriage bed:

> Corona un lascivo enjambre
> de Cupidillos menores
> la choza, bien como abejas
> hueco tronco de alcornoque.
>   *   *   *
> Todo es gala el africano,
> su vestido espira olores,
> el lunado arco suspende,
> y el corvo alfanje depone.
>
> Tórtolas enamoradas
> son sus roncos atambores,
> y los volantes de Venus
> sus bien seguidos pendones.
>
> Desnuda el pecho anda ella,
> vuela el cabello sin orden;
> si le abrocha, es con claveles,
> con jazmines si le coge.
>   *   *   *
> Cuevas do el silencio apenas
> deja que sombras las moren
> profanan con sus abrazos
> a pesar de sus horrores.
>
> Choza, pues, tálamo y lecho,
> cortesanos labradores,
> aires, campos, fuentes, vegas,
> cuevas, troncos, aves, flores,
> fresnos, chopos, montes, valles,
> contestes de estos amores, . . .[38]

A playful swarm of little Cupids crowns the hut, just like bees round the hollow trunk of a cork-tree. The African is all elegance, his clothes smell sweetly, he hangs up his crescent-shaped bow and puts aside his curved scimitar. Love-sick doves are his martial drums, and these birds of Venus are the standards that he follows. She goes with her breasts bare, her hair flies loose; if she clasps it, she does so with carnations, and with jasmine if she gathers it. Caves in which silence scarcely allows shadows to dwell are profaned by their embraces, despite the horrors aroused by the darkness. Hut, therefore, bridal bed, courteous peasants, winds, meadows, streams, plains, caves, trees, birds, flowers, ash-trees, poplars, hills, valleys, are the witnesses to these lovers' unions. . . .

Góngora brings sexual fulfilment nearer to reality in the world of pastoral. While describing nothing that was not present in the meadows, woods and shores of his own times, he achieves the distancing that equates sex and innocence, and he does so by the timelessness of his art which raises men, women and love to the perfection of the aesthetic. This was a form of idealization still possible as literature approached the Age of Disillusion.

One of the drawings illustrating the stage sets for the revival of one of Calderon's plays, *La fiera, el rayo y le piedra* ('The Beast, the Lightning and the Stone') to celebrate the marriage of Charles II. This performance was on the 4th June 1690 in the Royal Palace in Valencia; the play had been written in 1652 to celebrate the Queen's birthday. The floor of the stage represents the Earth with plants; the scenery represents the Heavens with the 12 Signs of the Zodiac. Above in the centre is Venus on a Star. Cupid is in the left foreground on a Rose and Anteros is in the right foreground on a Sunflower; these are the two sons of Venus, passionate and tender love, continually in conflict. In this scene from Act III, these three characters sang their lines from these positions.

FIVE.

IDEAL LOVE AND
THE PHILOSOPHY OF DISILLUSION

Neo-stoicism. QUEVEDO. CALDERÓN. *Ni amor se libra de amor.*
Violence and imprisonment. *la hija del aire. Eco y Narciso. El*
monstruo de los jardines. Apolo y Climene. El hijo del sol, Faetón.
Conclusion.

Neo-Stoicism

The Neoplatonist conception of ideal love could not withstand
the confrontation with reality. To maintain that human love
could be desensualized on the command of reason, transformed
into a spiritual attachment and then guided up the ladder of
Plato's heavenly eros until the mutual love of man and woman
merged without a break into mystical communion with the
Godhead: such a view of love represented an optimism about
mankind, and life in general, that could never have been
justified by experience. Hence, as we have seen, disillusion with
the ideal of love spread until the ideal became, like Don
Quixote's Dulcinea, hidden from sight, enchanted by evil
magicians, and unable to appear except symbolically as a
frightened, trembling hare fleeing from the huntsmen. This disillusion with the ideal of love because it is unattainable becomes
in the generations of Quevedo and Calderón disillusion with life
itself, since love promises men a happiness which life is radically
incapable of fulfilling.

The disillusion of Spanish literature in the seventeenth century
used to be seen as the result of Spain's political and economic
decline. There is a connection, of course, but the disillusion
would surely have been there even if the decline had been post-
poned for half a century, since pessimism was the air that most
Europeans breathed. There was certainly pessimism in England,
which was not in decline but, on the contrary, on the threshold
of imperial expansion. Renaissance humanists might have

celebrated man's dignity and his divine gift of reason, but a century later men were much more aware that primitive man had lost his first innocence and happiness, that this Hebraic and Christian conception of the Fall had been corroborated by the pagan idea of progressive degeneration from the Golden Age, and that the whole history of the human race was one of frustration and corruption.

Douglas Bush in his great work on English literature in the earlier seventeenth century writes of England: 'We find much disgust with men and society, much vague bitterness against a world that seems out of joint, against the apparent futility of life. . . . The young Sir William Cornwallis and the elder statesman Fulke Greville, to cite only two witnesses, see about them nothing but the corruptions of a sick time. Ancient heroes, Cornwallis declares in his essay on "Fame", searched for substance, modern men chase shadows: "we are walking Ghostes".'[1] This phrase of Cornwallis 'we are walking ghostes' is paralleled by the idea we find constantly expressed in Spanish literature. Francisco de Quevedo (1580–1645), for instance, in his *Sueño de la muerte* (Vision of Death) written 20 years after the publication of Cornwallis's *Essays*, says this of men:

> La muerte no la conocéis, y sois vosotros mismos vuestra muerte. Tiene la cara de cada uno de vosotros, y todos sois muertes de vosotros mismos. La calavera es el muerto, y la cara es la muerte. Y lo que llamáis morir es acabar de morir, y lo que llamáis nacer es empezar a morir, y lo que llamáis vivir es morir viviendo.[2]

> You do not know death and you yourselves are your death: she has the face of each one of you and all of you are the deaths of yourselves. The skull is the dead man; the face is death: and what you call dying is finishing dying, and what you call being born is to begin to die, and what you call living is to be dying in life.

For the Englishman men are walking ghosts; for the Spaniard they are walking death.

When applied to love of woman this idea takes a visible shape on the Spanish stage, first in 1612 in Mira de Amescua's play *El esclavo del demonio* (The Devil's Slave), then in Calderón's

El mágico prodigioso (The Wonder-Working Magician) of 1637, whence he repeats it with variations in his *autos sacramentales*. We may take it as a symbol of this new philosophy. The hero of *El mágico prodigioso*, Cyprian, is an earnest student of metaphysics, trying to work out the first and final causes of Being. The encounter with a woman distracts him from his studies and makes him fall so passionately in love that he offers to sell his soul to the Devil if the latter can bring the woman to his arms. This is symbolical of the surrender of the intellect to the senses. Surrendering himself to passion, Cyprian loses his freedom of will: a slave to the senses, he is a slave to the Devil. When the time comes to fulfil his part of the bargain the Devil brings him a phantom which, when embraced by Cyprian, turns into a skeleton. This symbolizes the fact that the material beauty which the senses reach out to is a phantom beauty because it is subject to decay and death. The man who so worships sensuous beauty that he surrenders to it his mind and his will courts ultimate frustration, for the time will come when, with the skeleton of material beauty in his arms and the bitter taste of disillusionment in his mouth, he will face emptiness with nothing left to live for. Men hunger for beauty, incarnate in supreme form in the beauty of woman, but in the course of Nature beauty dies. The goods of the world for which man yearns are frail and fleeting. Man's restless desire for happiness cannot find lasting satisfaction in their dust and ashes. Death casts its cold shadow over all the joys of life, and as they fade from sight, frustration is what looms.

Everywhere in Europe where this disillusion was strongly felt, individuals came to realize that help could come only from within themselves, and the philosophy that provided this help was a revived Stoicism. The chief propagator of neo-Stoicism in Spain was Francisco de Quevedo,[3] who has also been called the greatest love poet in the Spanish language. From one of his Stoic treatises we may extract the basic principles upon which the philosophy of disillusion was constructed. This is *La cuna y la sepultura* (The Cradle and the Grave).

The argument of the work is constructed on paradoxes such as these: life is death, wealth is poverty, wisdom is ignorance. Not only are these paradoxes true but their antitheses are also true. Not only is life death but death is life; not only is wealth poverty but poverty is wealth; not only is wisdom ignorance but to know that you are ignorant is to be wise: to know that you know nothing is to know everything. How are these paradoxes true? Because man is himself a paradox, compounded of contraries: matter and spirit, body and soul. These are contraries in two senses: first in the order of values, in that what is good for the body can be bad for the soul, and what is good for the soul can be bad for the body; secondly in the order of being, because the soul is the principle of life while the body is the principle of death. In consequence of this, man lives on two separate and contrary planes, and moves towards contrary ends: to begin to live is to begin to die. But to die is also to begin to live; it all depends upon the angle from which one interprets the fact. From the world's angle life is the gateway to death in the corruption of matter; from the soul's angle death is the gateway to life, eternal life in the incorruptible realm of the spirit. And so we read in the first sentence of the introduction: 'The cradle and the grave are the beginning of life and its end; and although they are judged by pleasure to be the two things furthest apart, the eyes of disillusion-ment see them to be not only contiguous but united and inverted, each being turned into the other; it being true that the cradle already begins to be the grave, and the grave to be the cradle to an afterlife.'[4]

Because of this dualism in man life is ambiguous and it is possible to interpret it in the form of contradictory concepts, both of which are true. To have great possessions is to be rich, but to have no possessions at all is also to be rich, because the soul is thereby given the opportunity of detachment from the world, the freedom of being unencumbered and unharassed. This does not mean that all judgements are relative and all values indifferent, because these contradictory statements are each true on a different level, that of body and that of soul, and the one is a more import-ant truth than the other. How are we to know which is which? By the light of reason. Reason is itself part of the paradox of human nature: it is both the only expression of true freedom and at the same time a bond of imprisonment. Thus Quevedo says of his intention in writing this work:

> e querido (viendo que el ombre es racional y que desto no puede huir) valiéndome de la razón, aprisionarle el entendi-miento en ella. Y para fabricar este lazo en que consiste su verdadera libertad, me e valido . . . de la doctrina de los estoicos.[5]

> Since man is rational, and cannot escape from rationality, I have sought to use reason in order to imprison in it his understanding. In order to manufacture this fetter in which alone true freedom consists, I have availed myself of the doctrine of the Stoics.

The paradoxes will have been noted: the understanding *imprisoned* in reason, true freedom in fetters. The idea of the un-fettered liberty of man is an illusion. Man must obey something and can only be a slave; he will obey either his instincts and passions or his reason. The moral of this paradox of man is that he is free only when he is a slave to reason.

Human life becomes clouded by ambiguity and disorder when the two levels of experience and the two orders of values, reason and sensual pleasure, are confused, and the lower not kept sub-ordinate to the higher. This is, in fact, what happens to the generality of men:

> Todo lo hazes al rebés, ombre: al cuerpo, sombra de muerte, tratas como a imagen de vida, y al alma eterna dexas como sombra de muerte.[6]

> You do everything the wrong way round, man: the body is the shadow of death, yet you treat it like the image of life; and you forsake your eternal soul as if it were the shadow of death.

When this happens, when reason obeys sensuality instead of commanding it, we have, as Quevedo puts it, 'a republic ruled by a slave'. That a slave should govern a state is an impossible concept, yet it is true on the spiritual level of human nature. Man alone in the whole of Nature makes the impossible actual.

Sexual love is of course a case of the human republic being ruled by a slave. Was this for Quevedo merely an abstraction, as we may suspect that Platonic love was for Castiglione and even for Bembo? I think not. We are forced to conclude that this Christian Stoicism of Quevedo was a profound conviction. What happens when an extremely intelligent man, of strong passions, converts this philosophy into experience? The result is a body of love poetry that is extraordinarily intense and anguished.

FRANCISCO DE QUEVEDO

Dámaso Alonso's study of Quevedo as a lyrical poet reversed in a revolutionary manner what had been the general consensus of previous critics. They had tended to deny that Quevedo was a true poet of love on the grounds that his poems lacked tenderness and understanding of the feminine heart, any ardent or melting rapture. Dámaso Alonso showed that idyllic sentiment was alien to Quevedo's experience of love, and, by stressing his 'desgarrón afectivo' (a phrase that became famous), he estab-lished him as a poet of an anguish that is very modern.[7] He did not, however, reach the heart of most of the individual poems he discussed, and this, it may be argued, is because he was not alerted to a certain quality in Quevedo's language, and in the pre-sentation of his poetic thought, that can be called metaphysical.

By a metaphysical quality in the language of Quevedo I mean, following James Smith,[8] a series of conceits formed of two opposing, contradictory or incompatible objects and ideas: while the two deny each other they yet support and complete each other. Such conceits depend upon metaphysical propositions being felt not as self-evident truths but as problems. To say that the spirit is superior to the body, and that the senses must be starved so that the spirit may be nourished, is a proposition to which it is possible to give a notional assent that makes it un-problematic; but to posit this as a truth of actual experience is to bring to the fore the problem inherent in the metaphysical pro-position. Do body and soul deny each other? Or support each other? Or do they do both at the same time? In this metaphysical problem there is inherent a moral problem: the clash between the claims of love as felt by passion and the claims of law as felt by reason, faith and conscience.

Where love poetry is concerned Quevedo does more than any other poet to transform hackneyed conventions into a living poetry close to experience. Many of his love poems can be individually traced back, sometimes as far as Petrarch, to particular traditions whereby a line of poets imitated their predecessors in order to improve on their treatment of a theme. This improvement undoubtedly exists in Quevedo. At the same time Dámaso Alonso is right in affirming that his poetry obviously has the stamp of sincerity and of personal experience. Taking this as axiomatic, and disregarding the element of improvement on what has gone before, each of the following sonnets will be presented as original and unique, which is in fact where the element of improvement lies in those that are derivative in theme.

The first sonnet is a direct statement of the Neoplatonic ideal:

Que vos me permitáis sólo pretendo,
y saber ser cortés y ser amante;
esquivo los deseos, y constante,
sin pretensión, a sólo amar atiendo.

Ni con intento de gozar ofendo
las deidades del garbo y del semblante;
no fuera lo que vi causa bastante,
si no se le añadiera lo que entiendo.

Llamáronme los ojos las faciones;
prendiéronlos eternas jerarquías
de virtudes y heroicas perfecciones.

No verán de mi amor el fin los días:
la eternidad ofrece sus blasones
a la pureza de las ansias mías.[9]

All I seek is to be admitted (to your service), and to learn to be courteous and a lover; I shun desire and, claiming nothing, I expect only to love in constancy. Nor do I offend the deities of form and face by any intention of sensual pleasure; what I saw would not be cause enough if there were not added to it what is understood by my mind. My eyes were summoned by her features, but what captured them were eternal hierarchies of virtues and noble perfections. Time will not see the end of my love, for eternity offers to emblazon the purity of my longing.

To *see* is to feel sensuous attraction; to *understand* is the Neoplatonic sublimation of this, whereby the facial features that attract the eyes are transcended in the spiritual qualities that the mind alone can grasp. Since this love is pure it is not subject to the ravages of time. Every lover hopes his love will never die: only the Platonic lover can have the assurance of this, because since sensuality must die with the body, it is only purity that can remain with the soul and be engraved in the heraldry of eternity.

The serene assurance of eternity in the perfection of one's love would be a splendid thing if it were real. This sonnet and one or two others like it may be taken as *prima facie* evidence that Quevedo's mind understood the ideal of purity and accepted it, but all the rest of Quevedo's poetry makes it clear that this understanding was notional only. Its acceptance in reality depends on the ability of the mind's understanding of a woman's spiritual perfection to blot out the visual image of her physical beauty, which is the starting point of love. Can understanding really dispense with sight? If it succeeds in doing so, what kind of beauty is it that it contemplates? The answer comes in:

> No es artífice, no, la simetría
> de la hermosura que en Floralba veo;
> ni será de los números trofeo
> fábrica que desdeña al sol y al día.
>
> No resulta de música armonía
> (perdonen sus milagros en Orfeo),
> que bien la reconoce mi deseo
> oculta majestad que el cielo envía.
>
> Puédese padecer, mas no saberse;
> puédese codiciar, no averiguarse,
> alma que en movimientos puede verse.
>
> No puede en la quietud difunta hallarse
> hermosura, que es fuego en el moverse,
> y no puede viviendo sosegarse.

Symmetry is not the craftsman who has constructed the beauty I see in Floralba; nor can this structure that outvies both the sun and the day be the triumph of number. Nor is it the result of musical harmony (despite the miracles this wrought through

Orpheus) although my desire does indeed recognize in it a hidden majesty that derives from heaven. It can be suffered but not known; one can covet but never fathom a soul that can be seen through its movements. Beauty cannot be found in deathly calm, for it is a fire in motion and can never while alive be tranquil.

To move from the sight of physical beauty to the abstract principles behind it is of course directly Platonic. Plato himself had asked whether beauty consists in symmetry, in harmony or in mathematical relations and proportions, and it had been asserted in the sixteenth century that the movement in fire is more beautiful than a static symmetry. Quevedo gives a special meaning to this. The mind can in fact never understand or fathom the beauty of woman, for her soul, which is the object of the mind, reveals itself in the woman's living movements, and this is the object of the eye. To contemplate beauty as symmetry and proportion is to reduce a woman to a lifeless statue. Beauty consists in life not death, and a beautiful woman is not an object that can be fathomed by the mind. Her beauty is seen, is suffered and is coveted. The fire in her movement thus becomes the fire of sensual passion which is the way that living beauty is apprehended and desired.

The previous theoretical harmony between the sight and the understanding has given way to an opposition, whereby the Platonic contemplation of the mind becomes a cold and lifeless activity. The suggestion is that the mind, in seeking perfection, in fact kills; that the restless flame of passion is what gives life. We cannot know, but we can suffer; and we have to suffer precisely because we cannot know. We can never while alive be tranquil. Otis Green says that this sonnet merely plays about with Platonic ideas on the nature of beauty, and Dámaso Alonso calls it 'cold' because it is abstract.[10] To me on the contrary there lies beneath the 'quietud difunta' of its calm abstractions a very disturbing quality that is far from cold and far from a mere playing about with ideas.

This sense of unease becomes more explicit in the further transformation of the Neoplatonic ideal which we find in:

Si mis párpados, Lisi, labios fueran,
besos fueran los rayos visüales
de mis ojos, que al sol miran caudales
águilas, y besaran más que vieran.

Tus bellezas, hidrópicos, bebieran,
y cristales, sedientos de cristales,
de luces y de incendios celestiales,
alimentando su morir, vivieran.

De invisible comercio mantenidos,
y desnudos de cuerpo, los favores
gozaran mis potencias y sentidos;

mudos se requebraran los ardores;
pudieran apartados verse unidos,
y en público secretos los amores.[11]

If my lids, Lisi, were lips, the visual rays of my eyes would be kisses and my eyes, which eagle-like gaze at the sun, would kiss more than they would see. Thirstily they would drink your beauty, and crystals thirsting for crystals, for light, for heavenly fire, they would live by nourishing their death. Maintained by invisible commerce, my powers and senses would enjoy your favours without the clothing of the body; our ardours would make love to each other silently, our two loves would be united while apart and would be secret though in public.

Instead of sight being raised to understanding, we have sight lowered to carnal possession. Sight is in fact half way between spirituality and carnality; it is not just that it can turn to either but that it can be both at once. We have here an experience that is both Neoplatonic and carnal, both chaste and sensual. The whole poem is in fact a metaphysical conceit, with a pair of opposites that support and complete each other while at the same time denying each other: eye-lids both are, and are not, lips. This is the basic conceit in the imagery. In the one direction the eyes that gaze at the beloved's beauty are eagles that soar into the sun, into the light and heavenly fire of the spirit; but in the other direction the lids that surround the eyes are lips that kiss with a thirst for a fire that will kill them. 'Cristales sedientos de cristales': the eyes are crystal balls that can reflect the light and fire of the heavens; but crystal is a common metaphor for water, and the eyes are crystal also because they are moist. Being moist they are lips, and being lips they thirst for the moisture of other lips in a kiss; but this is a thirst for fire, and the fire of the kiss kills the thirst for the heavenly fire of spiritual contemplation.

This basic conceit of lids is reinforced in the first tercet by an ambiguity in the language. *Gozar* (to enjoy) was a particularly ambivalent word: one could say either 'gozar de Dios' (see face to face in the beatific vision) or 'gozar a una mujer' (possess a woman in carnal union). The powers of the soul are what find enjoyment in spiritual contemplation, but the powers are *potencias*, and potency in Spanish is a sexual term as it is in English. 'Commerce' has the same ambivalence in both languages: in Spanish the sexual intercourse it can connote is generally of an illicit kind. Human life is maintained by the visible commerce of buying and selling: the powers and senses of the poet are maintained by an invisible sexual intercourse of the imagination, an illicit commerce because it is a betrayal of the aspirations of the spirit. The favours enjoyed by the Platonic lover, being spiritual, transcend the body; the body is the soul's clothing, these favours are therefore *desnudos de cuerpo* (literally 'naked of body'). This image functions like a conceit by suggesting the opposite of what it intends to say: not 'disembodied', but 'with the body naked'. It reinforces the strong sexual undertones of the first tercet, and the oppositions continue in the last tercet: this invisible commerce unites the lovers while they stay apart, it is a love-making that is secret precisely because it is in public. There is a suggestion of furtiveness here that contributes to the sense of unease this poem leaves one with, the furtive betrayal of the soul by an imagination that turns the mind's aspirations into an illicit sensuality.

Dámaso Alonso has called this poem 'suavemente conceptuoso, también muy de espiritual amor y de gran consuelo para muchos amores imposibles' ['gently conceptual, very much concerned with spiritual love and offering great consolation in the case of many an impossible love'].[12] Such an interpretation is only possible if the *conceptista* or metaphysical quality of the imagery is disregarded. Far from offering consolation of any kind, the sonnet seems to point to an existential anguish: the necessary co-existence of a soul and a body that try to deny each other unavailingly. The soul's powers (*potencias*) aim at an ideal of perfection that clashes with its opposite while the soul is tied to the potency of the body; the body aims at being nourished by a visible commerce that it knows will lead to the soul's death. This co-existence in opposition is a metaphysical problem as defined by James Smith; it gives rise to metaphysical poetry, namely to conceits that disclose the tensions inherent in experience. The basic tension becomes more explicit in:

> Mandóme, ¡ay Fabio!, que la amase Flora,
> y que no la quisiese; y mi cuidado,
> obediente y confuso y mancillado,
> sin desearla, su belleza adora.
>
> Lo que el humano afecto siente y llora,
> goza el entendimiento, amartelado
> del espíritu eterno, encarcelado
> en el claustro mortal que le atesora.
>
> Amar es conocer virtud ardiente;
> querer es voluntad interesada,
> grosera y descortés caducamente.
>
> El cuerpo es tierra, y lo será, y fue nada;
> de Dios procede a eternidad la mente:
> eterno amante soy de eterna amada.

Alas, Fabio, Flora asked me to love her and not to want her; and my love, obedient and confused and tarnished, adores her beauty without desiring her. What human emotion feels and laments the mind enjoys, wooed by the eternal spirit, imprisoned in the mortal chamber that guards this treasure. To love is to know ardent virtue; to desire is to have a selfish will, one that is decayingly discourteous and gross. The body is, and will be, earth, and was always nothing; the mind proceeds from God towards eternity: I am the eternal lover of an eternal beloved.

The opposition between the spirit and the senses is here based on the two words for 'to love': *amar* (in which is included reverence and divine adoration) and *querer* (literally 'to want' in which is included sexual desire). The key to the sonnet is the marvellous phrase 'el entendimiento, amartelado/del espíritu eterno' (6-7). The literal translation [the mind, wooed by the eternal spirit] cannot render the ambiguity, for *amartelado* means not only 'wooed', but 'in love with' and also 'tortured'. The human mind is wooed by God and responds by loving Him: God summons the mind to a spiritual good that is the mind's *gozo* (its joy). But this joy of the understanding is torture to the body, for this is what human feeling laments. Quevedo is summoned to be the eternal lover of an eternal beloved. His intellect and his conscience accept this as the true ideal: he must love in Flora what is eternal, her mind and her goodness. But to love her (*amarla*) eternally means never to be able to love her (*quererla*) at all. Although intellect and conscience can accept this, human feeling must weep for this condemnation of itself. Human feeling is of course the man of flesh and blood, and not a disembodied ideal being. Human feeling is confused, bewildered and tarnished (i.e. *deformed*) by this imperative (3) for the imputation of an almost worthless inferiority is a dishonourable insult. This is the paradoxical tension of man: to affirm a spiritual love, but to deny it in the act of affirmation. Existence is not a balanced harmony but an anguished tension, and Quevedo's poetry is full of the pain of having to live, of having to bear himself.

> A fugitivas sombras doy abrazos;
> en los sueños se cansa el alma mía;
> paso luchando a solas noche y día
> con un trasgo que traigo entre mis brazos.
>
> Cuando le quiero más ceñir con lazos,
> y viendo mi sudor, se me desvía,
> vuelvo con nueva fuerza a mi porfía,
> y temas con amor me hacen pedazos.
>
> Voyme a vengar en una imagen vana
> que no se aparta de los ojos míos;
> búrlame, y de burlarme corre ufana.
>
> Empiézola a seguir, fáltanme bríos;
> y como de alcanzarla tengo gana,
> hago correr tras ella el llanto en ríos.

Fleeting shadows are what I embrace; in dreams my soul tires itself out; night and day I struggle alone with a hobgoblin that I hold within my arms. When I want most to hold it tight, and when seeing my distress it slips away, I return with greater effort to my persistence, and these stubborn struggles with love undo me utterly. I turn to take vengeance on an insubstantial image that never leaves my sight; she mocks me and flees proud of her mockery. I start to follow her and my strength fails; and since I yearn to reach her I make my weeping flow in rivers towards her.

This sonnet exemplifies the Courtly Love tradition of love as suffering. Quevedo transforms it from a conventional statement into something real and urgent, with no complacency about it. Pure love, unfulfilled, desirable though it be on the spiritual plane, is an agony hard to bear. Deprivation of the physical fulfilment of love leads not to resignation and spiritual serenity but to a psychological obsession: the chasing of shadows and the embracing of a ghost. And to be reduced to this is a *burla*, the mockery of love. The *llanto* it produces is not the conventional poetic tears but a real anguish that condemns as an illusion the belief that there is anything noble in unfulfilled love.

The next sonnet in the same vein is more forceful still:

> Dejad que a voces diga el bien que pierdo,
> si con mi llanto a lástima os provoco;
> y permitidme hacer cosas de loco:
> que parezco muy mal amante y cuerdo.
>
> La red que rompo y la prisión que muerdo,
> y el tirano rigor que adoro y toco,
> para mostrar mi pena son muy poco,
> si por mi mal de lo que fui me acuerdo.
>
> Óiganme todos: consentid siquiera
> que, harto de esperar y de quejarme,
> pues sin premio viví, sin juicio muera.
>
> De gritar solamente quiero hartarme;
> sepa de mí a lo menos esta fiera
> que he podido morir, y no mudarme.

Let me shout out loud the good I lose if you can be stirred to pity by my grief; and let me perform a madman's actions, for it ill becomes me to be a lover and sane. The net I tear and the fetters

I bite, and the tyrannical cruelty that I experience and adore, do not suffice to reveal my suffering, if to my hurt I remember what I was. Listen to me all of you: permit me at least, tired of hoping and of complaining, to die insane since I lived unrewarded. I long only to wear myself out with shrieking; let this cruel woman at least know that I have been able to die but not to be faithless.

The last line asserts the convention of fidelity until death, but the expression, far from being conventional, is more intense than anything found in earlier poets, for constancy in a love that is compelled to be chaste is expressed not as a martyrdom of which the poet is proud but as a madness of which he is ashamed. Love and sanity are incompatible terms, and the madness is expressed in concrete images that denote a helpless frenzy: the tearing at the net in which he is entangled, the biting at the fetters that chain him (5). Unfulfilled passion for a woman is not here sublimated Neoplatonically into a rational devotion, but is represented as irrational: the adoring and clinging to one's own enslavement (6). The awareness of what one was when ruled by reason and not by passion brings not consolation but remorse (8); the laments of a chaste love are the shrieks of a madman (12). The last word of the poem, 'mudarme', is ambiguous. In this context its primary meaning is to 'be faithless', to 'prove inconstant', but its principal meaning is the normal one of 'to change' or be 'transformed'. The context of the whole sonnet reveals that the last line is not a conventional pledging of constancy until death but a statement that is ironical because of its ambiguity. The poet will die without ceasing to love (*mudarse*) but only because he is in fact 'mudado' in another way: *changed* from sanity into insanity. By its insistence on the irrationality of an enforced Platonic love this poem is in fact inverting poetic tradition while ostensibly re-affirming its basic concept.

These last two sonnets are 'metaphysical' only indirectly: rather than statements of the problem of soul and body they express the state of desolation that follows from the inability to resolve the problem. More characteristic of metaphysical wit, as defined by James Smith, is to state a problem, a *quaestio*, in the form of an argument leading to a conclusion. In the sonnet

'Mandóme, ¡ay Fabio! que la amase Flora', the distinction between *amar* and *querer* leads to the conclusion 'eterno amante soy de eterna amada'. But the argument as such is straight-forward, with nothing *agudo* or witty about it. An example of what Gracián calls 'un argumento conceptuoso' is the sonnet 'Si mis párpados, Lisi, labios fueran'. It is an argument from an impossible hypothesis, one that assumes a metaphor to be literally true: if eyelids were lips, what would follow? By its very nature the argument is fallacious, but it is poetically moving, even gripping; it leads to a conclusion that is illogical but nevertheless expressive of possible and tormenting but real experience. 'Argumentos conceptuosos', writes Gracián, are distinguished not by their logic or their eloquence but by their beauty. They are beautiful because their violation of logic leads to a surprising but satisfying conclusion; they are *poetically* true.[13] The theorist of wit who most clearly and fully analyses this kind of argument is not Gracián but the later Tesauro in his *Il cannochiale aristotelico* of 1654. He defines its structure as that of a 'sillogismo urbanamente fallace': logical in form but yet fallacious.[14] The fallacy, however, is 'urbane': subtle, poetically plausible, and thus capable of enchanting the mind. The following sonnet is a fascinating example of an 'argumento conceptuoso':

> Si hija de mi amor mi muerte fuese,
> ¡qué parto tan dichoso que sería
> el de mi amor contra la vida mía!
> ¡Qué gloria, que el morir de amar naciese!
>
> Llevara yo en el alma adonde fuese
> el fuego en que me abraso, y guardaría
> su llama fiel con la ceniza fría
> en el mismo sepulcro en que durmiese.
>
> De esotra parte de la muerte dura,
> vivirán en mi sombra mis cuidados,
> y mas allá del Lethe mi memoria.
>
> Triunfará del olvido tu hermosura;
> mi pura fe y ardiente, de los hados;
> y el no ser, por amar, será mi gloria.

If my death was daughter of my love what a happy birth that would be, the birth of my love at the expense of my life! What glory that dying should be born of loving! I would carry in my soul, wherever I went, the fire that burns me, and I would keep its faithful flame, with the cold ash, in the very tomb in which I was sleeping. On the other side of harsh death my love will continue to live in my shade, and my memory will go on living beyond Lethe. Your beauty will triumph over oblivion, my pure and burning faith will conquer Fate; and non-being, caused by love, will be my glory.

A conclusion is reached from a hypothesis based on a metaphor, and the metaphor itself is another commonplace of the Courtly Love tradition. If it is really true, asks Quevedo, that to love is to die and that love can cause death, what follows? The tone of the sonnet is triumphant and exultant. How glorious it would be to die of love! The poet would receive death in his arms as an exultant father opens *his* arms to receive a new-born child. If love causes death then it conquers it and survives both in the grave and beyond it. Like a martyr, finding in death his glorification, the lover, through death, will glory in the eternity of his love.

It is in this optimistic vein that the poem has been interpreted.[15] It certainly implies such optimism, but the way in which it expresses it seems also to imply something different. We should notice how the metaphor of love and death is developed. Love begets offspring; the poet's love begets death. The imagery is thus made concrete: *nacer*, *parto*, *hija*. Death is love's child and the birth of death, like the birth of every child, is a happy event (1-2). But love gives birth to the child 'contra la vida mía' (3). Emilia Kelley rightly interprets this *contra* as an exchange: love, she argues, exchanges life for something infinitely more valuable, for death, which is the assurance of love's immortality.[16] But the sense of aggression is also strong in this *contra*, and the image becomes startling when we realise that love is not a mother giving birth to life, but a mother who is in fact attacking and destroying life in order (the paradox continues) to put immortality in its place. The interplay of body and spirit, which is explicit in the second quatrain, produces the ambivalence of *gloria*: the human sense is uppermost in the fourth line, but the spiritual sense of salvation and heaven becomes uppermost in the last line, 'y el no ser, por amar, será mi gloria'. The surface meaning of *no ser* is to cease to live in this world: my salvation and my heaven consist in leaving the earth. But the fact that heaven is the perfection of being must give *no ser* the undertone of *non*-being: human love will find its heaven in non-existence. Is love's offspring, then, non-life in a deathly heaven?

The two great paradoxes of the sonnet, the 'parto contra la vida' (2-3) and 'el no ser será mi gloria' (14) are too startling and powerful to be given only a superficially optimistic, spiritual meaning. On the basis of the hypothetical love-death premise we can see that the conclusion 'our salvation will therefore lie in non-being' can be poetically true in two different ways. The 'urbanity' of this fallacy lies in our admission of its ingenuity, but also in our being startled and disturbed. That we are so is the result, I would contend, of an anguish at the heart of Quevedo's experience, a desolation of spirit at the moment of affirming the ultimate triumph of human love. This unresolved tension, this simultaneous affirmation and denial, is metaphysical poetry.

Another example of an 'argumento conceptuoso', and the most famous of the poems in which Quevedo develops the commonplace of constancy in love, is:

> Cerrar podrá mis ojos la postrera
> sombra que me llevare el blanco día,
> y podrá desatar esta alma mía
> hora a su afán ansioso lisonjera;
>   mas no, de esotra parte, en la ribera,
> dejará la memoria, en donde ardía:
> nadar sabe mi llama la agua fría,
> y perder el respeto a ley severa.
>   Alma a quien todo un dios prisión ha sido,
> venas que humor a tanto fuego han dado,
> medulas que han gloriosamente ardido,
>   su cuerpo dejará, no su cuidado;
> serán ceniza, mas tendrá sentido;
> polvo serán, mas polvo enamorado.

My eyes will be closed by the last darkness that will deprive me of the white day, and my soul will be set free by a moment of time that will be benevolent to its anguished anxiety; but not on that account will it leave on the other bank of the river its memory in which it used to burn: my flame knows how to swim across the cold water and how to show no respect for a stern law. My soul, for which nothing less than a god has been a prison, my veins which have given moisture to so great a fire, the marrow which gloriously burned (in my bones)—the former will abandon its body but not its love; the latter will be ashes, but it (the soul) will have feeling; they will be dust, but dust that is in love.

This is not just poetic hyperbole. The whole sonnet is imbued with feeling so passionate that it cannot but be genuine: this feeling is the impossibility of believing that a love that so fills his whole being could ever disappear as long as any part of his being exists spiritually or physically, alive or dead. But at the same time as this conviction is intensely felt, his mind knows, of course, that this cannot be. Passion affirms what reason has to deny. The poet is compelled, therefore, to affirm this by means of images that carry the tension within them, in other words by conceits that take the form of logically contradictory statements: the flame that can swim across the river without being extinguished, its fire being nourished not by anything combustible but by the liquid (*humor*) within the veins, ashes that can feel, dust that is in love. As concepts these paradoxical statements are false, but as conceits they acquire poetic truth through the passion that gives them life and through the unification of the poet's experience. Logic is violated in order to express one of the deepest paradoxes of human experience: that what one *knows* to be transient grips one in such a way that one *feels* it must be eternal. This is a basic human experience that can, of course, produce a natural need for religious faith. The opposition between transience and eternity is an existential, not just a theological problem, as Unamuno well knew. This, for Quevedo, is the human condition. The state of man is to be a lover but the condition of love is a state of anguish in the tension between the physical and the spiritual, the transient and the eternal.[17]

To conclude, I present a sonnet to which Dámaso Alonso so

rightly gave prominence, one that expresses in unrelieved form this desolation of the human condition:

> En los claustros de l'alma la herida
> yace callada; mas consume, hambrienta,
> la vida, que en mis venas alimenta
> llama por las medulas extendida.
>
> Bebe el ardor, hidrópica, mi vida,
> que ya, ceniza amante y macilenta,
> cadáver del incendio hermoso, ostenta
> su luz en humo y noche fallecida.
>
> La gente esquivo y me es horror el día;
> dilato en largas voces negro llanto,
> que a sordo mar mi ardiente pena envía.
>
> A los suspiros di la voz del canto;
> la confusión inunda l'alma mía;
> mi corazón es reino del espanto.

In the cloisters of my soul the wound lies silent; but it hungrily consumes the life which is nourished in my veins by a flame spread through the marrow of my bones. My life, parched with thirst, drinks the fire, which now, wan enamoured ashes, the corpse of a beautiful conflagration, displays its light expired in smoke and night. I shun people and the day is horror to me; my black weeping flows in long cries, sent out by my burning suffering to a deaf sea. To sighs I have surrendered my singing voice, confusion floods my soul, my heart is the realm of fear.

The cloisters are the centre of a monastery, the *clausura* into which nobody from the outside is normally allowed to penetrate; it is a place where silence is observed and where time is passed in meditation. The soul has its cloisters, a centre of seclusion and solitude, where the mind meditates on the silent wound of existence. Passion is a hunger and thirst that consumes man's being. But human life reciprocates by thirsting for passion's fire and seeking its own destruction in the beautiful conflagration of love which burns itself out into extinction. The consuming fire of passion is a negative existence in lonely darkness, communica-tion with life being only the river that flows into a deaf, unheeding sea. Existence is either heaven or hell. In heaven man sings; in hell he weeps and sighs. Subjection to passion is the negative state of being damned in the realm of fear. But hell is within man himself, it is the fire that feeds life within man's veins, and the fire that both nourishes and consumes is beautiful. The state of man is to be 'wan, enamoured ashes, the corpse of a beautiful con-flagration' (6-7) in the 'realm of fear' (14).

I have called the anguish of love in Quevedo existential, a condition of human existence. It is a permanent state of tension between passion and reason, a constant struggling awareness of the unbearable claims of the flesh and the unfaceable claims of the spirit. The tension could not be existential if it were not a tension of both thought and feeling. The tension is also one of language: for the sense of life as an anguish in face of the paradoxes of existence produced the images necessary to convey it. The conceits of Quevedo can be as aptly called metaphysical as those of Donne, even though the tension between body and soul be differently resolved in each poet. Donne may succeed in making body and soul serve each other and thus present the duality of love in an unanxious way. In this he is in one sense more modern than Quevedo, for the essential association of body and spirit rather than their century-long dissociation is a mark of much religious thinking today as it is of secular thought. Nevertheless, Quevedo's anguish, if not the particular form of the tension between body and spirit, makes him modern. His tension is that he cannot deny either the body or the spirit. To deny the spirit would not necessarily remove the tension, for it can bring the mind up against a meaningless and purposeless existence, and to face the loneliness of an absurd universe can also produce anguish, as our contemporary literature knows only too well. It is not this particular kind of anguish that Quevedo faced in the 'cloisters of his soul': his was specifically the loneliness of the believer who cannot make the spiritual conviction to which he holds firm in faith control his whole being and all his actions.

To say, as Otis Green does, that Quevedo's love poetry reflects a struggle between sin and repentance is to say what is obvious, but in an oversimplified way that cannot do justice to the depth of the poetry.[18] For sin has nowadays become a rather debased concept through association with prohibitions that seem arbitrary when they are not puritanical. Sin for Quevedo was an experience much deeper than mere prohibition or permission. It was a question of devaluing himself, proving unworthy of the best that was in him. He saw the condition of man as that of being 'amartelado del espíritu eterno', wooed by God with a love to which it was torture to respond, for the fire of his body, through the 'venas que humor a tanto fuego han dado', was not the fire struck from the spark of divinity that was in him as he believed it to be in all men. The devaluation of the human through betrayal of the summons to realize the best that is latent in our humanity is something that can take many agonising forms, and in the realization of the hurt that all these cause we may perhaps still respond to the anguish in the poetry of Quevedo, as well as to its technical skill, its intellectual depth and its emotional power.

CALDERÓN

The major dramatist of the Age of Disillusionment is Pedro Calderón de la Barca (1600–81). Thirtyfive years old when Lope de Vega died, he had already written some of his finest plays, such as *La vida es sueño* (Life is a Dream) and *El médico de su honra* (The Surgeon of his Honour). He was already established as the leading court dramatist and his art was moving away from Lope's technique and style into a tighter construction, a more formal or mannered diction and a less realistic presentation of the dramatic action. By 1635 his plots were tending towards abstraction and the themes and ideas underlying them were becoming more 'philosophical'. *Desengaño*, or 'disenchantment', is a keyword in his plays, practically from the very start; this concept colours the whole of his view of human life in its social setting and gives a characteristic note to his moral doctrine.[19]

In 1651 Calderón was ordained a priest and announced his intention to write no more plays. The decision to withdraw from society and the stage is plausibly attributed to the death of his 'commonlaw wife'. Nothing is known about her except the fact of her death, which was revealed when Calderón legitimized the son she had borne him, whom he at first called his 'nephew'. He did this before his ordination, making legal provision for the education and upbringing of the boy, who however died shortly afterwards. This liaison was probably a so-called 'clandestine marriage', which a couple contracted by secretly exchanging solemn promises to marry, while marriage remained economically difficult or socially impossible. Persons of quality could not marry unless the man was able to support his companion in the economic and social position that their 'honour' demanded.[20] Philip iv, however, would not countenance Calderón's decision to retire, and ordered him to continue to write plays for the Palace theatre. This he regularly did, on commission, until his death. He also wrote each year the two Corpus Christi festival plays for Madrid. These *autos sacramentales* are elaborate and highly skilful theological moralities expanding the medieval tradition of religious drama. In them his genius for giving dramatic form to personified ideas and conceptual abstractions reaches its height.

Calderón's gift for presenting dramatic concepts in universal terms means that in his drama we can properly find a philosophy of love, always within the traditions and forms of the secular theatre. To treat love in this way on the stage meant a move away from the 'natural' and the 'lifelike'. It meant imagining human actions and conflicts freed from verisimilitude and from the limitations of time and place which history and geography impose. Such conflicts and actions could be suggested by mythology. Interest in the classical myths had been revived in the fifteenth century, and the Renaissance gave them dominant roles to play in literature and art. They were part of the intellectual equipment of every educated man and provided a wealth of allegories, symbols and of what we now call archetypes. Generally there was, of course, no difficulty in making the necessary detachment from the mythological gods so that they should be seen only as allegories or moralities, and when there might be danger of taking them seriously the myths could be parodied or burlesqued. The dramatic genre of the *entremés* (Interlude) was a medium for poking fun at subjects for which decorum and convention demanded respectful treatment. The Church, and the clergy in particular, could not be satirized or criticized, but in the *entremés* the sacristan became a comic or even a malicious character; he was, of course, connected with churches and a cassock was his official attire. The classical gods, too, could be burlesqued in this genre.

In the seventeenth and eighteenth centuries mythology pro-vided popular subjects for court plays, masques and operas. Calderón's mythological plays were all commissioned by the Court and many of them were musical dramas, the sections that were sung varying in length from play to play. For a long period the emphasis on realism in drama made them appear meaning-less, if not ridiculous, but interest in them is now being shown. Sebastian Neumeister has studied this type of play as a specifically court genre, requiring a special relationship between the dramatic themes and the audience, with myths having a special relation to problems of State and political procedure.[21] And Robert ter Horst has praised the plays highly: 'Love as both a creative and a destructive force is the great theme of these plays, and they are mythological because in each of them the gods of classical antiquity meddle with men while, reciprocally, humans involve themselves with the immortals. Generally the emotion that brings gods and men together is sexual passion, so that Calderón is able to use the mythological as his psychological casebook. The seventeen *comedias* thus constitute a dramatic phenomenology of love. . . .'[22]

Ni amor se libra de amor. It may be argued that the plays which show the most characteristic features of Calderón's conception of love are nearly all ultimately based on what can be recon-structed as a personal experience. One of them that does not have this connection, and that can therefore serve as an illustration of his philosophy of love in the abstract, is *Ni amor se libra de amor* (Not even Love is Immune from Love), which treats the myth of Cupid and Psyche.[23]

This was a court play, performed on 19 January 1662 when Calderón was at the height of his powers. The style is elegant and the plot requires a complicated production with elaborate scenery. Like all the court plays of this period, it was intended mainly as a spectacle, and the non-specialist reader today is not likely to take it in any other way, for the two main characters, Cupid and Psyche, together with Venus and Jupiter who are also characters, are 'unreal', and the plot, as an action, bears no relation to real-life experience. But if the plot is examined as an ordered association of ideas, the play can acquire significance. Calderón is not a didactic dramatist (except in his *autos sacramentales*) and he gives no clue to the interpretation of his plot other than the associations that the story would already have aroused in his audience. The critic cannot therefore be certain that the interpretation he may extract from plot and characters is the one Calderón had himself read into the fable; he must rely only on its plausibility within the cultural period.

The fable of Cupid's love for Psyche is not part of the corpus of traditional Greek mythology. It was told by Apuleius and embedded in his second-century novel, *The Golden Ass*. Psyche, of course, means the soul, and in Greek poetry and philosophy the body was often considered the tomb of the soul. Moreover Psyche, the girl, became associated with Eros, the god of Love (who for the Romans was Cupid), and before Apuleius Eros had already been represented as inflicting many tribulations on the soul. Because the story in *The Golden Ass* is a conscious invention and of late origin, Jean Seznec excluded it from his study of the mythological tradition and its place in the Renaissance. He stated, however, that it was deliberately charged with spiritual implications and that on this account it profoundly influenced the period of Humanism.[24]

Most of the early interpretations of the fable were religious rather than humanistic, but the latter were foreshadowed by Fabius Fulgentius (467-532), known as Mythographus, whose interpretation may be summarized briefly. Venus, who is sensual love, jealous of the soul's beauty, sends her son Cupid, who is concupiscence, to attack her. But Cupid also bears within him the germ of true love which comes to the fore at the sight of the soul's purity and loveliness. He advises her not to see him as he is, for that would entail the corruption of her will which leads to lust. Her sisters, however, furnish her with the lamp of lust and, seeing Cupid for what he is, she destroys the purity of love within herself and is banished from the Palace of Innocence, only able to return after repentance and the toils of purification in exile.[25]

Calderón, as was customary with his sources, alters the Apuleius story in several significant ways. Such changes are always clues to the special meanings he sees in his historical or legendary materials. He retains the main point of the story, which is the conflict between Venus and Psyche, and although he does not specifically equate Psyche with the human soul, there are some pointers in this direction. He had already dramatized the fable in an *auto sacramental* written for the feast of Corpus Christi in Toledo (1640, according to the date on a surviving manuscript). After the production of his court play in 1662, he turned to the fable again and reworked his theological allegory in a more elaborate form for the Corpus Christi festivity in Madrid in 1665. In these *autos* Psyche was, of course, equated with the soul. In the *comedia* he had no need to make the equation because he was writing for an educated audience, but the fact that Apuleius (followed in this by Calderón) makes Psyche more beautiful than any woman, more beautiful even than the goddess Venus, is itself a pointer beyond the etymology of her name. The perfection of all human beauty can indicate only the soul.

Calderón's plot is set in Cnidus (or Gnidus) where Venus was the chief deity. The King, Atamas, has three daughters, of whom Psyche is the youngest. When she comes to place her offering on Venus's altar, the people acclaim her as more beautiful than the goddess. They affirm that her consummate beauty cannot be the handiwork of Nature, but must come only from heaven. Her signification is thus suggested. Psyche is therefore proclaimed the new goddess of love. The statue on the altar moves, announcing that Psyche's beauty will bring her unhappiness, since she will be possessed by a monster. Venus then calls on Cupid to avenge her. Angry at this insult to his mother he comes to kill Psyche, but he is unable to stab her, because Love is himself smitten with love.

In consequence of this Psyche has no suitors for her hand and (in Apuleius) the father invokes Apollo's oracle, which answers that the girl must be exposed on a mountainside, attired for her funereal marriage, and that her only offspring will be a monster. In Calderón it is Venus who foretells the monster as husband. A further innovation of his is that the father thereupon petitions Jupiter (not Apollo) to have Venus's prophecy revoked. Jupiter announces that the girl must expiate the outrage to Venus. Atamas shall take her to Mount Oeta, where he is to offer her in sacrifice. Calderón's version continues thus: the ship carrying them is swept by a storm on to an island, and Atamas sacrifices Psyche by abandoning her there. The terrified girl is led into a cavern by savages.

In Apuleius there is no decree by Jupiter and no demand for expiation: there are no caverns and no savages; on the contrary, it is Zephyr who wafts her on to a meadow, where she finds Cupid's palace. These Calderonian savages follow the traditional representation of lust in literature, but with the dramatic con‑ vention of comic relief, which Calderón never entirely forsakes, they are presented here with some burlesque touches. This is because Psyche is going to be led, not to the husband ordained by Venus, but to the union with Cupid in which there will be no savagery. The prophecy of disaster to Psyche and her imprison‑ ment in the mountain is associated, as we shall see, with a constant strand in many Calderonian plots, one that constitutes the most characteristic leitmotif in his thoughts. For the present it should be noted that the prophecy and the punishment indicate, on the conceptual level of myth and symbol, that human beauty is to be dominated by the lusts of the body.

There follows in Apuleius the well‑known episode of Psyche knowing Cupid only in the dark, forbidden by him ever to see his face. Psyche's sisters, finding her, persuade her to light a lamp at night to make sure that her lover is not the monster. Cupid upbraids Psyche for her infidelity and disappears with the palace. It is here that expiation enters into the original fable. In order to be reunited with Cupid, Psyche has to undergo a series of trials, at the end of which she finds him. Cupid then asks Jupiter, his father, to sanction his marriage to Psyche. He is reprimanded for causing so much trouble on earth with impurity and adultery, which are outrages to Jupiter's divinity, and the god affirms that Cupid will have to be married for his riotous nature to be tamed. The marriage is thus sanctioned and Jupiter states that the link will never be broken. Psyche is then raised to the ranks of the Immortals. Apuleius makes Jupiter scold Cupid playfully for being a mischievous boy. This playfulness gives a light touch to Jupiter's sanctioning of Cupid's marriage. The fable ostensibly presented the love of Cupid for Psyche as incompatible with divine authority, but this had never been a serious conflict, despite the trials to which Psyche is subjected. It is clear that this authority will finally sanction the union of the human soul to Love; all that is required at the end is that human love be disciplined and regulated within the social institution of marriage. This is the fable's way of reconciling the erotic and the spiritual sides of human nature.

Calderón alters and shortens the ending. When the palace disappears, Psyche finds herself on the sea shore in the company of her father and sisters. She explains what has happened and threatens to kill herself, since she cannot live without her lover. Cupid appears to announce that Venus has been mollified by Psyche's tribulation and has pardoned her. She will now become an immortal goddess of love, who will live for ever with the god of love. The reader may find this abrupt ending rather pointless. Its meaning can be detected by going back over the dramatization of the fable's main episode and examining the innovations that Calderón introduces into the story.

The inner meaning of the play emerges from four innovations, which are as follows. Psyche awaits in darkness Cupid's coming. When she hears a sound she asks, Who is that? Is it my love? He replies that he is the love of every human being, because by possessing her he possesses all the profundity (*abismo*) of love. This can be taken to mean that beauty in its perfection must inspire the totality of love, no part of it being left over for anything else. Psyche then asks him how he can be every man's love since his carrying bow and arrow must make him immune from loving. He replies that it is possible, when shooting an arrow, to hit a stone and for the arrow to ricochet and pierce him. In Apuleius the piercing of Cupid by his own arrow is accidental. Calderón must give some explanation for Cupid's falling in love because the title he has chosen for his play emphasizes it. The explanation he gives is not as pointless as it may seem. Nature is not inactive; she can guide the arrow to its proper object. Love is not immune from love because beauty of its very nature must be lovable, even to its creator. Man in loving the spiritual is responding to the call of the spirit.

Another innovation comes after Cupid forbids Psyche ever to look upon him, under pain of losing him and her happiness. Clearly this is loosely associated (as it was for Fulgentius) with the Garden of Eden, which was lost to Adam and Eve when they disobeyed the command laid upon them. Psyche will lose her paradise through disobedience, being tempted to that act by her envious sisters. There is a further association of ideas in that Satan tempted Eve by promising that she and Adam would be like God, knowing good and evil. The Fathers and the School men taught that curiosity, or the desire to plumb the depths of all experience, was sinful.

The next innovation enables Calderón to express Cupid's prohibition in a much more specific way than does Apuleius. When Cupid refuses to let her have a light he says that he will make her love him through hearing and not through seeing. This distinction between the ear and the eye is fundamental to Calderón's philosophy of love. What lies behind the prohibition is obvious. She must be content to believe what Cupid tells her about himself; her love will then be innocent. Sensuality would contaminate her love if she gazed upon his beauty and desired him on that account. The Earthly Paradise disappeared when mankind lost its innocence. Love is irresistible, but if it is to approach perfection it must enter the minds of men through the ear. Down the ages they have heard of perfect love from theo logians, philosophers and poets; to remain in the realm of the spiritual men must always hear their voices. The beauty of the body by itself will not penetrate the human mind, rather will it prevent men from listening.

Jupiter's removal from the final reconciliation is Calderón's last innovation. He has made the action a conflict, not between Cupid and Jupiter but between Venus and Psyche. Venus was the goddess of beauty until the arrival of Psyche (or the creation of the human soul) made her lose that status. The conflict is thus not between God and human nature, but within human nature itself. Men must strive so to love that, against the downward drag of the body, they succeed in refashioning to some extent humanity's innocence. The concepts implied in Calderón's reworking of the fable make it, strictly speaking, improper to speak of soul and body, for he has no dramatic character suggesting body as such. In his theological *autos sacramentales* he finds it difficult, indeed impossible, to give dramatic form to the Christian doctrine (as far as it had been developed) of the unity of body and soul. What we have in his Psyche play is not the Platonic dualism of the soul entombed in the body, but two different types of beauty existing together in mankind. This is facilitated by the mythological characters of Venus and Psyche, with Cupid, as the personification of love, torn between the different attractions of the two. To make beauty the motivating force of a love that leads to the spirit is, of course, Platonic, and insofar as Venus is at war with Psyche, she too fits into a general Platonic framework. It is, however, the modified Platonism of Calderón's age, which allows the body, under the control of the spirit, its worthy say in human love. The further modification by disillusionment enters with Psyche's fall into 'curiosity' and with the disappearance of Cupid and the palace. This threat lurks behind every formulation of the ideal.[26]

Calderón's general position thus fits into the Christianized Platonic thought of his age, and as such has progressed away from the medieval theological position that carnal love was fundamentally sinful, being at best only tolerated in marriage. Calderón, who in his *autos sacramentales* showed himself to be a Catholic theologian using allegorical drama as his medium for thinking and instructing, thus contributed in his secular plays to to the development of the concept of ideal love as elaborated in the literature to which he was heir. It is in him a theoretical ideal precariously balanced between soul and body, but affirmed as an ideal none the less. Within his own drama this represents a striking development from his early plays.

Violence and Imprisonment

Among Calderón's early plays there are themes of the traditional type with conflicts between love and honour, and love and duty, which take for granted an ethical imperative whereby the individual must fit into a rational social norm. There are, however, a few plays that are very different, whose themes contain a very strong element of violence far from any ideal world. They are characterized by a rebellious antagonism of sons, and in one case a daughter, to a father who in their eyes is a tyrannical destroyer of their freedom. A significant aspect of this theme is that the rebellious son is either illegitimate and a foundling, neither he nor the father knowing of the relationship, or he is virtually repudiated at birth by his father and brought up in confinement as well as in ignorance of his parentage.

The first of these plays (*c.* 1630) is *La devoción de la Cruz* (Devotion to the Cross), which has an important motif not subsequently repeated, that of the rebellious daughter who is placed by her father, despite her strong resistance, in a convent in order to prevent a union with a socially unworthy lover, who, unknown to the three of them, is her brother. This second motif thus shows that the passion of the two young lovers is, or would be if fulfilled, incestuous. In *La devoción de la Cruz* the son who rebels against his father's authority dies the violent death of a criminal, but not before repenting and not before his father, who has been hunting him down, comes to realize with remorse that he is a son.

The second play (*c.* 1632?) is *Las tres justicias en una* (Three Judgements in one Sentence). Here the son is illegitimate (an important new motif) but brought up as the child of a loveless couple, only the 'mother' knowing of this deception. The 'father' is a hard and cold disciplinarian, who shows no affection either to his wife or his 'son'. The boy grows up unruly, indulges in criminal behaviour and is publicly insolent to his father. Ultimately he is sentenced to death for banditry, and the man who has to sentence him is his real father who had thought to escape having to acknowledge him. A subsidiary motif, which is not developed, is that the young man had fallen in love with a girl who, unknown to both of them, was his half-sister. This is a more complicated plot and the family relationships are more tangled.

These plays develop one of Calderón's constant preoccupations; the fact, namely, that it is not possible in life to nail down sole responsibility for wrongdoing on the individual who commits it. Many others will have contributed to forming his character and placing him in situations whose pressures incline him to bad behaviour. What puts pressure on the character and behaviour of a young person is, in Calderón's drama as a whole, nearly always the result of other person's misbehaviour. It is ultimately impossible to pin responsibility for personal or social evil on any one human being; no individual is either totally guilty or totally free from guilt in any one of the misfortunes and calamities of human life. This has been called the concept of 'diffused responsibility' and has been seen as the key to Calderón's tragic sense of life.[27]

The third play exemplifying the antagonism and conflict between father and son is the most famous of all Calderón plays, *La vida es sueño* (Life is a Dream) which dates from 1635. There are two new elements here: the first, that a horoscope is cast at the birth of the son, and this is made historically plausible by the fact that the characters are a king and a prince. The horoscope foretells that the baby will grow into an anarchical young man who will plunge the kingdom into civil war, leading an army against his father, defeating him and having him kneel before him in humiliation. The second new element is this: in order to prevent the disaster to the kingdom and to himself, the king has the baby reared in imprisonment in a remote tower on a mountainside. Brooding over his decision to deprive his son of freedom, the king in due course comes to wonder whether he had not been too hasty and decides to administer a narcotic to his son, now a young man, to have him brought into the palace. He will then be able to show whether he will succumb to his predestined fate, or surmount it by the exercise of his free-will. When the young man awakens amid the splendour of royalty, he is told who he is and how he must belie the horoscope by his good behaviour, otherwise he will find himself again in prison. His reaction to his new situation is violently to exercise his power by asserting his will and by attacking his father in anger at the injustice done to him. Drugged again, and awakening in prison, he can only conclude that his experience of majesty and power must have been a dream.

The people, however, having learnt that there is a legitimate heir to the throne, refuse to accept any other and come to free him, asking him to lead them in insurrection against his father. This proves to the prince that his experience had not been a dream. He agrees to give battle though fearful of renewed disillusion. Before the battle is joined the prince reasons himself into the realization that he must act with responsibility for the good of others. He defeats the king and has him at his mercy. kneeling at his feet: the horoscope is thus fulfilled to the letter. The king expects to be killed, but this natural outcome was not in the prophecy; instead the wronged but victorious son publicly rebukes his father, telling him that, by depriving him of freedom in order to defeat a prophecy, he brought about the very conditions that made its fulfilment inevitable. The father is pardoned and reconciled with his son.

Although these plays have no direct bearing on the philosophy of love, their motif of an imprisonment that seeks unsuccessfully to forestall a prophesied violence, together with the nature of the violence itself, are crucial elements in Calderón's poetic and dramatic formulation of his philosophy of love. The violence, forming as it does the warp on an almost incredible woof of family quarrels and relationships, involving illegitimacy and incest, produces extraordinary plots which a young man could hardly have invented without some basis in his personal experience. The recurrence of this type of theme through the first ten years of his dramatic career points to an obsessive problem, and the repetition, down to the end of his life, of the motifs of prophecy, violence and the imprisonment of an adolescent, all suggest something of profound significance for the poet's life and thought.

It has been possible, with considerable plausibility, to recon-struct a traumatic event in the Calderón family. The reconstruc-tion is based on documents that can throw light on the plots of these early plays and on the remarkable coincidences that emerge between the plays and the biographical facts.[28] Calderón was born in 1600 and his father, Don Diego, died in 1615; an elder son (Diego) and daughter (Dorotea) were involved in the episode. Don Diego had had an illegitimate son, Francisco, who lived as part of the household with neither he nor the other children being aware of their kindship. Diego and Dorotea were born in 1596 and 1598 respectively. In 1611 an incident took place between young Diego, Dorotea and Francisco which had a shattering effect on the home. Diego, who was sixteen, was sent to Mexico to the care of a relative; Francisco was turned out of the home and disappeared, with his whereabouts unknown; Dorotea was enclosed in a convent. She was only thirteen, too early an age for normal admission; she did not profess as a novice until she was sixteen, the canonical age of consent. Her departure was shrouded in secrecy. The convent was not in Madrid where the family lived but in Toledo; she was conducted there, not by her father but by her godparents. All this points to something extremely grave.

In *La devoción de la Cruz* the unacknowledged son and the daughter fall in love; to prevent a marriage the daughter is forcibly enclosed in a convent, but her lover climbs in through the window with the thwarted intention of seducing her. In later plays of this type, shortly to be discussed, young women are confined in seclusion because prophecies foretell that they will be the cause of violence and havoc. In *Eco y Narciso*, for instance, a girl disappears from society and confines herself in seclusion because she has been raped. In other plays also the 'prisoner' is the offspring of a rape. The threat of incest in the early plays and the results of rape in the later plays are sufficiently numerous to point to a deep-seated obsession in the dramatist. A sexual mis-demeanour with Dorotea on Francisco's part, with the know-ledge or connivance of Diego, is indicated; that this might have been attempted rape is suggested by the violence of the horrified father who alone knew that it was incest.

Before the father's death Diego had returned from Mexico but Dorotea remained an enclosed nun for the rest of her life. Don Diego's will, drawn up shortly before he died in 1615, made public the existence of his illegitimate son, Francisco, whom he said he had disinherited and banished for violent behaviour; he now recognizes him as his son and makes provision for his inheritance, should he reappear. Pedro, the dramatist, was eleven years old at the time of this event. The emotional and psycho-logical shock must have been intense.

As Calderón grew into manhood the memory of this shock must have raised many moral and social problems in his mind, which he apparently proceeded to explore in his plays. The individual problem of Francisco's severe punishment raised the whole question of human guilt with the problem of justice or clemency in punishments. Was Francisco alone responsible for what had happened, or should the father share the guilt? In the first place he would have been punished for incest, but he did not know that Dorotea was his sister. The incest, if such it was, would have been prevented had the father acknowledged his illegitimate offspring as his son. This, over the years, made the dramatist elaborate plots in which shared guilt and diffused responsibility are the structural elements. He saw that there could properly be no question of an individual wrongdoer in human society; all men through the influence they exert on others and through the interlocking ramifications of all their actions share in the guilt of all men for the moral evils that beset human life. All men are born under the threat of violence. History has shown no way in which this can be prevented. Hence Calderón makes horoscopes and prophecies symbols of human proneness to wrongdoing and violence. All men are born, as it were, under the horoscope of violence, and are imprisoned in this violence until they are able to emerge in early adulthood as the makers of their own destinies.[29]

Horoscope and prison thus emerge in *La vida es sueño* as a potent symbol for Calderón's future thought and work. The violence of sex, most powerfully expressed by rape, forms the foundation of his philosophy of love. The prince is overcome by the beauty of the first woman he has ever seen, and since he is now wielding power and expecting obedience from everybody, he attempts to rape her. This is frustrated; but followed by the attack on his father the attempted rape leads to his being drugged again and returned to prison. In his disillusionment his reasoning on his broken 'dream' leads to the first inkling that freedom demands self-control and moral responsibility.

La hija del aire. The symbol of imprisonment became established through the existence in classical mythology of several myths in which imprisonment fails to forestall an oracle. A typical example is Danae. An oracle informs her father that she will bear a son who will kill him. In order to prevent her becoming a mother, he imprisons her in a tower. But Jupiter becomes enamoured of her and enters her prison as a shower of gold. She gives birth to Perseus, who in due course does become the instrument of her father's death. Myths like this one gave validity and universality to the situation and enabled Calderón to use it without stretching credulity, and even to impose it on fables and stories where it did not exist. He did this, for instance, in the legend of Semiramis, the warrior queen of Assyria, which he developed in the two parts of *La hija del aire* (pre-1650).

Semiramis is a woman who causes havoc and destruction, usurping the throne from her son, whom she imprisons, after rumour had it that she had murdered the king. This usurpation leads to war; she commands her army and is killed. The first part of the play had given the reason for her causing of havoc: an exceptional beauty that overwhelmed men. She was the offspring of a rape, daughter of a priestess of Diana who was profaned by a devotee of Venus. Above the human conflict lies a struggle between Diana and Venus (i.e. between chastity and sensuality). It is prophesied that she will cause violence and war, and will herself meet a violent death. She is therefore imprisoned in a cavern in a remote mountain to prevent this destructiveness and her own death. When she is accidentally found by the king's chief minister he is so overcome by her beauty that he frees her, undeterred by the threat of the prophecy. She herself faces it, confident that she will prevail. He attempts to keep her secluded from other men. The king, however, accidentally meets her. He too is overcome by her beauty, and her ambition is aroused when she sees the power she can have over him; she therefore does not scruple to betray the man who had rescued her. The passionate desire for the woman leads to fierce rivalry between king and minister, who previously had been devoted and loyal friends. The king claims Semiramis and when his minister resists, the king has his eyes taken out. This act of violence is the first of a series of acts of treachery and cruelty which lead to the queen's death. The prophecy is fulfilled and as Semiramis lies dying she shouts out that Diana has won. All this has followed from the fact that she was beautiful, yet her beauty has led only to destruc-tion and chaos. She has herself connived at this degradation of beauty by her own selfish ambition.

Within this framework of ambitious aims and violent acts beauty is neither Courtly nor Platonic. Nor could it be, for the enchantment of Semiramis's beauty is the fruit of a sacrilegious rape. The prophecy is thus allied in Calderón's mind with the doctrine of original sin, which in Christian eyes is the 'horoscope' under which all men and women are born. He never, however, makes this association explicit. He does not introduce any super-natural or dogmatic concept in these plays; he is developing the themes of beauty and love solely within the natural order. History does not need the help of Christian faith to tell us that human beings are not born in, nor grow up into, a state of natural innocence. Human love is threatened by degradation because sex breeds violence. Calderón's mind and heart may have been pierced in this respect by the experience that he could not banish from his memory; it is on record that he used regularly to visit his sister Dorotea in her convent.

Eco y Narciso. Only a few of the mythological dramas can be selected here to illustrate the philosophy of love that was evolved from continuous meditation on this family guilt. The fable of Echo and Narcissus gave rise to a beautiful play, *Eco y Narciso*, which was performed at Court on 12 July 1661. The story is related by Ovid in the *Metamorphoses* (Book 3) and the changes Calderón

introduced into the story are slight, except for one. In Ovid
Liriope is ravished under water by a river god; in Calderón she
tells how she was insistently wooed by a son of the Wind; on
her constantly rejecting his advances the Wind lifts them both up
and wafts them to a cavern on a mountainside, inhabited by
Tiresias, the seer. There she is raped and abandoned and gives
birth to Narcissus. This prison thus has two inmates, a mother,
victim of a rape, and a boy who will grow into adolescence under
the threat of a prophecy. Liriope in her misery cannot return to
her father. The woman is oppressed by shame and guilt, and by
the doom that her son will face as the result of her degradation;
the boy as he grows into puberty[30] is oppressed by the burden of
authority, by the ignorance of life in which it keeps him and by
the fetters it imposes on his movements. In Ovid the prophecy of
Tiresias takes this form: asked whether the child will reach a ripe
age, he replies 'if he never knows himself'. In Calderón Tiresias
tells Liriope that the boy will have to guard against a beautiful
face and voice, each of which will seek his destruction through
loving and hating.

The setting is Arcadia. Liriope is a shepherdess and not a
nymph. The play opens with the shepherds celebrating the birthday of Echo with songs and acclamations. All the young men
adore her for her beauty, but she is committed to none. The only
silent voice in the festive joy is that of Sileno, who explains that
it was twelve years ago that very day that Liriope, his daughter,
disappeared and she has not been heard of since. The songs in the
valley rise faintly up the mountainside and Narcissus, who has
never heard music, begins to move down to hear it better. Liriope
rebukes him for trespassing beyond the boundary she had set.
The fascination of the strange sound has made him rebellious
and he claims the freedom all other creatures possess. He had
watched an eagle feeding her young in the nest until they were
fully fledged, when she pushed them out to make them fly in
freedom. He had also watched a lioness suckling her cubs until
they too were able to be turned out of the lair to fend for themselves. Why cannot he be allowed similar freedom? Liriope says
she will give him the answer later; for the moment she must hunt

some food for their next meal. She is captured by one of the shepherds and when this Wild Woman, dressed in skins, tells her story Sileno acclaims her as his daughter. Together they follow her up the mountain to find Narcissus.

When Liriope was captured she had cried out to Narcissus that she was being forced to leave him. He heard her shouts and realized that the time had come for him to stand on his own feet. As she and the shepherd ascend, he with fear and trepidation begins his descent, venturing into the unknown. Puberty is thus represented as escape from captivity and a release from servitude to a parent. This had been presaged by his response to his first sensuous experience, that of music through the human voice. As he moves down to the valley his first need is to quench his thirst and he listens for the sound of running water. Here is one of Calderón's characteristically subtle touches. The first gratification of the human senses is through food and drink; this is followed by a gratification on a higher plane, that of the emotions. As Narcissus listens for the splashing of water, he hears the music of human song. Enticed downwards by this he forgets his physical thirst.

The shepherds have divided into groups, singing different songs alternately. In Ovid Narcissus is fascinated by Echo's broken speech and he follows her sounds and can never find her, for she is no more than Nature's echo. Calderón develops this fascination with echoes into a response to the allurement of music. Music is the most spiritual of the arts and thus closest to the call of love. Narcissus makes towards each song as he hears it, but it always gives way to another in a different direction. He is in a state of confusion because emotion needs direction. One song grows louder until Echo appears and Narcissus joins in it, the two singing a duet. Each is overwhelmed by the beauty of the other. The arrival of a particular woman gives his instincts and emotions the direction they require, but he has been brought up so selfcontained that he is as bewildered by her as he is at the world.

Once he is established in his society, which is dominated by the beautiful Echo, he begins to feel the social havoc that love can cause. He is reunited with his mother but the bond is no longer the same. She informs him of the prophecy that foretells his doom, warning him that since she can no longer protect him from seeing and hearing he must guard himself. With this warning his timidity before Echo becomes fear. So unresponsive is he that she is forced openly to declare her love and she is angered at the negative result. The passions of the shepherds, set aflame by Echo, now turn to jealousy of Narcissus and to anger at his slighting of Echo. Narcissus is attacked and would be stabbed but for the arrival of his mother and others. He is thus plunged by his first independent experience of life into a world of violence in which he sees hate as inseparable from love, as obverse and reverse. None of the shepherds explains to Sileno what has occurred, saying that this must be left to Narcissus, but he does not under⁄ stand what has happened to him. Liriope is aghast at what may well be the approaching fulfilment of the prophecy. Now that she knows the probable source of calamity in Echo's beauty she will be able to forestall it by means of the arts Tiresias had taught her.

A beautiful girl thus invites to love and a beautiful youth does not respond. Ovid's explanation had been this: 'Narcissus had reached his sixteenth year and might seem either boy or man. Many youths and many maidens sought his love; but in that slender form was pride so cold that no youth, no maiden touched his heart.'[31] This pride as the cause of frigidity is less comprehens⁄ ible today than the timidity that Calderón has been at pains to emphasize through rape, prophecy and imprisonment. Depart⁄ ing further from Ovid he proceeds to develop his characteristic opposition between seeing and hearing. A subtle touch intro⁄ duces this. Narcissus is out hunting in the heat of the day and goes to a stream to quench his thirst. As he approaches it he remembers how on his first experience of freedom he had been distracted by human voices in song. He wonders whether this time he will be able to see the nymph who inhabits the stream. Bending over the bank he sees a very beautiful face and thinks it to be the nymph looking up at him. Instantly enamoured of his own image, but knowing nothing about reflections, he woos the nymph but she does not reply. He sees, but there is nothing to hear. Wandering nearby Echo hears Narcissus and softly approaches to see whom he is addressing. She leans over him and Narcissus sees a second face in the water beside the first. This face, however, is speaking but in a very strange manner, for Echo is now affected by a potion administered by Liriope and can only repeat the last few syllables of each sentence of Narcissus' wooing of his nymph. These syllables, when put together, do make sense but it is a meaning unrelated to any context.

The whole concept is subtle. Love is a communication with both sight and speech, but love can have no direction if the communication by speech has no meaning. His mother's obsessive fears have made Narcissus afraid of a face that has both beauty and speech. He can turn only to the beautiful face that is silent and that does not therefore threaten him. Realizing that it is Echo above him who is speaking, he drives her away. Since her love has been requited by scorn, she succumbs to despair and melts into the air; her love is obliterated by Narcissus' hate. Narcissus, shunning an outward-going love and deaf to the voice of love, can communicate only with himself, with a self-love that follows from a frightened dislike of women and of any beauty other than his own.[32] Echo proves how right the poets were in maintaining that unrequited love was death-bringing, engendering solely a negative response to existence, since it shirks the whole of the spiritual side of human nature. Sex is inseparable from violence. Erotic passion breeds jealousy and hatred. Sex can be violent and murderous in seeking its satisfaction; 'seeing' breeds passion when it rejects the co-operation of 'hearing'.[33]

El monstruo de los jardines. Another mythological play by Calderón, *El monstruo de los jardines* (The Monster of the Gardens), which dates from before 1667, forms a thematic counterpart to *Eco y Narciso*, since its theme is the positive acceptance of the call of love despite all the dangers it threatens. Calderón expounds the legends concerning Achilles's boyhood and youth, according to which his mother Thetis, having been warned that he would die at the siege of Troy, attempted to prevent it by dressing him as a girl and placing him among the maidens in the court of King Lycomedes, where he gets one of the king's daughters, Deidamia, with child. This pregnancy is rejected by Calderón and everything preceding the 'monstrosity' of a man dressed as a woman is altered by him. He adds to the legend by making Achilles, like Narcissus, one of the 'prisoners' secluded by their mothers to avoid a prophecy of disaster.

The mother of Achilles was Thetis, a sea-goddess, who was compelled after long resistance to marry Peleus. This resistance was sufficient basis for Calderón to turn her into a raped virgin; what is more, he makes her, as he does the mother of Semiramis, kill her violator. At his birth Calderón gives as the prediction of the horoscope, which his mother casts, the threat that he will take part in the fiercest and bloodiest of battles. His mother brings him up in seclusion until he rebels against her tutelage; the oracle of Mars then affirms that Troy will be conquered and destroyed only if Achilles goes with the attacking army and kills Hector. Both prophecies are inconclusive, constituting a threat rather than a pre-destined fate, but they suffice to terrify Thetis, and she decides to hide him from the Greek military commanders, who have heard the prophecy that Troy will fall if Achilles fights on their side. She therefore dresses Achilles as a girl.

The second oracle does not state that Achilles will die, nor does it state that he will survive; the threat of disaster is there, but so also is a promise of victory and glory. This destiny is not fate in the normal sense, it is rather a summons to a positive endeavour; it is clearly Achilles's vocation in life. A man may seek to avoid his fate; he may also seek to deny his vocation if it threatens danger. In the course of the play none of the characters ever speaks of Achilles's fulfilling his destiny; he is told only that he should 'fulfil his own nature' (*cumplir con su mismo natural*). This sets the dilemma of Achilles and the course of the action, not within the duality of fate and freewill, but in that of the 'natural' and the 'unnatural'. The word 'monster' in the title refers to something that goes counter to Nature. Calderón's 'prisoners', whether male or female, are invariably called 'monsters' in the sense of being 'wild' men and women. Liriope, the mother of Narcissus, was a 'monster', or wild beast which had to be hunted, because after being raped and abandoned, she had to exclude herself from the society of civilized men. Thetis, in this next play, is in the same situation.

The boy Achilles, growing up in similar exclusion, is called the 'Monster of the Forests'; when he is placed in Deidamia's garden, he becomes the 'Monster of the Gardens'. This refers in the first place to the violation of Nature represented by a man dressing as a woman, but more particularly it means the violation of his own nature through his mother's refusal to let him face his vocation, which is to be 'Fame's Champion'. These titles are all in the play; they represent the gradations whereby Achilles fulfils his destiny by fulfilling his own nature. The passage from 'Monster of the Forests' to 'Monster of the Gardens' is effected by his responding to the call of love, which since the ages of Courtly Love had been considered, of course, the main civilizing force that could transform the human savage. The transition from 'Monster of the Gardens' to 'Fame's Champion' is, however, effected by abandoning love. It was unnatural for Narcissus and Achilles to reject love through timidity, the former through fear of women, the latter through fear of war. In both cases the fear is implanted in them by their mothers, who have themselves been made afraid by the violence they had suffered.

Achilles does not go counter to Nature by rejecting love because he is already, in the garden, the accepted suitor of Deidamia; he goes counter to Nature by giving love for woman the priority in life. The contradiction is apparent only, because 'nature' is used in two senses; in this latter case Calderón emphasizes that he goes against his *own* nature. Love, as literature had made all too apparent, can, of course, go counter to social obligations, but in such cases it was the obligations that literature generally presented as 'unnatural'. Love, as literature has made abundantly clear, can also go counter to moral duty; but it is morality that is 'natural' unless it is too rigorously defined. This is what moralists had always taught, but the earliest literature in the period covered by this book had presented love for woman as an all-absorbing, indeed all-consuming, passion that could not and should not be resisted; such infidelity would be worse than unnatural, it was treason against life itself. Celibacy in men and women who put the service of God above all else was justified as a divine calling or a vocation, but that, and moral duty, were the only considera‑ tions that justified the rejection of love of woman. Calderón now combines with social obligation and moral duty the new concept of fidelity to one's own nature, or to one's vocation, which, in effect, is fidelity to oneself in an unegotistical sense. Fidelity to oneself rather than fidelity to one's lady is a new concept. Courtly lovers were theoretically prepared to face suffering and death rather than prove false to their destinies by rejecting their ladies. This Calderonian hero must choose suffering and death rather than remain faithful to his lady.

Deidamia's conflict is the opposite one. She represents at first the woman who rejects love because she hates men, or rather, because she hates the subjection to men which love implies. She claims that this hatred of men, and this refusal to fall in love, is *her* 'natural condition'. Calderón's age could not take such feminism seriously because it was an open revolt against Nature, which was an impossible 'monstrosity'. Deidamia's destiny or vocation was the same as those of all women: to open her heart to love. Deida‑ mia first opens her heart to love when Achilles is dressed as a woman, a significant parallel to Serafina in Tirso's *El vergonzoso en palacio*, who first feels love when she sees a portrait of herself in men's clothes.

Deidamia's rejection of love is not, as she at first thinks, in answer to her own nature. It is a revolt against society, which had laid down rules for governing relations between the sexes; these rules, as women realized even then, discriminated unfairly against them. The breaking of one of these rules by Achilles dressing as a woman removes the cause of Deidamia's rebellion, and when Achilles is revealed as a man she realizes that the call of Nature is indeed the call of her own nature. There are, however, much weightier social barriers to the fulfilment of her love. There is first the opposition of her father who has chosen a husband for her; with this there goes the fact that she is no ordinary daughter but a princess, with an obligation to the State. Her honour is therefore implicated in the fullest sense. But when Achilles decides that he must accept the command of the Greek army, she pleads passionately with him, affirming that she will risk everything for his sake: father, husband, kingdom and honour.

Achilles' conflict is similar: the call of love to which he has responded is the only promise of natural happiness that his life offers him; the rest is hardship, suffering and probable death. This promises fame, but what is fame against happiness? Drums, trumpets and the call to arms in the service of the body politic and the common good (symbolized by the oracle of Mars) stir every fibre in his being more strongly than Deidamia, and he has to sacrifice love for the sake of the very duties which Deidamia had herself chosen in order to prove faithful to the love that she cannot sacrifice. Torn in opposite directions each lover is, in fact, following his and her own destiny, obedient to the call of their respective 'vocations', but in order to fulfil their destinies, Deidamia must sacrifice honour, which at that time meant sacrificing love; by sacrificing love he will sacrifice honour and eventually life also. Both must renounce happiness, and this tragic fate is, for each, the summons of love, which is the supreme promise of happiness to men and women in this life. Deidamia's passionate outburst reveals the previously secret relationship of the lovers, and each is faced by the anger of his society (Deidamia by her father and the kingdom; Achilles by the Greek army). Each is about to be killed, but the tumult is quelled by the voice of the goddess Thetis, who tells the Greeks not to destroy by the death of Achilles the happiness they had hoped to obtain by his life. The love of Achilles and Deidamia is thus accepted by all and she allows him to depart for Troy.

It is perhaps not accidental that it is a goddess who tells warring humanity that discord and the harsh subjection of women to the law of honour are not the purpose of human life. Happiness is what humanity must aim at and strive to achieve. The means, above all others, for achieving this is the love of man for woman. This, and not war, is the law of Nature. Nonetheless, men and women must live in political societies, and these must have rules which impose obligations and demand obedience. The State can have overriding claims on a man's loyalty, and it is man's nature to serve society and the State, which can rightly demand the sacrifice of his natural happiness. Love cannot mean self-absorption at the cost of all else, as Courtly Lovers had professed to believe. Woman's nature is to love, and to be totally receptive to the call of love. It would not be contrary to Nature if a woman's love were all-absorbing. It would be contrary to Nature (as the vital force of human civilization) if love became this for man; men and women must obey Nature by loving each other. Deidamia must not hate men, nor must Narcissus adore only himself. The image of humanity in the fountains of Nature is a double one. Echo's face is reflected beside that of Narcissus, and there must be no silence between them.

Nevertheless, the destiny of men and the destiny of women are not identical or equal. Underlying all Calderón's thinking on human love lies the thought of the raped virgin. Love does not bring happiness to everybody; through the drive of sexual passion there is a violence that can humiliate, degrade and dishonour, and the victim is always woman. This is expressed at its strongest by the raped woman who must seclude herself in a prison. But the concept is, in Calderón's dramatic thought, also at the heart of the innumerable ways in which society and masculine pride impose subjection upon women. For Calderón, they are the tragic victims of life because they are the tragic victims of love.

If the reconstruction that has been made above of the dramatist's family life is correct, Calderón had witnessed this fact in his own sister. Liriope, the raped mother, whose only anxiety is to save Narcissus from the destructive violence of love, is an example in his plays. Deidamia is another. Although *El monstruo de los jardines* has an ostensibly happy ending in that their societies recognize their right to love, the audience knows, as does his mother Thetis, that by sailing to Troy Achilles will sail to his death. Deidamia must face the death of her husband and the rupture of her happiness. Yet it is wrong for Liriope to bring up Narcissus in seclusion and fear of women; it is wrong also for Thetis to try to bring up her son 'as a woman' through fear of the wider violence in human society. Achilles will achieve fame, but for Deidamia there is only loneliness without her husband.[34]

Apolo y Climene. The most moving example in Calderón's mythological plays of a woman who is the tragic victim of love occurs in a drama that deals with the love of Apollo and Clymene, daughter of King Admetus of Pherae in Thessaly.[35] This play, *Apolo y Climene*, has a second part, *El hijo del sol, Faetón*, which tells the story of Clymene's son, Phaethon.[36]

Ovid records that Apollo and Clymene were the parents of Phaethon, but the love of the god for the woman is not recorded by him or by anyone else, although the myths of Apollo relate how he aroused the anger of Jupiter whose thunderbolt hurled him down to earth, where he was punished by having to tend the sheep in the sheepfolds of King Admetus (a year's hard labour, says Ovid). To the best of my knowledge, therefore, this myth in the form in which Calderón presents it is his own invention. It follows the pattern of the horoscope and the imprisonment of a girl, but gives it an original development. The girl is freed, but succumbs to love, which had been forbidden her because of her horoscope; she then returns to incarceration in another type of prison. This makes it the most elaborate and the most significant example of the mythical form that Calderón gives to the symbol of the prison, here more closely than ever related to a philosophy of love.

To summarize the plot in order to extract only what is essential for the philosophy of love does more violence to Calderón's stage artistry in the case of this play than in that of the others. Its action develops in a mysterious way that keeps the audience in suspense. A description of the staging and scenery is not extant; more imagination than usual is therefore required by the reader. The play opens at night which, since all plays were performed in daylight because there was no artificial lighting, had to be indicated by the slow and groping movements of the actors. An actor removes a screen of leaves and branches and comes out of an opening at the back of the stage, replacing the screen. A few moments later he returns and enters the opening, covering it again. The alarm is raised that a man has been in a forbidden garden. A woman comes on to the stage to bemoan her secluded existence in which 'she lives without living'. At the opposite end of the stage there is a slab which covers the mouth of a tunnel. In the next scene, two men are lifting this slab when there is thunder, lightning, an earthquake and the clash of arms in the sky; terrified, they make good their escape as a man falls from the sky on to the stage and then falls into the pit which the removal of the slab had opened up. It is a magnificently theatrical beginning, and not till well into the second act are these mysteries explained.

A daughter had been born to King Admetus; he learns from her horoscope that she will give birth to a son so arrogant and violent that he will cause a catastrophe and set the kingdom of Ethiopia on fire. To prevent this, the king has the girl, Clymene, kept in seclusion from her birth. He builds a temple to Diana, the goddess of virginity, consecrating the girl to her. Round the temple he lays out a beautiful garden and surrounds this by unscalable walls, which are patrolled on the outside by guards. No man other than himself is allowed in the temple precincts; even the gardener is a woman. He gives his daughter maidens as companions; they too are vowed to Diana. These precautions prove of no avail, for the king does not know of the existence of the tunnel which leads into the garden from outside the walls. The slab covers the entrance, and the tunnel terminates in a grotto inside the garden, which is hidden by the screen. The tunnel is called a *mina* or *sima*, an underground conduit.

This tunnel, anticipating the union of Apollo and Clymene is, to the modern mind, an obvious sexual symbol. Whether it was consciously so for Calderón can be determined only by the various ways it is described in the dialogue, and by the nature and activity of the men who use it; what it thus denotes in the action will point to its meaning in the theme. Numerous details of this kind make the conscious reference abundantly clear. In the first place its existence is known only to a character called Sátiro, and the mythical satyrs were of course renowned in antiquity for their lasciviousness. This character discloses the existence of the tunnel to Zephyr who passes through it for a tryst with one of the ladies-in-waiting, whom he deflowers, remaining her lover and having access to her only through the tunnel. When the slab at the other end has to be raised for entry into the garden, it is Satyr who gives assistance to the human lover.[37] In the second place Clymene refers to it as 'a mine whose mouth has been opened by Love, the engineer'.[38] In the third place, when Apollo is cast down to earth in the storm of lightning, Clymene is the only one of the women who claims that she saw the Sun fall from the sky and set the garden on fire. The sight had terrified her and later she says that she continues to feel a burning sensation from the heat of the falling Sun. This must represent the onset of adolescence, presaging the stirrings of sexual desire. It is at such a period of their lives that all these Calderonian 'prisoners' clamour for and obtain their freedom. In the case of Clymene the freedom is relative only. Lastly, when Apollo describes to Clymene how he came into the garden, he says that he fell 'into the conduit that leads a lover from outside into your gardens', and he asks how he was to know that a conduit tunnelled for water would lead to 'mines of fire'.[39]

The symbolism of the *mina*/*sima* seems obvious and intentional. The girl in the garden is Clymene. She has been agitated, first, by seeing a man (Zephyr), who cannot be found, and secondly, by seeing the startling disturbance in the heavens, and by the burning she has felt from the falling Sun. Alarmed by her agitation her father rushes to discover the cause. She then upbraids him for his treatment of her, and pleads passionately for the liberty that is her right. Sensing that she is confined in order to forestall a calamity, she demands to know why she should be made to suffer such grievous harm to prevent a harm she has not done. Her women corroborate her story about a man in the garden at night, and the king sees that all his precautions have proved fruitless. He tells her of her horoscope and decides now to allow her freedom of movement, but only on condition that she remains vowed to Diana as a virgin. Should she break this vow, Admetus will sacrifice her on Diana's altar. From being a physical constraint the prohibition becomes a moral one, which is to cause her a deeper anguish than before. Virginity is so contrary to Nature that it must be chosen voluntarily. None of the women in the forbidden garden remains a virgin.

While she is pondering in the evening on all these signs and portents, Apollo emerges from the tunnel, is struck by the beauty of the temple precincts and thinks that the silent and motionless Clymene must be a statue enhancing the beauty of the scene. When she moves and speaks he tells her that this first sight of her beauty has made him deeply enamoured. Her tragic conflict begins. She must not break her vow, nor can she love an unknown man, for Apollo has been forbidden by Jupiter to disclose his identity or use his divine powers. He can tell her only that he has fallen from the furthermost ends of the heavens into the depths of the earth (the brilliance of the Sun having been extinguished in the blackness of the tunnel). In the light of the developing theme these remarks, in Calderón's technique, have a much wider significance. They refer to the basic tenet of his philosophy, the indivisable unity of soul and body within their essential opposition. Love, which should shine with the light of the spirit, can be blackened with the brutishness of lust.

None of Clymene's companions experiences her tragic conflict. The fact that the tunnel has made the defending walls useless has meant that these other girls have already had their secret love affairs. It is even the case that Apollo himself has had an amorous encounter with one of them, though we are not told how and when. This does not point to any significance in the theme; it is needed for the plot, because when Apollo returns to seek Clymene his former love thinks he is returning on her account; an intrigue develops which is needed for the public disgrace of Clymene, since the girls, in order not to confess to their own transgressions, are able to place the blame on Clymene. She had raised the alarm and her agitation could point to guilt. Convinced that this is so, Admetus is about to hold her for the sacrifice when Apollo snatches her away, plunges into the river Erideron (which with poetic licence Calderón thus places in Ethiopia), and swims with her to the other bank, pursued in boats by the king and the others.

On the opposite shore they meet with the magician Fiton, named earlier as the soothsayer who had interpreted Clymene's horoscope to her father. The name associates the magician with Python, the serpent sent by Juno to persecute Latona before she gave birth to Apollo and Diana. This serpent was later killed by Apollo. The association of the names Python and Fiton is clear from the word *Fitonisa*, an alternative spelling in Spanish for the word *Pitonisa* (Greek—*pythonissa*), which means either the priestess who presided over Apollo's oracle at Delphi or a sorceress. Fiton tells Apollo that he can save Clymene. He makes her disappear within a rock and tells Apollo to hide. The pursuers arrive on the scene and Fiton tells Admetus that he had seen a man and woman in the river, struggling to reach the shore. This they failed to do and he saw them drown. Admetus is content with this report because he will no longer need to sacrifice his daughter. He departs, but the others do not accept Fiton's account, since they know the man was Apollo and therefore immortal. They determine to return and investigate further.

On their departure Apollo emerges from hiding and cries out for Clymene. Immediately Satyr appears. Apollo tells him he is going to free Clymene from within the rock, but when he hammers on it with his fists it disappears and in its place there is a magnificent palace with Clymene lying asleep. The lovers are reunited, but Clymene demands to know who Apollo is before she can marry him. When he insists that he cannot tell her more than that he emerged from the *minas de fuego* she thinks with terror that the fulfilment of her horoscope must be near. Fiton, however, assures them that he has the power to prevent it from coming true. He persuades Apollo to disclose his identity and tells the lovers that Apollo will be pardoned by Jupiter and that their marriage will be sanctioned. The two take him at his word, but Fiton comments how easily they have been deceived.

Later, in the cool of the evening Apollo falls asleep in the garden Fiton prepared for their love and Clymene retires without disturbing him. Apollo awakens when Mercury and Iris appear as the messengers of the gods to summon him back. Venus and Diana have taken pity on Apollo and have persuaded Jupiter to pardon him. Clymene, however, is not to be pardoned because she has broken her vow to Diana, and must remain secluded in the captivity that Fiton will prepare for her. Apollo will rather lose his godhead than forsake Clymene, and thus refuses to return. Clymene, realizing what the choice means for him, refuses to accept his sacrifice and pleads with him to go. Apollo, heartbroken at this dilemma, calls Mercury and Iris 'Cruel, merciful messengers of Good and Evil, announcing both joy and grief':

> Crueles piadosos nuncios
> del bien y el mal, pues a un tiempo,
> árbitros suyos, traéis
> juntos gozo y sentimiento:
> qué responderos no sé,
> porque dudo al responderos
> cuál pesa mas, la ventura
> que gano o el bien que pierdo.[40]

Cruel, merciful messengers of Good and Evil, since, as their arbiter you bring me both joy and sorrow: I do not know how to answer you for I am unsure what is harder to bear: the good fortune I gain or the good I lose.

All through the play Apollo has been conscious of the inseparability of good and evil in the world of men. He sees this now at its most harrowing: it is good for him to resume his rightful status in the world of the spirit, but evil for him to abandon Clymene to inescapable captivity in the domain of Fiton. He thinks to solve the dilemma by returning with the messengers, not to resume his divinity but to plead with the gods to show mercy to the woman he loves. He does return with them but will not be allowed to come back to earth. Clymene, for her part, is compelled to exchange the captivity of her vow to Diana for the captivity of Fiton. In between she has known only the brief period of freedom that enabled her to experience the love of a god and to conceive a son who will himself be the victim of a prophecy of doom.

Clymene is a tragic heroine in that she appears helpless in the grip of an adverse Fate. She is the victim of unjust confinement; she suffers from feelings and emotions she cannot explain; she tries to keep the vow imposed upon her, but what she does brings only further disaster; she denounces the presence of a man only to find that the revelation of his presence is turned accusingly against her. She becomes helpless: when about to be sacrificed to Diana by her father, she is rescued from his clutches in a manner that publicly seems to confirm the accusation of her guilt. She is trapped into acceptance of Apollo's love by Fiton's deceitful promise that Fate will now turn benign. Finally, she finds that Apollo himself has also been trapped and has promised more than he is able to fulfil. For his sake she accepts abandonment and is led by Fiton into a captivity gloomier than that of her father. Yet although her situation is entirely tragic it is not likely that the reader, even the most attentive, will be moved by deep tragic emotions. There is nothing of the passion and violence that fills the first part of *La hija del aire* or of the fury that grips the two men who fight for the hand of Semiramis. As befits both Calderón's approaching old age and the type of theatre for which he was writing, the mood of the work is reflective, the tone more detached. The play is poetically elegant and dramatically refined rather than passionate and violent.

The reader may well ask why is it that happiness seems unattainable and suffering inevitable and enduring. Satyr and Fiton are intended as the instruments of suffering and tragic doom, yet they are not made repellent, and only after the final calamity does Satyr appear dressed as such to frighten those who behold him. When Clymene first sees Fiton she is struck by the severity of his appearance from which she cannot judge whether he is man or beast, yet she follows him passively and accepts his word. There is thus little or no tragic evil in the normal or dramatic sense although the play is full of sadness. Fiton is not a satanic character, though he can play like the Serpent on human weakness.

Moreover, although Satyr is present whenever Apollo seeks Clymene in pursuit of his love, there is nothing lustful in Apollo's words or in his treatment of her; nor is anything approaching lust discernible in Clymene's attitude towards Apollo. The two could not love more chastely, yet their love is somehow 'evil' and cannot endure. Dramatically the only evil apparent in the action is Fiton's admission, in asides, that he is deliberately deceiving them into thinking that their love will be acceptable to the gods and to Fate. That he comments how easily they are taken in is an indication that they ought not to have been. Even the breaking of their vows by Clymene's three companions is not presented as in any way vicious. Their only real offence is subterfuge and secrecy, for in asserting the claims of love they are asserting the rights of Nature. What, then, is the 'evil' that Calderón is attempting to convey? The answer follows from the myth's point of departure. What can the love of a god for a woman signify?

The answer lies once more in the fact about human nature that has been so often emphasized throughout these pages. Calderón is by virtue of mythology giving it a new emphasis. The need to love, and the capacity to love, come down to mankind from heaven. This is the primary significance of the Christian doctrine of the Incarnation, but that is not what Calderón has in mind here. It is not only Christians who can hold that humanity has a spark of the divine. It shines in self-abandonment to the good of another; it lies in a capacity for altruism and self-sacrifice; it lies in men's urge to search for the ideal and to live by it. The vitality and the ardour of human love, when directed outward, are god-given and the spirit in man responds to this. God and man meet in love, and man yearns instinctively for a vision of, and contact with, the spiritual. But the love of man and woman for each other must express itself through the body as well as through the spirit. The suffering that could follow from the inability to achieve the balanced harmony between the two was evident in the literature that nurtured Calderón and evident in his own response to the existential problem. Clymene, still uncorrupted by human society, must respond to the love of a god for her, but she cannot love divinely. The deception that Fiton practises is to instil in Clymene and Apollo the belief that their love will endure under the sanction of heaven, but what Satyr represents makes this impossible. The existence of the body makes human love ultimately unspiritual. Apollo can return to heaven to plead for Clymene but he cannot come back to her. She, for her part, cannot keep him. The material body represents an imperfection in the world of spirit and men must not delude themselves into the belief that no imperfection, and therefore no evil, exists. The Palace of Pure Love is an illusion, the creation of human imagination.

This does not mean that Calderón holds there is in the moral sense anything intrinsically evil in sensuality; moral evil for him does not lie in acts as such but in intentions and in the degree of self-seeking involved. But although love comes down from heaven and man must respond by his very nature, only in the mystical relationship can the response be god-like. For Apollo to come down to earth he must shed his divinity, and for Clymene to love him she must allow herself to respond sensually: this is what makes the Palace of Pure Love a delusion. It must be emphasized, however, that there is no wickedness involved, which is why there is no tragic horror or violence in this play, only the sense of sadness and frustration which belongs to the human condition and not only to dramatically imagined men and women. That is why the play may be called 'philosophical' and why the appropriate conceptual and narrative mode is myth.

El hijo del Sol, Faetón. In the sphere of human love within social relationships Clymene may indeed be seen to epitomize Calderón's view of woman's lot, centred in the suffering of oppression and repression. Her son, Phaethon, for his part, may be seen, to some extent, as epitomizing the male role in human life. The two plays together can give us Calderonian symbols of the human tragedy.

In *El hijo del Sol, Faetón* (Phaethon, Son of the Sun) the boy, born and brought up in Fiton's cave, grows up not knowing who his father was, and therefore not knowing who he is himself, and what role he is to play in the world. He is another of the Calderonian fatherless sons, imagined extensions of Calderón's own illegitimate half-brother. Calderón follows Ovid closely. Phaethon has been told by his mother that Apollo was his father. He tells this to his companion, Epaphus, when the latter taunts him with his fatherless condition, but Epaphus only laughs at the answer, saying that this cannot be proved. Clymene tells her son to seek out Apollo and demand proof of his parentage. Phaethon finds him, and arrogantly claims the right to drive his father's sun-chariot for incontrovertible proof of his divine descent. Apollo concedes his demand; Phaethon mounts the chariot but cannot control the fiery horses, comes too close to the earth, scorching the lands of Thessaly and crashing to his death in the River Erideron. With overweening pride in his divine origin and in order to prove his worth, he harnesses the energy of the Sun only to destroy himself and to threaten the destruction of the earth. Man, because of his need to prove his worth throughout history, because of the boundless energy which characterizes his achievements, and because of the astounding products of his reason, is indeed of divine origin, but with overbearing pride he usurps divine powers which ultimately he cannot control.[41]

Arrogance, ambition, violence and a desire for domination were, for Calderón, the masculine traits, in love as well as social activities, just as long-suffering patience, even victimization,were for him the marks of womankind.[42]

CONCLUSION

At the beginning of this book the following passage from George Santayana's *Life of Reason* was quoted: 'There can be no philosophic interest in disguising the animal basis of love, or in denying its spiritual sublimation, since all life is animal in its origin, all spiritual in its possible fruits.'[43] The dichotomy between the animal origin and the spiritual sublimation of human love has been the central thread of this chapter. The sublimation had been stressed virtually exclusively in the sixteenth century. The Age of Disillusion brought the animal side of love into confrontation with the ideal and posed the enduring existential problem. After a period of transition in which the Real and the Ideal are placed side by side, body and spirit are seen as presenting an indissoluble union and their contradiction is shown to be at the core of human experience.

Quevedo's poetry expresses this paradox most uncompromisingly. One of his collections of maxims contains the following: 'jamás blasoné del amor con la lengua, que no estuviese muy lastimado lo interior del ánimo' ('I have never praised love with my tongue without feeling deeply hurt in the innermost part of my mind').[44] It was hurtful for him to have to praise the un-praisable, and this was because his conscience could not remove the hurt from his experience. He inherited from centuries of Christian belief and practice the conviction that sexual love was by its very nature demeaning to the dignity of a being created in the divine image, with reason and an immortal soul. The ideal of Platonic love, although it could not satisfy the urge of appetite, could not destroy or kill desire. On the plane of his poetic imagi-nation, which would have been the plane of his conscience, though not necessarily of his actual experience, he could not deny the instrinsic 'sinfulness' of sexuality. Great poet and fine thinker that he was, he did not see sin as the breaking of rules that might seem arbitrary and external: sin for him was everything that deeply degraded the dignity of man.

Quevedo and his age were able to express an inner turmoil of this kind through the development of imagery known as 'meta-physical conceits'. What lyrical poetry could accomplish so movingly could not be so easily communicated through drama. Calderón, it might be thought, was particularly hampered by the formality and ceremoniousness of the court theatre; he could not in that medium express the anguish of Quevedo. Nevertheless, he could with the help of myths create a medium, detached and not intimately personal, to express his own philosophy of love.

In this philosophy the sense of sin is not absent by any means, but the stress is on the physical violence and the social upheavals that untamed sexuality can cause. Nothing is more degrading to human dignity, whether to man or to woman, than the act of rape. It is the extreme expression of self-seeking pleasure, and thereby the total negation of the social bond. Sexual passion breeds jealousy, which can also lead to violence and murder. Violence of these kinds, together with the treachery and deceit that rivalry in love can engender, are the sins of love that Cal-derón's plays stress. But the deeper problem concerning the dig-nity of human nature remains. In a Christian culture this was not only a problem of reason to be answered by philosophy, the prevailing philosophy in Calderón's lifetime being Stoicism; it was also a problem of theology.

Calderón was a recognized theologian after his ordination to the priesthood at the age of fifty-one. All his *autos sacramentales*, which he began to write probably in his middle thirties, are testimony to his high theological competence and to the sincerity of his religious faith. This religious faith was always held and expressed intellectually, and, wherever possible, with rational argument. Perhaps the existence of nearly eighty *autos*, but more probably nineteenth-century liberal hostility to the Spain of the Inquisition and of the Counter-Reformation, branded Calderón as an intransigent anti-humane dogmatist and distracted attention away from his secular *comedias*, which are actually far more numerous than his religious ones. Nowadays the balance is being righted, and his late court plays, which are in no sense dogmatic, are receiving attention. It must be emphasized that Calderón as a whole is a humanist, a Christian one of course like the great majority of his contemporaries in Europe This survey of his philosophy of love has emphasized the point What he finds sinful and degrading in human love is what no man of reason could defend.

Yet despite the disillusionment that colours (but does not blacken) Calderón's view of man's moral and social life, in the sphere of human love the element of idealism still remains, as it does in Quevedo. This is most evident in those plays where the passion of love, which he constantly suggests has no sinfulness in it (unless abused), is put side by side with the call of divine love. In *Ni Amor se libra de amor* the acceptance by both Jupiter and Venus of the marriage of Cupid and Psyche suggests on the plane of 'philosophy' that there is no essential antagonism between the love of the body and the love of the spirit. Nevertheless, as the analysis suggested, there was no way of subordinating one to the other and of course no necessity. When Calderón brings about a direct confrontation between human love and divine love, he does so by means of a special kind of plot in which a man feels the powerful attraction of both kinds of love and is finally faced with a choice. This plot, which he uses on two occasions, requires both a freely given conversion to the God of Christianity and the free acceptance of martyrdom at the hands of a persecuting

State. The significance of this in relation to human love may be indicated briefly.

Los dos amantes del Cielo (The two Lovers of Heaven) dramatizes one of the most 'romantic' of the legends of the saints, that o Chrysanthus and Daria who were martyrs in early Roman times.[45] In his free elaboration of the legend Calderón makes Chrysanthus, son of a powerful Roman senator, an incipient philosopher. His studies have led him to the Gospel of John and his mind is bewildered. What is the 'Word', that 'was with God' and at the same time, 'was God'? How could this 'Word be made flesh'? His mind is irresistibly drawn to these intellectual enigmas, but is also drawn to beauty. This is of three types, each represented by a young woman. One sings a song, and the beauty of music captivates his ear; another recites a poem which appeals to both his ear and his mind, because it is a poem in the 'metaphysical' style, with 'witty' conceits and reasoning; the third girl captivates the eye with her physical beauty. This third beauty is the one that is irresistible, but Daria scorns all offers of love; her pride is such that she could only love a man who would die for her. Chrysanthus vows that he could and would. Here the extravagant concept of Courtly Love is brought up against religion. His mind, however, is brought back to the mysterious 'Word'. A convert Christian elucidates the meaning of the Gospel and begins to instruct Chrysanthus in the new faith. Here Chrysanthus learns that there was a Man who could and did die for love of every man and woman, and he thereby realizes what a sacrificial love can mean.

Christians are being persecuted, and the persecution is being directed by Chrysanthus's own father, who attempts to distract his son by persuading him into marriage. Daria, however, is determined to defend the honour of her pagan gods by attempting to overcome Chrysanthus's new faith by arguments. When eventually she is overcome by the realization that a Man had in fact died for her, she can accept Chrysanthus's love, and she gives him her hand in the promise of marriage, already calling him husband. The two are captured and are martyred by being buried alive. The points to be noted are, first, that the appeal of intellectual argument is stronger than the sensuous appeal of music: secondly, that the mind is driven towards God by the desire to pierce mystery (the riddle of existence expressed in para-doxical, enigmatic imagery); thirdly, that the attraction of physical beauty can overcome the attraction of intellectual poetry, but not the urge to penetrate the mysteries of life.

These points are expressed more maturely and much more convincingly in *El mágico prodigioso* in which the theme of human love is again bound up with a legend of martyred saints. Cyprian and Justina were reputedly martyred in Antioch during the per-secution of Christians under Diocletian in the third century.[46] Calderón's Cyprian is absorbed in the attempt to comprehend the elder Pliny's definition of God and to square it with the pagan religion. He refuses to take any part in social life or festivities until he comes face to face with Justina, when his intellectual activity crumbles away under the surge of sensual passion, and God is forgotten. She is secretly a Christian and cannot respond to his advances, for this would mean the abjuration of her faith. She tells him that it is 'impossible to love him until death', by which she means that the impossibility will exist until she dies. He takes this to mean that she will love him when he is at the point of death and claims to rejoice at this confession, for his love for her is bringing him death already. So much is his intellect now in abeyance that he discards his student's clothes, dresses as a gallant, suffers the pangs of irrational jealousy and even fights duels with Justina's other suitors. Finally he plumbs the depths of unreason when he cries out that in order to possess Justina's beauty he would willingly sell his soul to the Devil. The latter appears and accepts the bargain. Cyprian does not know who he is and had actually encountered him previously without know-ing who he was.

The Devil, as the active principle of Evil, is in Cyprian's case the outward representation of the irrationality that subordinates everything to the 'living death' of sexual passion. He undertakes to bring Justina to him. Her temptation is poetically one of the most beautiful scenes in all Calderón's drama. She becomes aware for the first time in her life how all Nature around her responds to the call of love: the sunflowers longingly follow the sun its course, birds sing amorously to each other, and vines entwine lovingly around trees. She alone has not experienced love, but now, under the stress of this sensuous awareness, she thinks of Cyprian and confesses that she would go to him if she knew where he was. At this confession of love the Devil tugs at her but reason, momentarily weakened, becomes active again and her will can reject the temptation.

All that the Devil can take to Cyprian is a cloaked and hooded figure, which he avidly embraces in what is symbolically a rape. He tears off the hood and cloak and finds that he is embracing a skeleton. Underlying this powerful dramatic moment is the sudden realization (the essential beginning for Calderón of moral and religious conversion) that the subjection of the reason and the will to a pleasure that cannot endure is in effect to love death instead of life. By beginning to love he had, it is indeed true, begun to die. He wrings from the Devil the admission that Justina could resist temptation because her will, unlike his own, was free. And immediately Cyprian's intellect begins to function again. How could her will resist passion, while his could not? From this he reasons to the conclusion that faith in her God gave her the strength to resist. He is back again at the search for God, able now to identify his abstract First Cause, omniscient and omnipotent, with the personal God of the Christians. Proclaiming himself to be one, he is cast into the prison where Justina is awaiting her execution. She completes his conversion. Cyprian follows her in proclaiming his willingness to die for the spiritual love that now fills his mind and heart; whereupon Justina says she can fulfil what she told him, that she would love him at the time of death. They are thus united in their human love by being united in the love of God, the love that can survive the body's transformation into a skeleton.

Drama thus enabled Calderón to overcome the dichotomy of body and spirit, of human love and divine love. Martyrdom, so important a factor in the history of Christianity, made it possible to represent the primacy of divine love over human love, because the fact that death follows the mutual confession of love means that this divine love cannot be betrayed: death makes both loves absolute. Yet Calderón so arranges his two plots that religion does not supplant the human. The love of God complements and perfects the love of woman, which in both these plays is the beginning of the search for God, and which is crowned when God is found and accepted. Human love starts with the response of the senses to physical beauty, but is perfected in the response of the mind to the thirst for a truth that can give meaning to existence, a truth that is indestructible in death.[47]

In the first chapter it was suggested that the equating of human love with suffering and death was basically a religious concept, since only poetic hyperbole could relate it to human experience. In these martyr plays Calderón reveals how the association of love and death could, within a religious context, be intimately bound to human experience. By implicitly affirming that religion does not override human values but perfects them, Calderón was pointing in the direction that Christian theology was to follow. For centuries theology had held that the justification of sexual love lay essentially in the procreation of children. Calderón, however, gave it, when properly expressed in an altruistic (and therefore 'ideal') manner, a spiritual orientation and justification.

In a sense, therefore, Calderón did spiritualize human love. Although as a dramatist he was close to the reality of experience in a way that the court poets of the latter half of the fifteenth century did not need to be, he was still in the tradition of idealizing human love, a tradition that they, in the special way of that age, had carried to extremes. In his thought, however, the idealization of love was related to religious experience in a way that was not extravagant and that did not lessen the priority of religion.

Calderón's plays mark the end of the connection between literature and philosophies of love in the sense that this book has tried to illustrate. He died when the age of Rationalism and Enlightenment was about to begin, rather later in Spain than elsewhere. Although human love was still to be portrayed in literature as idealistic in a romantic sense, it was no longer to be associated with a religious sense of life. The problems of love became restricted to the rules of a repressive moral code as well as the restrictions of the legal system and of social traditions. Not till about the middle of the nineteenth century did love in Spanish literature come into direct conflict with religion, but not on the existential plane of a Quevedo or the metaphysical plane of a Calderón. It became in the individual a conflict of conscience: the conflict between the individual's claim to freedom and the claim of the Church to the possession of a divine right to restrain that freedom.

The idealization of love, as traced in this book, bears no relation to love as dealt with in contemporary literature, and little relation to it as dealt with in modern philosophy. But for over two centuries it helped to inspire a great literature whose loss would impoverish our culture. For this literature to be valued as it deserves, it is necessary to understand, with as much sympathy as the passage of time permits, the contrasting theories of love which helped to give it substance. It may even be that the comprehension of these older theories of love may help us to evaluate the place given to human love in our society and culture today. As a woman writer has put it:

> The fear of love grows as the hunger for it becomes un-appeasable. The slow growth of feeling between two people used to be what drew bodies together, along with minds. One result of the new permissiveness is that the first tremor of genuine emotion is apt to send people scurrying for cover —in opposite directions. Mind and body are not to be taken lightly. Their connection is intimate and mysterious and better mapped by poets than pornographers.[48]

NOTES

Introduction

1. N. S. Trübetzkoy, quoted by Robert Scholes, *Structuralism in Literature* (New Haven 1974), 6.
2. Scholes, 4.
3. A good history of the philosophy of love is Irving Singer, *The Nature of Love: Plato to Luther* (New York 1966).
4. I shall refer to St John's mystical 'philosophy' instead of 'theology' to bring his poetry into line with the theme of this book. The distinction between philosophy and theology is not material in the intellectual exploration of the human experience of love. It matters not whether this exploration is founded on reason or on the supernatural because we are dealing with the expression of love in literature, in actual experience filtered through the imagination, and union with God in love was as real an experience for St John as the sexual union of man with woman was for others. When, in expounding elements of his poetry, I stress its precision in the conformity of symbols and metaphors to his concepts, and the intellectual grasp shown in the ordered structure of his poems, I write as a literary critic, and my use of 'symbols' and 'metaphors' is not that of a linguistic philosopher, who would look for precision of another kind and not find it. For a modern exposition of mysticism and language see W. T. Stace, *Mysticism and Philosophy* (London 1961), 277-306 (especially 284-94).
5. *The Life of Reason*, second edition (New York 1905), 9.
6. On Courtly Love as the beginning of Romantic Love see C. S. Lewis, *The Allegory of Love. A Study in Medieval Tradition* (Oxford 1936).
7. Logan Pearsall Smith, *Little Essays Drawn from the Writings of George Santayana* (London 1920), 5-6.
8. The critical principle was outlined by T. S. Eliot in his essay 'Tradition and the Individual Talent' of 1919 (reprinted in *Selected Prose of T. S. Eliot*, edited by Frank Kermode (London 1975), 37-44): 'The mind of the poet ... may partly or exclusively operate upon the experience of the man himself; but, the more perfect the artist, the more completely separate in him will be the man who suffers and the mind which creates; the more perfectly will the mind digest and transmute the passions which are its material' (41); 'The business of the poet is not to find new

216

emotions, but to use the ordinary ones and, in working them up into poetry, to express feelings which are not in actual emotions at all. And emotions which he has never experienced will serve his turn as well as those familiar to him' (43).

Chapter One. *The Religious Language of Human Love*

1. Theories about the origin of Courtly Love are classified and discussed by Roger Boase, *The Origin and Meaning of Courtly Love. A Critical Study of European Scholarship* (Manchester 1977).

2. Boase, 62–75.

3. Boase, 83–6.

4. Denis de Rougemont, *L'Amour et l'Occident* (Paris 1939); *Passion and Society*, translated by Montgomery Belgion (London 1940; revised edition 1956).

5. *L'Amour et l'Occident*, 155.

6. *L'Amour et l'Occident*, 153. The unchristian or anti-Christian nature of Courtly Love was developed in a wider context by A. J. Denomy, *The Heresy of Courtly Love* (New York 1947).

7. M. C. D'Arcy, *The Mind and Heart of Love. Lion and Unicorn: A Study in Eros and Agape* (London 1945).

8. In Chapter 3.

9. Eduard Wechssler, *Das Kulturproblem des Minnesangs. Studien zur Vorgeschichte der Renaissance* (Halle 1909).

10. Peter Dronke, *Medieval Latin and the Rise of the European Love Lyric*, second edition, 2 vols (Oxford 1968).

11. D. R. Sutherland, 'The language of the troubadours and the problem of origins', *FS*, 10 (1956), 199–215 (212). Cited by Dronke, i, 49.

12. Boase, 33. See, too, H. J. Chaytor, *Troubadours of Dante* (Oxford 1902), 173–6.

13. René Nelli, *L'Érotique des troubadours* (Toulouse 1963).

14. Nelli, 64. 'Amour courtois' is defined (64) as, 'espèce d'amitié amoureuse—platonique ou semi-platonique—mais de toute façon excluant le "fait"'. 'Platonic' in the strict sense is of course inaccurate here; what is meant is a love that no longer stresses the need for its own physical consummation.

15. Nelli himself argues (329–32) that both strands continue into the sixteenth century, when 'amour courtois' fuses with Neoplatonism.

16. Pedro Salinas, *Jorge Manrique o tradición y originalidad* (Buenos Aires 1948), 23; see, too, Otis H. Green, 'Courtly Love in the Spanish *cancioneros*', *PMLA*, 44 (1949), 247–301, reprinted in *The Literary Mind of Medieval and Renaissance Spain* (Lexington 1970).

Notes

17. *Spanish Literary Historiography: Three Forms of Distortion* (Exeter 1967); *La poesía amatoria de la época de los Reyes Católicos* (Durham 1981). See, too, Professor Whinnom's introductions to the works cited in footnote 27 below.

18. 'Bembo, Gil Polo, Garcilaso; Three Accounts of Love', *RLC*, 40 (1966), 526‑40.

19. On the dating of the *Cancionero de Palacio* see Brian Dutton, 'Spanish fifteenth‑century *cancioneros*: a general survey to 1465', *KRQ*, 26 (1979), 455‑60; and his *Catálogo‑Indice de la poesía cancioneril del siglo XV* (Madison 1982).

20. *Cancionero de Palacio*, edited by Francisca Vendrell de Millás (Barcelona 1945), 87.

21. *La poesía amatoria*, 29.

22. Crisógono de Jesús Sacramentado O.C.D., *Vida de San Juan de la Cruz*, edited by Matías del Niño Jesús O.C.D. (Madrid 1982), 181, n.31.

23. José M. Blecua, 'Los antecedentes del poema del *Pastorcico* de San Juan de la Cruz', *RFE*, 33 (1949), 378‑80; reprinted in *Sobre poesía de la Edad de Oro* (Madrid 1970), 96‑9.

24. Melvin W. Askew, 'Courtly Love: Neurosis as Institution', *PsR* 52 (1965), 19‑29 (19, 27).

25. Evelyn Underhill, *Mysticism. A Study in the Nature and Develop‑ ment of Man's Spiritual Consciousness*, thirteenth edition (London 1960), 265.

26. Or else, as Patrick Gallagher has put it, the aspiration is the painful awareness of sinfulness on the part of the poets: 'The ideal of Courtly Love is in fact atonement for adultery, and the atone‑ ment is envisaged, as it must be in a Christian society, in terms of suffering, penance, self‑denial, martyrdom' (*The Life and Works of Garci Sánchez de Badajoz* (London 1968), 288). From the point of view of understanding the minds and sensibilities of the Courtly Love poets I am sure this is a correct approach, but I suggest that the different one I am putting forward, the aspiration to a perfect love, is, so to speak, the other face of the coin. Religious writers, and specifically mystics, who accepted the language and emotions of Courtly Love, could not have been interested in it as atonement for adultery. What lay behind this poetic language had to have another meaning for them. From either angle, in inter‑ preting both aspects of this literature, the use of religious concepts is crucial.

27. *Diego de San Pedro, Obras completas, ii: Cárcel de amor*, edited with an introduction and notes by Keith Whinnom (Madrid 1971); *Prison of Love, together with the continuation by Nicolás Núñez*, trans‑ lated with an introduction and annotations by Keith Whinnom

(Edinburgh 1979). On San Pedro's life, background and other works see Keith Whinnom, *Diego de San Pedro* (New York 1974).

28. On its printing history see Whinnom's edition of the *Obras completas*, ii, 67⁄70, and the additional information in vol. iii, edited with Dorothy S. Severin, 323⁄4.

29. The lover is led into an allegorical 'prison of love' by a hairy savage who represents Desire, and who entices men into imprisonment by carrying the statuette of a beautiful woman. This symbol of the Wild Man is the connecting link between the medieval idea of Courtly Love in its fifteenth⁄century form and the Renaissance ideal of Platonic love; what they have in common is the aspiration for a perfect love to be achieved by the permanent chaining of the Wild Man. On this and other occurrences of the Wild Man in medieval works see A. D. Deyermond, 'El hombre salvaje en la novela sentimental', *Fi*, 10 (1964), 97⁄111, and, on the later period, *The Wild Man Within. An Image in Western Thought from the Renaissance to Romanticism*, edited by Edward Dudley and Maximillian E. Novak (Pittsburgh 1972); Oleh Mazur, *The Wild Man in the Spanish Renaissance and Golden Age Theater* (Ann Arbor 1980).

30. The recantation of San Pedro occurs in his poem *Desprecio de la fortuna*, in *Obras completas* iii, 271⁄97; the *Cárcel de amor* is referred to as 'salsa para pecar' in verse 2, 276.

31. Modern editions include Juan del Encina, *Eglogas completas*, edited by H. López Morales (New York 1968); *Obras dramáticas*, edited by R. Gimeno, 2 vols (Madrid 1974⁄7). For a different approach to the treatment of love in these plays see Antony van Beysterveldt, *La poesía amatoria del siglo XV y el teatro profano de Juan del Encina* (Madrid 1972), and the general study by H. W. Sullivan, *Juan del Encina* (New York 1976).

32. *Amadís de Gaula*, edited by E. B. Place, 4 vols (Madrid 1959⁄69). Vol. i (reissued in enlarged form in 1971) gives a survey of early editions, translations and adaptions. The most recent English version is *Amadís of Gaul*, translated by E. B. Place and H. C. Behm, 2 vols (Lexington 1974⁄5).

33. The surviving fifteenth⁄century fragments, discovered in 1955, were published and discussed in *El primer manuscrito del 'Amadís de Gaula'*, edited by A. Rodríguez⁄Moñino and others (Madrid 1957). On the controverted question of the text's sources and history see Grace S. Williams, 'The *Amadís* Question', *RH*, 21 (1909), 1⁄67; María Rosa Lida de Malkiel, 'El desenlace del *Amadís* primitivo', *RPh*, 6 (1952⁄3), 283⁄9, republished in *Estudios de literatura española y comparada* (Buenos Aires, 1966), 149⁄56. A general survey of the matter is provided in Frank

Pierce, *Amadís de Gaula* (New York 1976); see also the works cited in Daniel Eisenberg, *Castilian Romances of Chivalry in the Sixteenth Century: A Bibliography* (London 1979).

34. Northrop Frye, *Anatomy of Criticism* (Princeton 1957), 136.

35. Yolanda Russinovich de Solé, *El elemento mítico simbólico en el Amadís de Gaula: interpretación de su significado* (Bogotá 1974).

36. In the traditional form of the story Amadís did accede to Briolanja; it was Montalvo who kept him faithful and chaste. Referring to the version of the story that he is rewriting, Montalvo recalls that Prince Alfonso of Portugal was so sorry for Briolanja that he ordered his scribes to make Amadís her lover (Chapter 40). Probably in that version, which may have been the original story, Oriana's outrage at the infidelity of her knight was so great that Montalvo retained it but made her jump to the wrong conclusion: she becomes subject to the stress of jealousy which forces Amadís to expiate his imagined fault by penance at Beltenebros, an episode well-known to readers of *Don Quijote*.

37. On secret marriage in the Middle Ages, and its application to *Amadís*, see Justina Ruiz de Conde, *El amor y el matrimonio secreto en los libros de caballerías* (Madrid 1947). A good survey of the variety of love relationships in the story may be found in Pierce, 95-106.

38. Gil Vicente, *Tragicomedia de Amadís de Gaula*, edited by T. P. Waldron (Manchester 1959).

39. Cervantes, for example, satirized Don Quixote's shortcomings as a heroic champion of justice (in order to satirize the literary shortcomings of the novels of chivalry) but he did not satirize the chivalresque ideals *per se*.

40. Gil Vincente, *Tragicomedia de Don Duardos*, edited by Dámaso Alonso (Madrid 1942). See, too, Thomas R. Hart, *Gil Vicente: Casandra and Don Duardos* (London 1982).

41. Stanislav Zimic, '*Don Duardos*: espiritualisación de la aventura caballeresca', *BBMP*, 57 (1981), 47-103, is struck by the similarity of language, imagery and tone of the poetry of *Don Duardos*, especially in the descriptions of Flérida's garden, with the *Song of Solomon* in the translation of Fray Luis de León. His analysis of the play is an interesting sidelight on the close relations between divine and human love in the literature of the period. It shows how natural it can be for a critic who is not averse to making this association to read of the one love in terms of the other. It might be noted, however, that the 'chivalresque' love of *Don Duardos* is closer to Courtly Love than to Neoplatonism. Zimic suggests rather daringly that Luis de León could have read the collected plays of Gil Vicente and been influenced by *Don*

Duardos in his commentary on the *Song*. He makes his point about the similarity between the two poems without needing to stretch it this far.

42. The first extant edition (Burgos 1499) was entitled *Comedia de Calisto y Melibea* and consisted of sixteen acts; before 1502 the text was extended to include five more acts and the title was changed to *Tragicomedia*. The critical edition to which reference is made here is Fernando de Rojas, *La Celestina. Tragicomedia de Calisto y Melibea*, edited by Dorothy S. Severin with an introduction by Stephen Gilman (Madrid 1969, 1971, 1974). The classic translation into English is that of James Mabbe (1631). There are modern versions by P. Hartnoll (Everyman 1959) and J. M. Cohen (Penguin 1964).

43. The absence of any thought of marriage throughout the work has been taken to reflect Rojas's Judaism. It has been assumed that Melibea's father, like Rojas himself, was a *converso*, and that his daughter would have been socially unacceptable to the social class to which Calisto belonged. This surmise is an historical extrapolation from the text, where there is no mention or suggestion of Melibea's Judaism. Within literary tradition there was no need for any thought of marriage; indeed, it would have been an intrusion, for no Courtly Lover could ever think of marriage. The work's tragic sense of life would have been diminished by an explicit context of social conventions and prejudice. The thesis of Jewish influence has been advanced by, among others, Fernando Garrido Pallardó, *Los problemas de Calisto y Melibea, y el conflicto de su autor* (Figueras 1957); Segundo Serrano Poncela, *El secreto de Melibea y otros ensayos* (Madrid 1959); Stephen Gilman, *The Spain of Fernando de Rojas: The Intellectual and Social Landscape of 'La Celestina'* (Princeton 1972).

44. See Martín de Riquer, 'Fernando de Rojas y el primer acto de *La Celestina*', *RFE*, 41 (1957), 373-95.

45. On the treatment of Courtly Love see J. M. Aguirre, *Calisto y Melibea, amantes cortesanos* (Saragossa 1962); John Devlin, '*La Celestina*', *A Parody of Courtly Love: Towards a Realistic Interpretation of the 'Tragicomedia de Calisto y Melibea'* (New York 1971); June Hall Martin, *Love's Fools: Aucassin, Troilus, Calisto and the Parody of the Courtly Lover* (London 1972).

46. It seems natural from the context to take this as an indictment; but it is possible to interpret it in another way. Love, though seeming beautiful, can become ugly when it transgresses morality and flouts the social laws. Melibea 'loved in an ugly fashion' by secretly hiding her actions from her parents and thus disobeying them. Calisto 'loved in an ugly fashion' by not proceeding to win

her hand by announcing his suit to her father and obtaining his consent; then by employing a bawd, by secret nightly meetings and by seduction. Spanish literature naturally continued to condemn such transgressions for being anti-social while sympathizing with the embraces of the lovers for being in accordance with the law of nature. As the ballad of Conde Claros put it: 'que los yerros por amores/dignos son de perdonar' (Errors committed by love deserve to be pardoned). See Colin Smith, *Spanish Ballads* (Oxford 1964), 177 and R. Menéndez Pidal, *De Cervantes y Lope de Vega*, fourth edition (Madrid 1948), 74-7. What Rojas is saying through Pleberio goes much deeper than this.

47. Act 21, 233: 'Cébasnos, mundo falso, con el manjar de tus deleites; al mejor sabor nos descubres el anzuelo: no lo podemos huir, que nos tiene ya cazadas las voluntades'.

48. *La Dorotea* is discussed in Chapter 4.

49. They have been studied by Pierre Heugas, *La Célestine et sa descendance directe* (Bordeaux 1973).

Appendix

50. *La poesía amatoria de la época de los Reyes Católicos* (Durham 1981). Professor Whinnom states (93, n.29) that I had sent him the first chapters of a book that was about to appear, whereas what he received was the first draft of the first of three lectures on which the present book is based. This lecture was itself merely an outline of the possible relation of Courtly Love to Mysticism; as such as it was never published.

51. *Spanish Literary Historiography: Three Forms of Distortion* (Exeter 1967).

52. *La poesía amatoria*, 21: 'Para Parker, es más bien el instinto religioso pervertido el que produce el amor cortés, amor que intenta deificar a la amada, amor que dicta una sumisión completa a otra voluntad, amor cuya expresión más típica es la del sufrimiento causado por el amor no correspondido y por el deseo de lo imposible, de fundirse y perderse en otro ser'.

53. *La poesía amatoria*, 22: 'Visto desde esta perspectiva, el autor de *Cárcel de amor* llega a ser una especie de místico descaminado'.

54. *La poesía amatoria*, 22: 'la curiosa coincidencia del lenguaje del amor humano y del divino se puede explicar de una manera menos transcendental'.

55. The reader, it is to be hoped, will have excused at the start of this book the presumption in applying the latter term to myself.

56. Professor Whinnom attributes to me the statement that modern critics cannot understand the type of idealism associated with Courtly Love in general: 'En primer lugar, dice (Parker),

algunos críticos de hoy en día estamos tan imbuidos de los modernos conceptos materialistas que somos incapaces de comprender bien lo que era el idealismo de épocas antiguas' (21). I cannot find this statement in the original lecture and I do not think that I made it. I did, however, state the following view: 'idealism of this kind is not easily accepted as a serious concept, and among literary critics there is, in fact, a strong tendency against idealizing any of the cultural values of the past that cannot be squared with the values of contemporary "humanism"'.

57. In a work that appeared after Chapter 1 was completed (*The Courtly Love Tradition* (Manchester 1982)), Bernard O'Donoghue describes the use of religious language of human love as a 'recurrent issue in criticism of medieval literature' and concludes (12): 'the use of religious parallels and terminology was thought to elevate its context in secular literature without prejudice to its religious source'.

58. Some of the variety and ambiguity of meaning possible in a *cancionero* poem is discussed by Professor Ian Macpherson in a forthcoming article ('Secret Language in the *Cancioneros:* Some Courtly Codes') which he has been kind enough to send me.

Chapter Two. *Ideal Love and Neoplatonism*

1. *The Dialoghi d'amore* were translated into Spanish twice during the sixteenth century; the second and better known version was by Garcilaso de la Vega el Inca (Madrid 1590; reprinted in Madrid 1948). The celebrated translation of Castiglione by Juan Boscán (Barcelona 1534) was edited by M. Menéndez Pelayo as *Anejo* 25 of *RFE* (Madrid 1942).

2. The standard biography is still Hayward Keniston, *Garcilaso de la Vega: A Critical Study* (New York 1922). The importance traditionally accorded to Isabel Freire has been questioned by Frank Goodwyn, 'New Light on the Historical Setting of Garcilaso's Poetry', *HR*, 46 (1978), 1-22, and by Pamela Waley, 'Garcilaso, Isabel and Elena: The Growth of a Legend', *BHS*, 56 (1979), 11-15; but see Elias L. Rivers, *Garcilaso de la Vega, Poems: A Critical Guide* (London 1980), 15 n.1.

3. On Garcilaso's poetic development see Rafael Lapesa, *La trayectoria poética de Garcilaso* (Madrid 1948; second edition 1968), and the anthology of modern studies *La poesía de Garcilaso: ensayos críticos*, edited by Elias L. Rivers (Barcelona 1974).

4. All references to the poems are to Garcilaso de la Vega, *Obras completas*, edited by Elias L. Rivers, second edition (Madrid 1968).

5. Renato Poggioli, *The Oaten Flute: Essays on Pastoral Poetry and*

the Pastoral Ideal (Cambridge, Massachusetts 1975); Darío Fernández-Morera, *The Lyre and the Oaten Flute: Garcilaso and the Pastoral* (London 1982).

6. Lapesa in *La trayectoria poética* follows the old method of looking for biographical identification of the poem's shepherds and shepherdesses. Such identifications may well exist but they are not required for an understanding of the poem's 'philosophies'. It makes better sense if the characters are seen not as distinct individuals but as different phases of experience which can succeed each other in an individual's life. Albanio, Salicio and Nemoroso are three projections of Garcilaso himself, as they can be of any man. This was persuasively argued by R. O. Jones, 'The Idea of Love in Garcilaso's Second Eclogue', *MLR*, 46 (1951), 388-95. See also the studies by Elias L. Rivers, 'Albanio as Narcissus in Garcilaso's Second Eclogue', *HR*, 41 (1973), 297-304; Darío Fernández-Morera, 'Garcilaso's Second Eclogue and the Literary Tradition', *HR*, 47 (1979), 37-53; Inés Azar, *Discurso retórico y mundo pastoral en la Égloga segunda de Garcilaso* (Amsterdam 1981).

7. I have discussed this at greater length in 'Theme and Imagery in Garcilaso's First Eclogue', *BSS*, 25 (1948), 222-7; a different approach to the poem is suggested by M. J. Woods, 'Rhetoric in Garcilaso's First Eclogue', *MLN*, 84 (1969), 143-56.

8. The following studies may be particularly mentioned: Elias L. Rivers, 'The Pastoral Paradox of Natural Art', *MLN*, 77 (1962), 130-44; Alan K. G. Paterson, 'Ecphrasis in Garcilaso's *Egloga tercera*', *MLR*, 72 (1977), 73-92; P. Gallagher, '*Locus amoenus:* The Aesthetic Centre of Garcilaso's Third Eclogue' in *Hispanic Studies in Honour of Frank Pierce*, edited by John England (Sheffield 1980), 59-75.

9. The reading 'degollada' (literally 'beheaded') and its interpretation have been subjects of controversy since the sixteenth century.

10. His poetic craftsmanship has been studied by A. D. Kossoff, *Vocabulario de la obra poética de Herrera* (Madrid 1966); W. Ferguson, *La versificación imitativa en Fernando de Herrera* (London 1981); M. J. Woods, 'Herrera's Voices', in *Medieval and Renaissance Studies on Spain and Portugal in Honour of P. E. Russell*, edited by F. W. Hodcroft and others (Oxford 1981), 121-32.

11. The critical edition followed is Fernando de Herrera, *Obra poética*, edited by J. M. Blecua, 2 vols (Madrid 1975).

12. There is a variant reading for lines 6-7: 'sufrid, qu'un ora alegre 'n tantos días / tristes meresca un triste descontento': 'permit a sad, unhappy man to deserve an hour of joy among so many days of sadness'.

13. The most notable feature about this poem, however, is its form. In

lines 7 and 8 the repetitions first of *perdí* and secondly of *cobré* are, as it were, two rhythmical hammer blows which convey the sensation of increasing anguish. Then line 10, by means of the two rhythmical stresses in *umor / ardor*, accentuates a further contrast which continues the staccato effect of *perdí / cobré*. The rhythmical contrast exists also in 'es llama, es fuego' in line 11, which repeats the sensation of urgency. At the close, the contrast between *espiro* (breath out) and *respiro* (breathe in) which are the rhyming words of the tercets is also remarkable: one *exhales* fire because passion is in the body; one *inhales* the eternal longing of the flame that aspires upwards because the life-giving force which is desired is outside man. There is a forcefulness here that is both intellectual and linguistic; at his best Herrera is a splendid craftsman of style, expressing emotion through ideas, sounds and rhythm.

14. The stars in the first quatrain are the poetic hyperbole for eyes; the sense is that the blue of the sky is set against her green eyes.

15. *Sonnet 10* is another flight into Neoplatonism through the contemplation of the Lady's beauty which still shows at the close (12-14) the contamination of Petrarchan Courtly Love. The Lady is Light, her eyes are stars, hers is a cosmic beauty (1-11). The whole sonnet breathes serenity. The final lines are no cry of anguish, or even of unhappiness.

16. This sonnet is perhaps informed by the Scholastic doctrine that it is the nature of good to communicate itself, that God created the Universe because he wanted creatures to share his goodness: 'bonum est diffusivum sui'; Aquinas, *Summa Theologica*, 1. q. 5 a. 4.

17. The critical edition used here is Francisco de Aldana, *Poesías*, edited by Elias L. Rivers (Madrid 1957), who is also the author of the standard study *Francisco de Aldana: el divino capitán* (Badajoz 1955).

18. *Aborio*: a neologism from the Italian *avorio*.

19. See Rivers's note in *Poesías*, 14.

20. Francisco de Aldana, *Epistolario poético completo*, edited by A. Rodríguez-Moñino, second edition (Madrid 1978), 98 (ll.442-5).

21. The love of friends engaged in joint contemplation of existence is celebrated in the *Carta a Galanio*. It also informs Fray Luis de León's ode to Francisco Salinas, as L. J. Woodward argued, though line 43, 'amigos a quien amo', cannot be emended to 'amigo', as he suggested, because the plural is required for the heptasyllable: L. J. Woodward, 'Fray Luis de León's *Oda a Francisco Salinas*', *BHS*, 39 (1962), 69-77.

22. Line references are to the text of the poem in A. Rodríguez-Moñino, *Epistolario poético completo*.

23. On the image of the circle in Aldana's poetry see M. Louise Salstad, 'Francisco de Aldana's Metamorphoses of the Circle', *MLR*, 74 (1979), 599-606.

Chapter Three. *The Human Language of Divine Love*

1. Dámaso Alonso, *La poesía de San Juan de la Cruz (desde esta ladera)* (Madrid 1942; fourth edition 1958). The parenthesis 'desde esta ladera' served to indicate that the mystical subject matter of the poems was excluded. Part of it was republished with some expansion in the same author's *Poesía española. Ensayo de métodos y límites estilísticos*, fifth edition (Madrid 1976).

2. Alan Watt, 'Psychedelics and Religious Experience', in *The Religious Situation: 1969*, edited by Donald R. Cutler (Boston 1969), 615-31 (621); see also Aldous Huxley, *The Doors of Perception* (London and New York 1954), and *Moksha: Writings on Psychedelics and the Visionary Experience, 1931-1963*, edited by Michael Horowitz and Cynthia Palmer (London 1980). The relation between drug-stimulated experience and traditional mysticism has been studied by R. C. Zaehner, *Drugs, Mysticism and Make-Believe* (London 1972).

3. *Noche oscura*, ii, 18:5; *Llama de amor viva* (B), 3:49; *Cántico espiritual* (B), 27:5; *Subida del Monte Carmelo*, ii, 5. These and further references may be seen in Crisógono de Jesus, Matías del Niño Jesús, Lucinio Ruano, *Vida y obras de San Juan de la Cruz*, seventh edition (Madrid 1973), which contains a useful index to the Saint's writings.

4. On the relation between Courtly Love and Mysticism in the earlier medieval period see Etienne Gilson, 'Saint Bernard and Courtly Love', in *The Mystical Theology of St Bernard*, translated by A. H. C. Downes (London and New York 1940), 170-97; Marina Warner, *Alone of All Her Sex* (London 1978), 121-74; Jean Leclercq, *Monks and Love in Twelfth-Century France: Psycho-Historical Essays* (Oxford 1979).

5. On the *alumbrados* and the Inquisition charges against them see A. Márquez, *Los alumbrados. Orígenes y filosofía 1525-1559*, second edition (Madrid 1980), and, for further studies, A. Gordon Kinder, *Spanish Protestants and Reformers in the Sixteenth Century: A Bibliography* (London 1983).

6. See Chapter 2, footnote 1.

7. The penultimate line does not mean 'pasar al dulce amado centro del alma', but 'pasar desde el alma al dulce amado centro': i.e., the physical point of unity of the two bodies. Love is born in the souls of lovers but its spiritual nature is incapable of passing from their souls to the bodies, and that is why the bodies lament their deprivation.

8. On the doctrine of the Dark Night see E. W. Dicken, *The Crucible of Love* (London 1963); Federico Ruiz Salvador, *Introducción a San Juan de la Cruz. El hombre, los escritos, el sistema* (Madrid 1968).

9. *L'Amour et l'Occident*, 40.

10. In line 11, 'hábito' can mean either 'clothing' or 'custom'; an alternative translation would be 'my love for you is the habitual longing of my soul'. Sebastián de Córdoba wrote a divinized version of this sonnet with relatively few changes in its basically 'religious' language: see Sebastián de Córdoba, *Garcilaso a lo divino*, edited by Glen R. Gale (Ann Arbor and Madrid 1971), 97.

11. *Llama de amor viva (B)*, 3:69⁄76.

12. *Llama*, 3:79⁄80.

13. See Evelyn Underhill, *Mysticism. A Study in the Nature and Development of Man's Spiritual Consciousness*, thirteenth edition (London 1960), 413⁄43.

14. *Moradas* 7, 2:14: Santa Teresa de Jesús, *Obras completas*, edited by Efrén de la Madre de Dios and Otger Steggink, third edition (Madrid 1972), 443.

15. See Emilio Orozco, *Poesía y mística* (Madrid 1959); Margaret Wilson, *San Juan de la Cruz: Poems* (London 1975). Dámaso Alonso, in *La poesía de San Juan de la Cruz*, argued that the Saint was influenced by Garcilaso indirectly through the divinized versions of Sebastián de Córdoba. This view, which won general though not universal acceptance, must now be revised in the light of Colin P. Thompson, *The Poet and the Mystic* (Oxford 1977), which seriously questioned the evidence in favour of Córdoba's influence.

16. The *Cántico espiritual* exists in two versions, in the second of which there is an additional stanza and some of the other stanzas are in a different order. The first version (A) is preferred by several literary critics as being more 'dramatic', but the second version (B) presents the mystical experience and teaching in a more logical sequence; it is the version to which reference will be made here. The text of *Cántico B* is reproduced in the edition of the *Obras* mentioned above (footnote 3), 704⁄6.

17. Dámaso Alonso has shown how the originality and special quality of St John's verse derive from his avoidance (with only one exception) of the usual positioning of the three beats of the hendecasyllable line, together with a marked paucity of adjectives and a scarcity of principal verbs (several stanzas have no verbs at all). These original characteristics combine to give a sense of speed and urgency, hastening on too swiftly to pause.

18. On the origins of this tradition and its broader context see Pierre Grelot, *Man and Wife in Scripture*, translated by Rosaleen Brennan (London 1964); Richard A. Batey, *New Testament Nuptial Imagery* (Leiden 1971); and the article by various authors on 'Cantique des Cantiques' in *D S*, ii, cols 86-109.

19. On the poetry of Fray Luis see Elias L. Rivers, *Fray Luis de León: The Original Poems* (London 1983). It has been conjectured that St John may have known some of the poems of Fray Luis which circulated in manuscript in Salamanca during his lifetime but the evidence is not convincing: F. García Lorca, *De Fray Luis a San Juan: la escondida senda* (Madrid 1972).

20. Luis de León, *Obras completas castellanas*, edited by Félix García, 2 vols (Madrid 1957), i, 652. Theodoretus (*c.*393-*c.*458) was Bishop of Cyrus in Mesapotamia. He played a leading part in the Nestorian controversies but held back from actually denouncing Nestorius with whom he was on friendly terms. He was denounced as a heretic but the condemnation was later withdrawn.

21. Luis de León, i, 753.

22. Only translations of the *poems* are here in question: it is they, and not the prose treatises, that pose the special difficulties. The principal translations are: E. Allison Peers, *The Poems of St John of the Cross* (London 1947), and Roy Campbell, *The Poems of St John of the Cross* (London 1951). There are also versions by Willis Barnstone, *The Poems of St John of the Cross* (New York, 1972); Lynda Nicholson in Gerald Brenan, *St John of the Cross. His Life and Poetry* (Cambridge 1973); and in *The Collected Works of St John of the Cross*, translated by Kieran Kavanaugh and Otilio Rodríguez (Washington 1973). A faithful translation of the *Cántico espiritual* (*A*) may be found in Colin Thompson, 173-7. The finest version I know of the three major poems is Edward Sarmiento, *Three Translations from St John of the Cross and other Poems* (privately printed at the Carmel, Ware 1976).

23. *Cántico*, 18:4.

24. Lynda Nicholson also has, 'O daughters of Judaea'; Kavanaugh and Rodríguez give, 'You girls of Judea'; and Barnstone, 'O virgins of Judea'.

25. Nicholson has, 'On the outskirts keep repose', and Kavanaugh and Rodríguez, 'Stay away, there on the outskirts'; Barnstone misses the sense with, 'live in some far-off place'.

26. *Cántico*, 2:3; 13:10. In the Western United States such hills are numerous and are denoted by the French word *butte*.

27. *Cántico*, 2:6. Knowledge of the truth is the health of the mind; the understanding is therefore ill if it does not know him. The

will's function is to love the good and to possess it; possession of its good brings pleasure and delight, as in love; without the God whom it loves but does not possess the will therefore suffers. Memory only remembers that it has never know God or possessed him; since God is the promise of life the memory that he is lacking is tantamount to death.

28. Jean Vilnet, *Bible et Mystique chez Saint Jean de la Croix* (Paris 1949); Henri de Lubac, *Exégèse médiévale. Les quatre sens de l'Écriture*, 4 vols (Paris 1959/64), iv, 500/5.

29. As Colin Thompson has written of the *Cántico* (139), 'The tendency has been to force poem and commentary so far apart that there is no meeting/ground between them. That surely is an unacceptable position. They interact constantly, and it is only on rare occasions that San Juan loses sight of the poem altogether'.

30. *Subida del Monte Carmelo*, i, 2:4; ii, 5:3.

31. On the influence of the *Song of Solomon* see José L. Morales, *El Cántico espiritual de San Juan de la Cruz: su relación con el Cantar de los Cantares y otras fuentes escriturísticas y literarias* (Madrid 1971); Fernande Pepin, *Noces de feu. Le symbolisme nuptial du Cántico espiritual de Saint Jean de la Croix à la lumière du Canticum Canti/corum* (Paris, Tournai and Montreal 1972).

32. The poem follows the three stages of the mystical way: purgation, illumination and union. In these early stanzas the need for purgation, or mortification, is stressed: the soul must steel herself to prepare to know God directly.

33. The stage of illumination that begins here is marked at first by visions and trances: *Cántico*, 13:6, 7. These are transient pheno/mena to which St John attaches no importance. They represent a revelation of the world of spirit that still retains contact with sensible experience, although this ecstasy does represent the first loosening of the chains that bind the soul to matter.

34. *Cántico*, 14 and 15:25/7.

35. *Cántico*, 14 and 15:8.

36. *Cántico*, 16:9.

37. Since Aminadab denoted a charioteer, and a *cerco* or 'surrounding wall' could also mean a 'siege', it is natural to translate *caballería* as 'cavalry', but it could also mean 'horses' in a collective sense.

38. *Cántico*, 40:3. The Vulgate text is sufficient justification for St John's symbol of the cavalry horses as the sensuous passions, but there is a wider justification for the symbol than this. The horse is ambivalent in ancient mythology, signifying either good or evil, either the white horses of the Sun's chariot or the black horses of Chaos: '. . . the horse could be ridden by the Devil and then becomes phallic . . .' (J. C. Cooper, *An Illustrated Encyclopaedia of*

Traditional Symbols (London 1978)). The unruly horse is a not-uncommon symbol in modern literature and films: a striking example occurs at the end of D. H. Lawrence's *The Rainbow*, where the frightened Ursula is enclosed in a field with a horse that stampedes round her. See also C. G. Jung, *Man and His Symbols* (New York 1964), 174.

39. *Cántico*, 40:6. This selective analysis of the *Cántico espiritual* will have demonstrated, it is hoped, that the commentary is not an extraneous adjunct to the poem but something intrinsically united to it, like the air which the poem must breathe in order to communicate its full significance, which no literal interpretation can give. The commentary adds 'philosophy' to the human experience, and life without explanation and meaning is empty. The meaning of life that the mystic mines from his experience is also the poetry of existence. It matters little whether the 'philosophy' is true or false, provided the poetry has the special beauty that poetry alone can give, and provided the poetry and the 'philosophy' are in harmony. The symbolism and allegory revealed by the commentary are no pedestrian addition rendering it lifeless; on the contrary, they make the poetry glow with a heightened radiance of mind and heart.

Chapter Four. *Ideal Love and Human Reality*

1. Pietro Bembo, *Gli Asolani*, translated by Rudolf B. Gottfried (Bloomington 1954).
2. Flaminio Nobili, *Il trattato dell' amore humano* (Lucca 1567), facsimile reprint (Rome 1895).
3. Jorge de Montemayor, *Los siete libros de la Diana* (Valencia 1559?), edited by F. López Estrada (Madrid 1946); Gaspar Gil Polo, *Diana enamorada* (Valencia 1564), edited by R. Ferreres (Madrid 1953). On the background to these works see F. López Estrada, *Los libros de pastores en la literatura española* (Madrid 1974), and, for a sensitive analysis, A. Solé-Leris, *The Spanish Pastoral Novel* (New York 1980).
4. Luis de Granada, *Introducción del símbolo de la fe* (Salamanca 1583), in *Obras de Fray Luis de Granada*, edited by Justo Cuervo, 14 vols (Madrid 1901-8), vi, 156-7.
5. It is included in Luis de León, *Obras completas castellanas*, edited by Félix García, 2 vols (Madrid 1957), i, 243-538.
6. P. Malón de Chaide, *La conversión de la Magdalena*, edited by F. García, 3 vols (Madrid 1930). A less successful instance of criticism of secular fiction is Bartolomé Ponce de León's *Primera parte de la Clara Diana a lo divino* (Saragossa 1599?). Intended as a rebuff to Montemayor's *Diana* it is of little literary value.

7. Among the many studies in which Cervantes's philosophy of love is treated the following in particular may be mentioned: Marcel Bataillon, 'Cervantes y el matrimonio cristiano', in *Varia lección de clásicos castellanos* (Madrid 1964); Robert V. Piluso, *Amor, matrimonio y honra en Cervantes* (New York 1967); A. J. Close, 'Don Quixote's Love for Dulcinea: A Study of Cervantine Irony', *BHS*, 50 (1973), 237-55; F. Márquez Villanueva, *Personajes y temas del Quijote* (Madrid 1978); J. Herrero, 'Arcadia's *Inferno*. Cervantes's Attack on Pastoral', *BHS*, 55 (1978), 289-99, and 'Sierra Morena as Labyrinth: From Wilderness to Christian Knighthood', *FMLS*, 17 (1981), 55-67.

8. *Don Quijote de la Mancha*, edited by Martín de Riquer (London 1958), Part I, Chapter 25 (245-6).

9. Part II, Chapter 73 (1057).

10. *La Galatea*, edited by J. B. Avalle-Arce, second edition, 2 vols (Madrid 1968). The concept of love in this novel is discussed by A. Solé-Leris in the work cited in footnote 3.

11. *Novelas ejemplares*, edited by F. Rodríguez Marín, seventh edition, 2 vols (Madrid 1975), i, 221-324. There is an English version in Cervantes, *Exemplary Stories*, translated by C. A. Jones (London 1972). See J. Lowe, *Cervantes: Two novelas ejemplares: La gitanilla and La ilustre fregona* (London 1971), and Ruth El Saffar, *Novel to Romance: a study of Cervantes's Novelas ejemplares* (Baltimore 1974).

12. Alban K. Forcione, *Cervantes' Christian Romance. A Study of Persiles y Sigismunda* (Princeton 1972), 31-2.

13. *Los trabajos de Persiles y Sigismunda*, edited by J. B. Avalle-Arce (Madrid 1969), 51.

14. Cervantes remained firm in the traditional belief that literature should be instructive as well as pleasing. Both ends were attained for him on the traditional level of the 'high' style, distinguished from the 'low' style not only in its artistic tone but also in its avoidance of the crudeness and vulgarity of 'real' life. The high style demanded a 'serious' theme and tone; the low style was 'comic'. We now see the former as the romantic mode and the latter as ironic. Cervantes's comic writing was for him also exemplary on its lower level. We see it, of course, as a far more serious vision of life than his romantic idealism, and we can recognize that he, with a greater literary artistry than the writers of contemporary picaresque novels, broke down the distinction between the high art of the 'serious' and the low art of the 'comic'. He thus stands as one of the pioneers of modern literature. On his literary theory see E. C. Riley, *Cervantes's Theory of the Novel* (Oxford 1962).

15. The standard biography is Hugo A. Rennert, *The Life of Lope de Vega* (Glasgow 1904), revised and brought up-to-date in its Spanish version: Américo Castro y Hugo A. Rennert, *Vida de Lope de Vega*, con notas adicionales de Fernando Lázaro Carreter (Salamanca 1969).

16. The definitive study of Lope's poetry remains to be written. Crucial for its interpretation are the critical essays of Dámaso Alonso, 'La correlación poética en Lope (de la juventud a la madurez)', *RFE*, 43 (1960), 355-98, and *Poesía española. Ensayo de métodos y límites estilísticos*, fifth edition (Madrid 1976). See also José F. Montesinos, *Estudios sobre Lope de Vega* (Salamanca 1967), and the introductions by J. M. Blecua to his editions of the *Obras poéticas, I* (Barcelona 1969) and *Lírica* (Madrid 1982).

17. *Poesías líricas*, edited by José F. Montesinos, 2 vols (Madrid 1925-1926), i, 38-40. All references are to volume i of this edition.

18. Sonnet 7 (119-20).

19. See Sonnet 191 (151-2).

20. See Sonnet 50 (126-7).

21. Sonnet 61 (129).

22. When Lope writes poems that on the surface are closer to the old tradition, his imagery emphasises the concept of guilt and the sense of remorse: an example is Sonnet 175 (147-8) which has echoes also of Neoplatonism.

23. The vast corpus of Lope's poetry does contain poems that are academic exercises, or that exemplify particular stylistic fashions. He showed that he could do what others did, but this 'artificial' poetry is not central to his work.

24. Sonnet 1 (117-18).

25. *La Dorotea*, edited by E. S. Morby, first edition (Berkeley and Los Angeles 1958), second edition (Madrid 1968). On the genesis of the work, and its interpretation, see Alan S. Trueblood, *Experience and Artistic Expression in Lope de Vega: The Making of La Dorotea* (Cambridge, Massachusetts 1974).

26. On the social and psychological aspects of love in the drama see Melveena McKendrick, *Woman and Society in the Spanish Drama of the Golden Age* (London 1974).

27. Francisco de Quevedo, *La hora de todos y la Fortuna con seso*, edited by Luisa López Grigera (Madrid 1975), 208.

28. *El caballero de Olmedo*, edited by Inés I. MacDonald (London 1962). There is an English version in *Lope de Vega (Five Plays)* (New York 1961), translated by Jill Booty, with an introduction by R. D. F. Pring-Mill. On some of the critical problems involved in its interpretation see J. W. Sage, *Lope de Vega. El caballero de Olmedo* (London 1974).

29. *El castigo sin venganza*, edited by C. A. Jones (Oxford 1966). There is an English translation in *Five Plays*. On this and other honour plays of Lope see Donald Larsen, *The Honor Plays of Lope de Vega* (Cambridge, Massachusetts, and London 1977).

30. The general features of Tirso's drama are surveyed in M. Wilson, *Tirso de Molina* (New York 1977).

31. On the tension between Old and New Christians and its social background see J. H. Elliot, *Imperial Spain 1469-1716* (London 1963), and J. Lynch, *Spain under the Hapsburgs I. Empire and Absolutism 1516-1598*, second edition (Oxford 1981).

32. *Antona García*, edited by M. Wilson (Manchester 1957). Isabella was the half-sister of the King of Castile, Henry IV, who was firmly believed to be impotent. Either she or her younger brother Alfonso was expected to succeed him, when the Queen eventually gave birth to a daughter who was christened Juana (1462). Public opinion refused to accept her as the legitimate offspring of the King and ascribed her paternity to the King's favourite, Don Beltrán de la Cueva, whereupon the unfortunate child was given the derogatory cognomen of *La Beltraneja*. Alfonso died in 1468, leaving Isabella as Juana's only rival. On Henry IV's death in 1474, the King of Portugal saw the opportunity of uniting the kingdom of Castile with his own by marrying Juana, and invaded the sister kingdom without waiting to accomplish the union. At the same time most of the Castilian nobility, knowing that their feudal privileges would be more secure under Juana than under Isabella, declared in the former's favour. Isabella therefore had to conduct both an international and a civil war.

33. *El burlador de Sevilla*, edited by G. E. Wade and E. W. Hesse (Salamanca 1978). There is a critical guide by D. Rogers, *Tirso de Molina. El burlador de Sevilla* (London 1977).

34. The play is included with *El burlador* in Tirso de Molina, *Comedias, I*, edited by Américo Castro (Madrid 1910) and frequently reprinted. There are more recent editions by Francisco Ayala (Madrid 1971) and E. W. Hesse (Madrid 1976).

35. In *Obras dramáticas completas*, edited by Blanca de los Ríos de Lampérez, 3 vols (Madrid 1946-58), i, 794-838.

36. Dámaso Alonso, *Góngora y el 'Polifemo'*, fifth edition, 3 vols (Madrid 1967): the poem is edited with a commentary in vol. 3. See also Alexander A. Parker, *Luis de Góngora: Polyphemus and Galatea: A Study in the Interpretation of a Baroque Poem*, with verse translation by Gilbert F. Cunningham (Edinburgh 1977).

37. *The Solitudes of Luis de Góngora*, translated by Gilbert F. Cunningham (Baltimore 1968), 75-7.

38. The poem is edited, with a commentary, by Dámaso Alonso in *Góngora y el 'Polifemo'*, ii, 36‑45.

Chapter Five. *Ideal Love and the Philosophy of Disillusion*

1. Douglas Bush, *English Literature in the Earlier Seventeenth Century*, second edition (Oxford 1962), 3.
2. Francisco de Quevedo, *Sueños y discursos*, edited by Felipe C. R. Maldonado (Madrid 1972), 195.
3. See H. Ettinghausen, *Francisco de Quevedo and the Neostoic Move‑ment* (Oxford 1972); K. A. Bluher, *Seneca in Spanien: Unter‑suchungen zur Geschichte der Seneca‑Rezeption in Spanien vom 13. bis 17. Jahrhundert* (Munich 1969).
4. *La cuna y la sepultura*, edited by Luisa López Grigera (Madrid 1969), 16.
5. *Ibid.*, 16‑17.
6. *Ibid.*, 30.
7. Dámaso Alonso, 'El desgarrón afectivo en la poesía de Quevedo' in *Poesía española* (Madrid 1950), 531‑618. A guide to criticism of Quevedo's love poetry may be found in James O. Crosby, *Guís bibliográfica para el estudio crítico de Quevedo* (London 1976), *Francisco de Quevedo*, edited by Gonzalo Sobejano (Madrid 1978), 381‑9, and Francisco de Quevedo, *Poesía varia*, edited by James O. Crosby, second edition (Madrid 1982), 27‑40, 579‑90. The subject has been studied by my former pupil Julián Olivares, *The Love Poetry of Francisco de Quevedo. An Aesthetic and Existential Study* (Cambridge 1983). See also José María Pozuelo Yvancos, *El lenguaje poético de la lírica amorosa de Quevedo* (Murcia 1979).
8. James Smith, 'On Metaphysical Poetry', *Scrutiny*, 2, no. 3 (December 1933), 222‑38, republished in *Shakespearian and Other Essays* (Cambridge 1974), 262‑78.
9. The sonnets considered here may be found in Francisco de Quevedo, *Obra poética*, edited by José Manuel Blecua, 3 vols (Madrid 1969‑71), and in *Obras completas, 1: Poesía original*, edited by José Manuel Blecua, fourth edition (Barcelona 1973).
10. Otis H. Green, *Courtly Love in Quevedo* (Boulder 1952), 26; Alonso, 557.
11. On the punctuation of this sonnet see Olivares, 163 n.4.
12. Alonso, 556.
13. Baltasar Gracián, *Agudeza y arte de ingenio*, edited by Evaristo Correa Calderón, 2 vols (Madrid 1969), ii, 80‑93.
14. A facsimile reprint of *Il cannochiale aristotelico* in the edition of Turin, 1670 has been published with an introduction by August Buck in *Ars Poetica, Texte und Studien zur Dichtungslehre und Dichtkunst*, 5 (Berlin and Zurich 1968).

15. See Emilia Navarro de Kelley, *La poesía metafísica de Quevedo* (Madrid 1973), 119-23.
16. Kelley, 120.
17. A guide to critical interpretations of this poem may be found in Crosby's edition of *Poesía varia*, 587-8; see also Olivares, 128-41. Most critics do not interpret tension in this poem but interpret it instead as triumphantly affirming the victory of love over death and time. For me, I repeat, there is tension in Quevedo's imagery: no flame can swim across water without being extinguished; no flame can be formed by any liquid, even though it be the blood that boils in passion. And the phrase 'polvo enamorado' is surely as much a denial of *amor* as it is of *polvo*, for it can be not only 'polvo *enamorado*' but '*polvo* enamorado' (i.e. 'amor hecho polvo'). Love triumphing over death and time is also love triumphed over by death and time.
18. Green, 72-9.
19. The plays discussed here may be found in Pedro Calderón de la Barca, *Comedias*, a facsimile edition prepared by D. W. Cruick-shank and J. E. Varey with textual and critical studies, 19 vols (London 1973), and in *Obras completas, 1: Dramas*, edited by Ángel Valbuena Briones (Madrid 1959), to which page numbers refer.
20. See A. A. Parker, 'Los amores y noviazgos clandestinos en el mundo dramático-social de Calderón', in *Hacia Calderón. Segundo coloquio anglogermano, Hamburgo 1970*, edited by Hans Flasche (Berlin 1973), 79-87.
21. *Mythos und Repräsentation. Die mythologischen Festspiele Calderóns* (Munich 1978).
22. Calderón, *The Secular Plays* (Lexington 1982), 5. This section of ter Horst's excellent book is a much wider study of Calderón's theory and treatment of love than I attempt here. See also A. Valbuena Briones, 'Eros moralizado en las comedias mitológicas de Calderón', in *Approaches to the Theater of Calderón*, edited by Michael D. McGaha (Washington 1981), 77-94, and William R. Blue, *The Development of Imagery in Calderón's Comedias* (York, S. Carolina 1983). Thomas Austin O'Connor ['On Love and the Human Condition: A Prolegomenon to Calderón's Mytho-logical Plays', in *Calderón de la Barca at the Tercentenary: Proceedings of the Comparative Literature Symposium*, vol. xiv (Lubbock 1981), 119-34] makes 1651 a watershed in Calderón's output by remark-ing on the subsequent preponderance of mythological themes. He makes a sharp division, however, not only between types of theme and staging (which is of course legitimate) but also between two opposing philosophies of life (which is doubtful). The one is a

belief in reason and in its ability to produce harmonious social living, the other a concern with violence and disaster in which man is no longer master of his fate. O'Connor calls the first view Thomism and the second Augustinianism, but this opposition between Aquinas and Augustine is simplistic for as Christian theologians both held that man could act reasonably or unreasonably and that success or moral failure would normally follow. The distinction that should be made is between the social harmony produced by Comedy and the disasters produced by Tragedy. These are not necessarily conflicting views of life, although temperament and experience may make a writer incline more to one than to the other. Mythology, as the pages that follow will argue, enables Calderón to give a symbolical, more universal significance to tragic themes, but his tragic view of life is not essentially changed.

23. Lope de Vega also wrote a play about Cupid and Psyche, *El Amor enamorado* (1625-35), in which the fable is burlesqued. It shows that the age did not treat its conventions solemnly, even though it could take its 'philosophy' seriously.

24. *The Survival of the Pagan Gods*, translated by Barbara F. Sessions (New York 1953), 121.

25. *Mythologiae*, Book III, Chapter 7. This Fulgentius has been identified with St Fulgentius, the famous bishop of Ruspe, but the identification is not certain.

26. To the best of my knowledge the interpretation I suggest has not been given before. Ter Horst calls the play 'wonderfully erotic' (5) but it is not one of the plays that he analyses. O'Connor's view is that 'Calderón shows us that love leads to pardon and restores harmony to human affairs disrupted by the hostile proclivities of our nature and our world. In this view of life, Calderón affirms that love and forgiveness must work hand in hand, for only love offers us any solution to the myriad problems our weak nature creates for us' (132). This is applicable only if Cupid and Psyche are taken to be 'human' characters. On the symbolical plane the theme is arguably more significant. The approach of Neumeister (who discusses the play at length in his fourth chapter) is not literary criticism in the traditional sense but structuralist with a sociological bias. He is not interested in the 'plot' or in the 'meaning' to be extracted from it but in the function that the mythological plays could perform in court life. Such an approach constitutes a contribution to the social history of Spain rather than to the history and evaluation of its literature.

27. See A. A. Parker, 'Towards a Definition of Calderonian Tragedy', *BHS*, 39 (1962), 222-37.

28. The basis of this reconstruction, with all the steps in the argu-
    ment, has been set out in A. A. Parker, 'Segismundo's Tower:
    A Calderonian Myth', *BHS*, 49 (1982), 247-56. An earlier
    paper had developed the theme of antagonism between sons and
    fathers throughout Calderón's career: 'The Father-Son Conflict
    in the Drama of Calderón', *FMLS*, 2 (1966), 99-113.

29. There has been much misunderstanding of Calderón's position
    as regards the concept of Fate. It has generally been thought that
    he was an unequivocal champion of the ability of men through
    the exercise of an untrammelled free-will to be the sole architects
    of their fate. Calderón believes in free-will but also in pre-
    destination (i.e. divine foreknowledge); both were doctrines held
    by the Roman Catholic Church. The problem to which they
    gave rise was the impossible one of formulating definitions to
    safeguard one doctrine as against the other. Of the very many
    prophecies in Calderonian drama there is not a single one that
    is not fulfilled. Freedom consists in a man's recognition of where
    his temperament and actions can carry him, and in cooperating
    with Fate at the end instead of struggling against it, in other words
    in accepting God's will. Thus Segismundo, the prince in *La vida
    es sueño*, having fulfilled the horoscope, rejects the vengeance he
    was seeking against his father and pardons him. His fate is to be
    the vehicle of justice not of injustice.

30. In Ovid he is sixteen when he meets Echo; Calderón makes him
    between eleven and twelve.

31. Ovid, *Metamorphoses*, translated by Frank Justus Miller, third
    edition, 2 vols (Cambridge, Massachusetts, and London 1977),
    149.

32. This contrast between the positive love of Echo and the negative
    love of Narcissus parallels on an abstract and more sophisticated
    level the contrast between the two sisters in Tirso's *El vergonzoso en
    palacio*.

33. The critics who have written on this play are few. They have,
    naturally enough, centred attention on the psychology, noting how
    the severity with which the frightened mother brings up her son
    produces timidity in him. The best of these interpretations is by
    O'Connor (121-31). An exception is Charles V. Aubrun, who
    produced the first handy edition of the play [second edition (Paris
    1963)]. Rather than analysing the play in itself, he looks at the
    totality of Calderón's treatment of classical mythology within the
    wider context of Calderón's philosophy of life in general. He has a
    particular view of Calderón as a dramatic poet whose mind was
    formed in the concept of a confused and disturbed world in which
    men can be guided only by an awareness of spiritual forces

beneath the chaos and by the need of salvation. None of this is specific to Calderón's response to the fable of Echo and Narcissus. He makes the surprising suggestion that Calderón wrote the play for the 'pagans' of his day (king, ministers, courtiers) to recall them to the Christian verities they were neglecting (xxvi). His final conclusion is difficult to square with the text: 'N'y suffisant pas et rien n'y suffisant, oui, tout de même, si la quête de la Loi peut seule nous acheminer auprès de la fontaine où Narcisse, tragique/ ment, s'éprit de la Vérité insaisissable et ineffable, de l'âme cristalline de l'Univers' (xxviii).

34. The interpretation advanced here is a modification of my paper 'El monstruo de los jardines y el concepto calderoniano del destino', in *Hacia Calderón. Cuarto coloquio anglogermano, Wolfenbüttel 1975* (Berlin 1979), 92/101. The ambivalent erotic situation of Achilles and Deidamia is the subject of two papers by E. W. Hesse, 'Calderón's *El monstruo de los jardines* and its sexual problems', in his *Essays on Spanish Letters of the Golden Age* (Potomac 1981), and 'Calderón's *El monstruo de los jardines*: Sex, Sexuality and Sexual Fulfilment', *RCEH*, 5 (1981), 311/19. Ter Horst refers to the play briefly (133). Neumeister, who deals with it at length (137/200), takes as certain that it was performed in the Royal Palace in 1661 together with *Eco y Narciso* as a 'double/bill'. This was originally suggested by Aubrun in the first edition of his text of *Eco y Narciso*. Noting the repetitive plot structure of the two dramas he had thought it 'probable' that they were performed one after the other. In the second edition (vii n.13) this hypothesis became a certainty without further explanation. There is no documentary evidence of a performance of *El monstruo de los jardines* in 1661. The earliest evidence is of a performance in Seville in 1667 (Emilio Cotarelo y Mori, *Ensayo sobre la vida y obras de D. Pedro Calderón de la Barca* (Madrid 1924), 322), it being claimed at the time that the play was a 'new' one. This probably meant that it was new to Seville: provincial performances of Madrid plays were usually a few years later. The repetitive plot structure will be apparent from the account given of the two plays but it does not mean necessarily the same year of composition or performance. Repetition of dramatic patterns is fairly frequent in Calderón, and the primary interest lies in the differences of mean/ ing suggested by the modifications each time the pattern is repeated. Comparisons and contrasts are also a notable feature of Calderón's technique, and the structural similarity of these plays points to an intended contrast in the two themes despite their similar patterns. The contrast can in fact be accentuated by the similarity, and this is what the above analyses have sought to

bring out. The plays may have been performed close together in time but they need not have been, for they are thematically independent and distinct, and although they do constitute a contrasting pair each exists as a unity in its own right. Assuming an intentional and very close connection Neumeister enters into structural analyses that do not, to my mind, illuminate the meaning, and, although some interesting points are made, his approach does not shake my conviction that each of the plays is independent as a dramatic construction, and that each interprets a particular fable within the particular terms of reference it imposes.

35. In the myth of Phaethon his mother, Clymene, is married to Merops, king of Ethopia. That is why in *Apolo y Climene* Calderón makes Admetus king of Ethiopia instead of Pherae or Thessalonika. But in *El hijo del sol, Faetón* he is 'rey de Tesalia'.

36. It is not clear when the two plays were staged. There is no reason why they should have been performed in the same season, but obviously there should not have been a long interval between them. I am indebted to Dr D. W. Cruickshank for the following observations. The fact that *Faetón* is promised in the penultimate speech of *Apolo y Climene* makes it likely that they were performed in close sequence. According to Cotarelo (313) *Faetón* was played on 1 March 1661, but Cristóbal Pérez Pastor's transcript of the document in question (*Documentos para la biografía de D. Pedro Calderón de la Barca*, vol. 1 (Madrid 1905) 280-1) refers only to a 'fiesta grande'. A performance was planned for 14 February 1662 (see N. D. Shergold, *A History of the Spanish Stage from Medieval Times until the End of the Seventeenth Century* (Oxford 1967), 325-7) but this was the occasion when the Marqués de Heliche attempted to blow up the stage, and it is not known when the performance eventually took place. There was a performance for Mariana's birthday, but this was 22 December 1679.

37. *Sátiro* acts the part of *gracioso*, the indispensable jester or fool. He is grotesquely dressed and makes a number of silly jokes. This is not a serious dramatic representation of Lust. The character does not clown; his dress and jokes define him rather as Folly. Only at the very end when Clymene is abandoned and Apollo has returned to the heavens does Satyr appear dressed as such.

38. Page 1885: 'Hacia la mina / que amor ingeniero tiene / abierta contra la plaza / de mis vanas altiveces, / he de acercarme' ('I must approach the tunnel that Love the engineer has opened up towards the fortress of my vanity and haughtiness'). In *El galán fantasma*, an early comedy, the lover enters the lady's garden through a tunnel or *mina*. But this *mina* has no erotic symbolism. It was built as part of a plot by the future *galán*'s father to avenge an insult to his

honour; and there is no *sátiro* who alone knows of its existence and raises and lowers the covering slab.

39. Page 1902: Pues entre la tempestad, / que de sí me arroja, hube / de caer (imaginando / que aun los montes no me sufren), / sin saber dónde, en la sima / que a tus jardines conduce / ajeno amor. ¿Quién creerá / que equivocando arcaduces, / de minas que fueron de agua, / minas de fuego resulten? ('For during the storm which spat me out I was destined (imagining that even the mountains rejected me) to fall I knew not where into the conduit that brings to your gardens an outside love. Who would believe that mines designed to carry water would (belying the nature of aqueducts) lead to mines of fire?'). The phrase 'la sima que a tus jardines conduce ajeno amor' is not easy to construe. It may be translated 'the conduit that brings to your gardens the love of another person', but it also carries the suggestion that this love, which comes from outside, is in some sense 'foreign' to the place, that it violates Diana's sanctuary.

40. Page 1905.

41. In an early study of Calderón's symbol of the Sun ('Metáfora y símbolo en la interpretación de Calderón', in *Actas del primer congreso internacional de hispanistas*, edited by Frank Pierce and Cyril A. Jones (Oxford 1964), 141-60) I likened the conflagration and destruction caused by Phaethon to an atomic explosion, itself the proof of man's god-like powers (160). When I sent the typescript of this study to my friend, the late Edward M. Wilson, he advised me to remove the reference to an irrelevant nuclear explosion. I did not do so. It is reintroduced now in this footnote as a sign of the universality and relevance to human life of much of classical mythology.

42. With a virtually exclusive emphasis on his wife-murder plays, previously sadly misunderstood, Calderón was supposed to be an anti-feminist playwright. This emphasis is being righted: 'Calderón strikes a responsive chord in many of us today by his affirmation of a woman's dignity through his positive affirmation of her God-given liberty' (O'Connor, 132).

43. *Reason in Society*, second edition (New York 1905), 9.

44. *Sentencias* (no. 1111) in *Obras completas: prosa*, edited by Luis Astrana Marín, third edition (Madrid 1945), 987b. I am grateful to Dr R. M. Price for the information that this *sentencia* was drawn from Antonio de Guevara, *Reloj de príncipes*, edited by Angel Rosenblat (Madrid 1936), 142: 'jamás blasoné del amor con la lengua que no estuviese muy lastimado de dentro en el ánima'. Quevedo's debt to Guevara (1480-1545) is a further illustration of the link between his philosophy of love and the Courtly Love

tradition of the late fifteenth and early sixteenth centuries.

45. See *Butler's Lives of the Saints*, revised by H. Thurston and D. Attwater, second edition, 4 vols (London 1956), iv, 196⁄7. The date of the play is unknown, but it is dramatically so immature that it must be early. Its immaturity consists in the number of supernatural events that, against all probability, help to bring the two lovers together in faith and martyrdom. These are intrinsically absurd and mar the good points of the play. But they do have a dramatic function. Religious faith holds that divine Providence and not a purposeless Fate guides men's lives by what, although they do not see it, is ultimately for their good. Such a belief cannot easily be *enacted* on the stage before an audience of ordinary people, the majority probably uneducated. If supernatural intervention is shown by a miracle, then the audience will grasp the idea. Calderón, however, soon abandoned this simple-minded device.

46. See *Butler's Lives of the Saints*, iii, 652⁄4. The play was originally composed for the Corpus Christi festivities of 1637; a revised version was printed in 1663.

47. On the typically Calderonian character of the student who reasons his way towards Truth see José María de Cossío, *Notas y estudios de crítica literaria: siglo XVII* (Madrid 1939), 73⁄109.

48. Shana Alexander, 'At the Sexual Delicatessen', *Newsweek*, 5 February 1973, 43.

INDEX